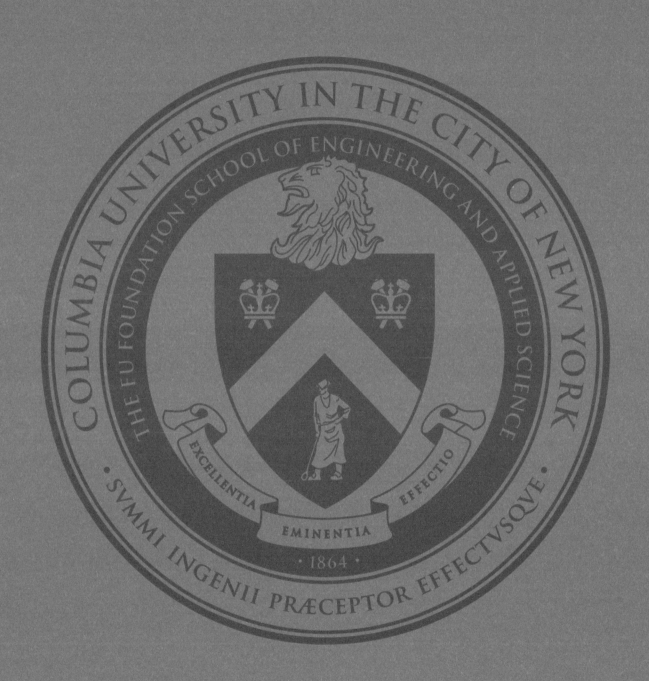

COLUMBIA|ENGINEERING
The Fu Foundation School of Engineering and Applied Science

# EXCELLENTIA
Excellence

# EMINENTIA
Leadership

# EFFECTIO
Impact

*Photography by Eileen Barroso*

Printed by Kirkwood Printing Company, in cooperation with Columbia Engineering.

Printed in the United States of America.

For information, contact the Office of the Dean, Columbia Engineering, Columbia University, The Fu Foundation School of Engineering and Applied Science, 500 West 120th Street, Room 510, New York, NY, 10027.

Library of Congress Control Number: 2011938259

ISBN: 978-0-9839511-0-0

"Inspired by the scientific breakthroughs of their predecessors, Columbia Engineering's faculty provide the same inspiration for our students throughout our classrooms and laboratories, educating them to be engineering and applied science leaders who will address some of the world's most challenging problems and develop solutions for the betterment of the human condition." —Feniosky Peña-Mora
Dean and Morris A. and Alma Schapiro Professor

## SUSTAINABILITY

# INFORMATION

## Educating Socially Responsible Global Engineering and Applied Science Leaders

Since 1754, Columbia has been educating socially responsible engineering and applied science leaders whose work has resulted in the betterment of the human condition around the world. One notable early graduate of Columbia includes John Stevens, Class of 1768, whose technology made possible early steamboats and steam locomotives. Following in his footsteps at Columbia was his son, John Cox Stevens, Class of 1803, a builder of yachts and also an inventor.

That spirit of entrepreneurship and innovation spurred the founding of Columbia Engineering as a separate school in 1864, to provide a sense of independent community for like-minded faculty and students. Early graduates of the School included Michael Pupin, Class of 1883, inventor of long-distance telephony and many other transformational technologies, who joined the faculty in 1889. His most famous pupil was Edwin Howard Armstrong, inventor of the FM radio and father of the broadcast industry. Armstrong joined the faculty upon his graduation in 1913, the same year he applied for his first patent, the audion tube, considered to be the first radio amplifier, which, interestingly enough, he developed during his junior year at the School.

While some early faculty leaders were Columbians, our School has benefited over the years by attracting many of the most distinguished engineering and applied science professors in the world. The Columbia Engineering faculty have always represented the most brilliant minds of each academic generation and they have chosen Columbia Engineering as the place where they are doing their very best work, making an impact on our world and that of future generations.

In these pages, you will learn about the research that each of our faculty members is undertaking. While we have divided their work into the broad groupings of health, sustainability, and information, we recognize the imperfect nature of categorizing research that by its very nature is pandisciplinary, particularly in the area that I call CyberBioPhysical Systems™, where the biological, physical, and digital worlds integrate and fuse.

It is within this area where many of our faculty are working to find innovative solutions to the most challenging problems of modern society. As our professors investigate complex problems across the research spectrum, they are developing the breakthroughs that will improve the way we live our lives today, tomorrow, and beyond.

Feniosky Peña-Mora

Dean and Morris A. and Alma Schapiro Professor

# HEALTH

Interdisciplinary approaches to improving public health began with the School's first dean, Charles F. Chandler, a chemist, who, in 1866 began to improve standards in New York City for milk and water purity. Then, in 1896, electrical engineering professor Michael I. Pupin created a fast-exposure X-ray that was first used by a surgeon to locate buckshot in a patient's hand. The following pages present a sample of the work of current faculty from many of our departments, all making discoveries that improve human health at a local and global scale.

# Building Disposable Surgical Robots

## PETER K. ALLEN

Professor of Computer Science

Minimally invasive, or laparoscopic, surgery has many advantages. By using several small incisions rather than one large cut, it reduces patient trauma and pain while speeding recovery and lowering costs. Yet it remains a niche procedure. Peter Allen, who likens it to pushing long sticks through small holes, sees several reasons why.

First, laparoscopic tools move counter-intuitively. Surgeons must move left to go right, or up to go down, for example. That means extensive training to learn to make precision cuts or tie sutures. The use of long, rigid sticks also limits the complexity of potential procedures. Finally, laparoscopy demands a high level of teamwork by surgeons inserting tools through several incisions.

Allen's solution is much simpler: small, intuitive robotic tools that provide a single surgeon with everything he or she needs to conduct a procedure through a single incision. He has already taken the first step, licensing a small robotic imaging system co-developed with Columbia physician Dennis Fowler. The device pans, tilts, and zooms to generate 2-D or 3-D images, and tracks surgical instruments automatically. The system has been tested in vivo on animals.

Building the device presented many engineering challenges. The package's high-resolution camera, bright lights, powerful motors, and control system had to fit through a single half-inch incision. "We want to create a robotic surgical platform that is so small, it can perform surgeries through natural orifices without an incision," said Allen. "That's the way surgery is moving. We could move it through the esophagus to the stomach, perform the operation, stitch it up, and take it out again."

To control costs, Allen opted for common off-the-shelf parts that he could buy through catalogs. He assembled the device from five-millimeter watch motors, small surveillance cameras, and LED lights. "The idea was to keep costs down," Allen said. "Ultimately, we want to drive component costs under a few hundred dollars so we can make it disposable."

Automated tracking is one of the device's most innovative features. Physicians manually box an image of whatever they want to track. The software keeps the camera aligned. "It's a challenging environment, with blood spills and occlusions. If the camera loses the target when it moves behind an organ, it does an intelligent search to reestablish its position," Allen said.

"What we have now is a robotic platform inside the body that can move a camera," he continued. "We want to extend that by adding more tools and creating a small, affordable platform for robotic surgery."

*B.A., Brown, 1971; M.S., University of Oregon, 1976; Ph.D., University of Pennsylvania, 1985*

Little is known about the biological causes for psychiatric disorders like schizophrenia and bipolar, which combined afflict an estimated 10 million people nationwide. Columbia researchers are working hard to change that by exploring the role of genetics from a multidisciplinary approach.

Dimitris Anastassiou's aim is to discover novel biological mechanisms responsible for psychiatric disorders. Given the limited success of identifying significant individual risk-conferring genetic variants, such as single mutations in DNA, Anastassiou says discovery of responsible interactions among multiple genetic variants may reveal new disease mechanisms.

Anastassiou and Maria Karayiorgou, professor of psychiatry and medical genetics at the Columbia University Medical Center, are principal investigators on a project that will identify single nucleotide polymorphisms (SNPs, pronounced "snips") that are jointly, rather than individually, associated with disease.

A SNP is a small genetic change that can occur within a person's DNA sequence. The genetic code is specified by the four nucleotide "letters" A (adenine), C (cytosine), T (thymine), and G (guanine). SNP variation occurs when a single nucleotide, such as an A, replaces one of the other three nucleotide letters—in this case C, T, or G.

An example of a SNP is the alteration of the DNA segment AAGGTTA to AAGTTTA, where the fourth letter in the first snippet, G, is replaced with a T. On average, SNPs occur in the human population more than one percent of the time, but because neighboring SNPs are statistically linked, researchers only need about one million of them to analyze our genomes.

The traditional approach looked only at individual SNPs. Anastassiou's research investigates the possibility that a person may be predisposed to a disease if two SNPs at different locations in the genome have the unusual letter combinations, rather than each one of them alone, a phenomenon called "synergy." There is a huge number (about a million squared) of "synergy" pairs of SNPs, resulting in significant computational and statistical challenges for this project. To perform this research, Anastassiou has a high-performance computer cluster containing 800 processors at his disposal.

"The aim is to discover the biological mechanisms responsible for psychiatric disorders," said Anastassiou. "Once such mechanisms are discovered, the ultimate vision is to develop drugs that would interfere with these mechanisms."

Anastassiou is a prominent leader in digital technology. His research has resulted in Columbia being the only university in a consortium that licenses MPEG-2, the technique used in all forms of digital television transmission, including DVDs, direct satellite TV, HDTV, digital cable systems, personal computer video, and interactive media.

*Dipl., National Technical University of Athens (Greece), 1974; M.S., University of California-Berkeley, 1975; Ph.D., UC Berkeley, 1979*

## *Finding the Mechanisms of Psychiatric Disorders*

# DIMITRIS ANASTASSIOU

Charles Batchelor Professor of Electrical Engineering

## *Trying to Grow Strong Cartilage*

# GERARD A. ATESHIAN

Professor of Mechanical Engineering
and of Biomedical Engineering

About 25 million U.S. adults suffer from osteoarthritis, a debilitating degeneration of the joints that can cause extreme pain and limit mobility. Cartilage, the thin, white connective tissue lining the ends of the bones, normally works as a cushion that redistributes stresses and reduces friction. But with osteoarthritis, it wears away. As a result, bones rub directly against each other. The problem is getting worse as the U.S. population gets older and heavier. (Extra weight puts more pressure on joints.)

Gerard Ateshian and his team are trying to understand how normal cartilage provides lubrication. That way, they can slow down the degeneration of the cartilage or come up with substitutes to repair worn joints. Cartilage is a highly hydrated tissue. In fact, nearly 90 percent of the cartilage located near the articular surface consists of water. This fluid pressurizes upon loading and supports most of the load transmitted across the joint. As a result, there is very little friction and wear of cartilage under normal conditions.

Traditionally lubrication has been an engineering topic. So this research, which applies engineering to a problem related to physiology, is a perfect marriage of engineering and medicine. The goal: to use tissue engineering techniques to grow artificial cartilage that's as strong and resilient as the native tissue, and equally able to reproduce low friction and wear.

In adulthood, the biological triggers that tell cartilage to regenerate are turned off. Therefore, human cartilage cannot restore itself once it has deteriorated in the joints. But fortunately, the body is unlikely to reject the lab-grown tissue since adult cartilage does not contain blood vessels.

As a result, it is unlikely that recipients of engineered cartilage would need anti-rejection drugs, providing a viable alternative to joint replacement surgery or debilitating pain. In collaboration with Clark Hung from biomedical engineering, Ateshian has applied insights gained from cartilage mechanics and lubrication studies to develop better and stronger engineered cartilage.

Ateshian is director of the Musculoskeletal Biomechanics Laboratory, which he founded in 1996. The lab's fundamental philosophy is that major scientific breakthroughs can be achieved in biomedical engineering by judiciously combining theoretical analyses with experimental studies. The lab's research efforts have expanded toward modeling of solute transport and growth processes in biological tissues, the development of computational tools that can address these mechanisms, and the extension of insights gained from musculoskeletal studies to cardiovascular tissues and reproductive cells.

*B.S., Columbia, 1986; M.S., Columbia, 1987; M.Phil., Columbia, 1990; Ph.D., Columbia, 1991*

In medical imaging, physicians need high-resolution images with high contrast, so they can see what's inside the body, down to the submillimeter level. Such images allow physicians to pinpoint treatment, so they can eradicate disease-causing tissue without harming healthy tissue that surrounds it. Researchers use varying techniques to create images of what's inside the body. Ultrasound techniques, for example, produce high-resolution images but sometimes with little contrast, so it's hard to discern healthy from unhealthy tissue. Optical tomography, which uses infrared light, produces images with high contrast but poor resolution. Photoacoustic tomography is a new multi-physics modality for obtaining high-contrast, high-resolution images of human tissues.

Guillaume Bal specializes in the field of mathematical inverse problems, working in the theoretical realm and collaborating with scientists and engineers who are exploring ways to develop new methods for imaging. He has developed mathematical models for several modalities of medical imaging, including optical tomography, photoacoustics, and several other novel multi-physics modalities combining ultrasound with optical or elastic waves. Photoacoustics is seen as a promising modality for obtaining accurate imaging of tissue in the human brain. His work also helps inform applications in earth science, where researchers work to create images of what exists below the surface of Earth.

Bal also develops mathematical models to analyze equations with random coefficients. He uses such equations for problems involving water or seismic waves moving through geologic formations, sound waves moving through the ocean, or light streaming through the atmosphere. These models look at phenomena at the macroscopic scale, which is more amenable to computations and parameter estimation. Such analyses are crucial in the field of uncertainty quantification with a wide array of applications ranging from dynamics in nuclear waste disposals to uncertainties in climate modeling.

Bal joined Columbia Engineering in 2001 as an assistant professor of applied mathematics. In the fall of 2003, he was a visiting scholar at the Institute for Pure and Applied Mathematics at the University of California-Los Angeles. Bal has also taught at the University of Chicago and was a postdoctoral research associate at Stanford University. He is the recipient of the 2011 Calderón prize. Other awards include an Alfred P. Sloan Fellowship in 2003 and an NSF Career Award, also in 2003.

*Diplôme, École Polytechnique (France), 1993; Ph.D., University of Paris VI (France), 1997*

*Sharpening Images Through Mathematics*

# GUILLAUME BAL

Professor of Applied Physics and Applied Mathematics

## *Delivering Drugs Faster*

# SCOTT A. BANTA

Associate Professor of
Chemical Engineering

People suffering from brain diseases and conditions ranging from traumatic brain injury to brain cancer to progressive brain disorders could be helped if therapeutic drugs could be easily delivered to the affected areas. The blood-brain barrier (BBB), composed of tightly interacting cells, acts as part of the body's defense system to block bacteria and other substances carried in the blood from invading the brain. It is extremely effective, which makes it very difficult to deliver important diagnostic and therapeutic agents to the brain.

Scott Banta is working toward solving this problem by using a biochemical engineering approach, creating specific cell penetrating peptides (SCPPs) that can cross the BBB and target specific brain cell populations. Banta and his research group are engineering new peptides that are specific for different cell and tissue types. The plasma membrane protects cells by regulating the access of molecules to the cellular cytoplasm. Only compounds within a narrow range of size, charge, and polarity are able to cross the membrane.

Using the process Directed Evolution, the Banta group is creating new SCPPs that are able to both target and penetrate specific cells. These peptide sequences can deliver therapeutic cargos, such as DNA, proteins, drugs, or other exogenous materials, to the targeted cellular cytoplasms.

Collaborating with Barclay Morrison of the Department of Biomedical Engineering, Banta is seeking to create SCPPs that are specific for different brain cell types. There is a narrow window of time following a brain injury where the targeted delivery of neurotrophic agents to injured cells could provide a significant benefit to the head-injured patient. In addition, delivery of neurotrophic factors via SCPPs could be beneficial in slowing down the progress of diseases such as Parkinson's, Alzheimer's, and Huntington's. This project has been supported by the National Institutes of Health and the National Science Foundation.

Banta's interests and expertise extend beyond the human body. In 2010, Banta was awarded an ARPA-E grant from the U.S. Department of Energy to launch new research on using genetic engineering to create renewable biofuels in collaboration with Alan West (Chemical Engineering) and Kartik Chandran (Earth and Environmental Engineering).

"We are going to use genetic engineering to incorporate a new metabolic pathway into an organism that is currently used for wastewater treatment," he said. "The bacterium, N. europaea, has the ability to grow on ammonia, oxygen and $CO_2$. We will engineer it to create isobutanol, which is a biofuel that is compatible with the existing transportation infrastructure. The cells will fix $CO_2$ from the atmosphere, and the ammonia will either be generated electrochemically, or it will be obtained during wastewater treatment."

*B.S., University of Maryland (Baltimore County), 1997; M.S., Rutgers University, 2000; Ph.D., Rutgers University, 2002*

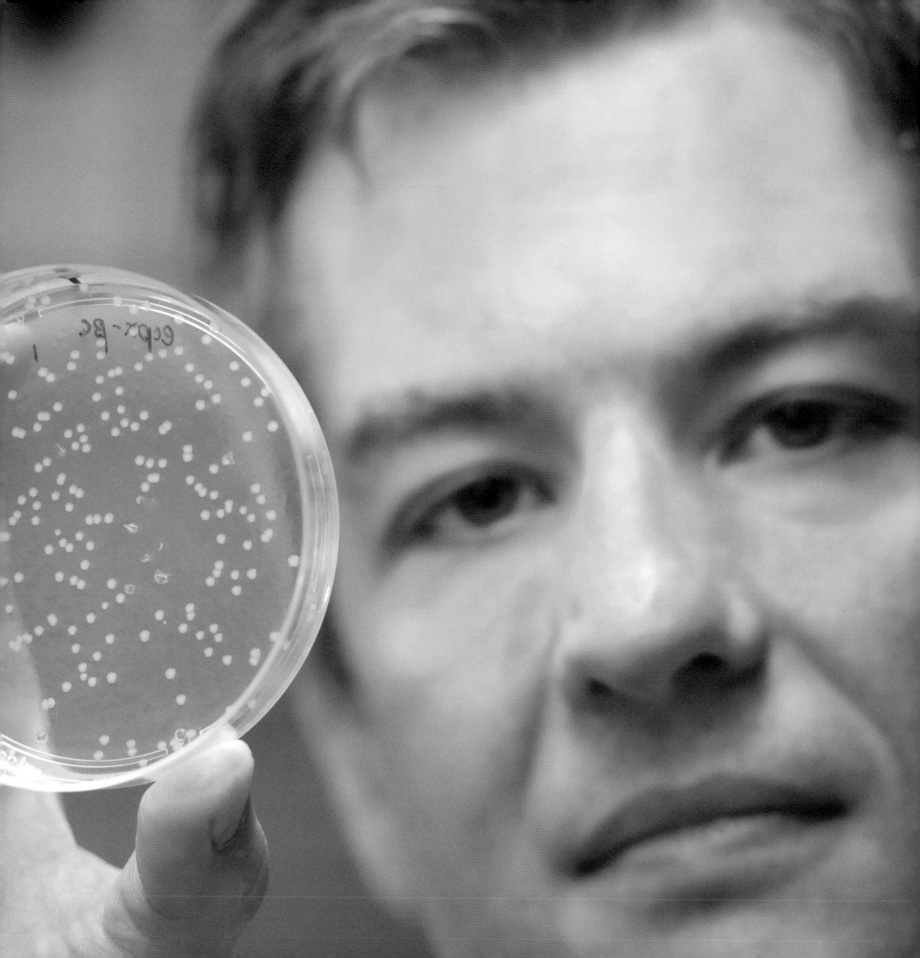

Malaria kills one million victims each year in tropical countries, most of them children. While drugs exist to combat the disease, the malaria parasite develops resistance to these drugs. An effort is now underway to harness a noninvasive electromagnetic-based treatment in the fight against this disease.

The electromagnetic field used in this innovative treatment is the same that is produced in lightning, is responsible for the Northern Lights, and also causes compasses to point in a north-south orientation. It is also found in high-frequency radio waves that bounce from one part of the world to another via antennas to phone networks, TV pictures, and the Internet.

Understanding electromagnetic fields allows scientists to develop smaller and more powerful antennas useful in emergency communication devices and portable radar, or those made flexible with new alloy materials and applied to implantable medical devices. Electromagnetics also has a direct application at the biological level—as in the treatment of parasitic diseases like malaria.

Malaria is caused by a parasite that is transmitted from one human to another by the bite of mosquitoes. In humans, the malaria parasite travels to the liver, where it invades a red blood cell. There, it consumes the cell's hemoglobin and produces hemozoin, an iron crystal, as a waste product. It then divides into many more daughter parasites that invade other red blood cells. Researchers now understand that the iron crystal remains with the parasite within the host cell. By applying a suitably designed magnetic field, the iron crystals can be made to agitate, rotate, and churn, destroying the parasite before it can multiply further.

Paul Diament is the lead inventor of the magnetic resonance method of treating the malaria parasite, and is working with biologists at the Columbia Medical Center in pursuing this application. He is an eminent researcher in electromagnetics and wave propagation. His teaching and research focus includes microwaves, antennas, optics, radiation statistics, plasmas, wave interactions, relativistic electron beams, and transient electromagnetic phenomena. Along with biomedical applications, his research interests include attempts to make mutual coupling among antennas beneficial rather than detrimental, potentially achieving smaller antenna size.

Diament is a member of the Institute of Electrical and Electronics Engineers, the American Physical Society, the Optical Society of America, Tau Beta Pi, Eta Kappa Nu, and Sigma Xi.

*B.S., Columbia, 1960; M.S., Columbia, 1961; Ph.D., Columbia, 1963*

# Employing Electromagnetics to Treat Malaria

# PAUL DIAMENT

Professor of Electrical Engineering

## *Predicting Bone Strength, Preventing Osteoporosis*

# X. EDWARD GUO

Professor of Biomedical Engineering

Ten million Americans suffer from osteoporosis, a gradual weakening of the bones that can lead to fractures, loss of mobility and independence, and depression. Another 18 million suffer from low bone mass. No cure exists for either condition. Doctors simply tell patients to consume enough calcium and vitamin D, to do weight-bearing exercise, and to avoid smoking. Sometimes they also prescribe medications, including bisphosphonates (Fosamax, Actonel, and Boniva), selective estrogen receptor modulators (Evista), or hormones such as parathyroid hormone (Forteo). But all come with side effects, and none are free. The only bone builder on the market, Forteo, costs $8,000 a year and requires daily shots for two years.

X. Edward Guo, director of Columbia's Bone Bioengineering Laboratory, is trying to figure out how to prevent and treat osteoporosis from both engineering analysis and biological perspectives. To do so, he and his team are analyzing high-resolution 3-D images of bone from both laboratory samples and non-invasive patients' images to figure out how to better predict fracture risk in patients and monitor efficacy of anti-osteoporosis treatment. With several multi-million-dollar grants supported by the National Institutes of Health (NIH) and working with endocrinologists Drs. Elizabeth Shane and John Bilezikian at Columbia University's College of Physicians and Surgeons, and Dr. Felix Wehrli at the University of Pennsylvania, they have developed novel imaging analysis and modeling techniques to identify microstructural deteriorations in bone and have translated these technologies in clinical assessments of osteoporosis. Guo and his team also plan to use their knowledge to better understand osteoporosis and bone loss experienced by astronauts in outer space.

During the last two years alone, Guo, as principal investigator, has received four new NIH grants totaling $6.3 million to support his innovative bone bioengineering research. These include a highly competitive NIH Challenge Grant, which was ranked in the top two percent in the review process. This two-year $915,108 grant will support Guo's work in testing the novel hypothesis that an osteocyte network may function in a similar way as a neuronal network and plays an important role in mechanical memory. The current yearly research expenditure in Guo's laboratory is over $2 million, one of the top funded bioengineering laboratories in the country.

In the future, Guo and his team hope that doctors can prescribe drugs that would help mature bone cells recruit more bone-forming cells and snub the bone-destroying ones. Such drugs would be a boon to an aging population. After all, women over 50 can lose as much as 20 percent of their bone mass around menopause. Perhaps someday everyone could get drugs at a younger age to prevent later bone loss.

*B.S., Peking University, 1984; M.S., Harvard-MIT, 1990; Ph.D., Harvard-MIT, 1994*

Artificial limbs are being used with increasing frequency to replace missing body parts, such as arms and legs. Typically, patients need them because of infection, circulatory disease, congenital defects, accidents, cancer, or, increasingly, war-related injuries. Right now, nearly four million Americans have a prosthetic device.

Henry Hess and his collaborators are working with molecules to figure out how to build artificial muscles that are as good as the real thing. In a system that's far more efficient than anything manmade, the human body takes glucose and uses the sugar to power muscles that enable people to move and talk. But if Hess and his team can figure out how to duplicate Mother Nature, they can make better prostheses, and ultimately, better car engines, too. Imagine a car engine that worked like a big, artificial muscle.

The team is also working on novel "smart dust" biosensors, which may be used to detect cancer earlier or detect pathogens like anthrax in the environment. In these devices, the artificial muscles play the role of miniature pumps that collect and transport the molecules of interest.

Hess, who was raised in East Germany, joined the Columbia Engineering faculty in 2009 and teaches Tissue Engineering. The course introduces students to the field of biomaterials, and in particular to the many factors important in the selection, design, and development of biomaterials for clinical applications.

He directs Columbia's Hess Laboratory on Nanobiotechnology – Synthetic Biology. His lab focuses on the engineering applications of nanoscale motors. Such microscopic motors with the ability to create forces and drive active movement with high efficiency enable new approaches to a wide range of nanotechnologies, including biosensing, drug delivery, molecular assembly, and active materials.

"We have successfully utilized motor proteins in synthetic environments for the controlled transport of nanoscale cargo," said Hess, "and continue to advance the design of such hybrid bionanodevices and materials.

"The hybrid approach has the advantage that techniques, materials, and devices unique to either biology or technology can be merged into a revolutionary combination. Applications particularly suited to hybrid systems are found in medicine and biotechnology, where biocompatibility is critical and the environmental conditions are favorable for biological nanomachines."

His other research interests include engineering at the molecular scale, in particular the design of active nanosystems incorporating biomolecular motors, the study of active self-assembly, and the investigation of protein-resistant polymer coatings.

*B.S., Technical University Clausthal (Germany), 1993; M.Sc., Technical University Berlin, 1996; Ph.D., Free University Berlin, 1999*

*Building Tiny, Muscle-Like Engines*

# HENRY HESS

Associate Professor of Biomedical Engineering

## *Imaging Diseases in New Light*

# ANDREAS H. HIELSCHER

Professor of Biomedical Engineering, of Electrical Engineering, and of Radiology

Rheumatoid arthritis (RA) is an autoimmune disease that affects nearly 20 million people worldwide, striking young people as well as old, causing pain, stiffness, and swelling of the joints. Early diagnosis and treatment can slow or prevent joint damage and increase the likelihood of leading an active and full life.

Leading an international team of engineers, scientists, and physicians from Germany and the United States, Andreas Hielscher has developed a 3-D optical tomographic (OT) imaging system that displays disease activity in joints. "Shining light through the finger allows us to see the disease before X-rays can find any changes," explained Hielscher, showing the latest results from a recent clinical trial.

In another project that relies on the same harmless light transmission measurements, members of his laboratory have built an optical imaging system for the diagnosis of breast cancer. Breast cancer afflicts one in nine women during their lifetime and is the second leading cause of cancer deaths in women. Hielscher's patented imaging technology has been licensed by a New York company and promising clinical pilot studies using the new imager are underway.

Hielscher also employs OT imaging to localize green fluorescent proteins (GFPs), developed by Columbia's 2009 Nobel laureate Martin Chalfie. GFPs and their derivatives make it possible to see and monitor cell and tissue behaviors during development, including observation of cancerous tumors in vivo. Hielscher and his colleagues use GFP to study the growth of cancers in the stomach, liver, and brain. Most recently, he is applying this technology to monitor drug effects in difficult-to-treat early childhood cancers, such as neuroblastoma and Wilms tumors.

Before joining Columbia Engineering in 2001, Hielscher was a postdoctoral fellow at Los Alamos National Laboratory and was on the faculty at the State University of New York Downstate Medical Center. Now he directs Columbia's Biophotonics and Optical Radiology Laboratory, which works towards establishing optical tomography as a viable biomedical imaging modality. To this end, Hielscher's team is developing state-of-the-art imaging hardware and software that provide 3-D distributions of physiologically relevant parameters in biomedical systems. The work of the laboratory is supported, among others, by the National Institute of Arthritis and Musculoskeletal and Skin Diseases, the National Institute of Biomedical Imaging and Bioengineering, the National Cancer Institute, and the New York State Foundation for Science, Technology and Innovation.

*B.S., University of Hannover (Germany), 1987; M.S., University of Hannover, 1991; Ph.D., Rice University, 1995*

Light Detection Unit

- Detection Board

1 Detection Channel

Gain Stage (TIA)

Gain Stage (PGA)

Anti-aliasing low-pass filter

2 ADC chips

Gain Bit Logic

Voltage Regulators

W alk into any clinical research lab and you will undoubtedly find one or more microscopes. The problem with conventional microscopes, however, is they can only show images of thin slices of dead tissue or cells in a dish. It takes a special kind of instrument to produce images from inside the living body, which is exactly the kind that Elizabeth Hillman is building.

"It is a significant technical challenge to build imaging systems capable of studying cellular or molecular processes in living organisms," said Hillman. "You need devices that can image very fast and in 3-D and that show you lots of different things at once. It's a complex problem, one that forces you to think about physiology and physics at the same time."

One such optical imaging technique is microscopy to investigate the brain, particularly the relationship between blood flow and neuronal activity. Functional magnetic resonance imaging (fMRI), one of the most ubiquitous tools used to investigate neuronal activity, relies on detecting subtle changes in blood flow in the brain.

"The problem is, we really don't understand why these changes in blood flow occur," said Hillman. "Even the best neuroscience textbooks only devote a page or so to blood flow in the brain."

Hillman's work is beginning to tease out this complex process, improving our fundamental understanding of how the brain functions, and also raising the possibility that fMRIs will one day prove even more useful and revealing. In another project, she is developing a technique that permits her to create images of the organs in live lab mice, which she hopes will allow pharmaceutical companies and researchers to study diseases and treatments without sacrificing large numbers of animals. She has also developed techniques to make images of living human skin and is using optical imaging to investigate how the electrical activity in cardiac tissue changes during a heart attack.

Because all of these measure different wavelengths of light, none require the heavy shielding or careful dose monitoring necessary in radiologic imaging. Hillman hopes that ultimately many of her imaging tools will prove useful in the clinic and as laboratory research tools. She is quick to point out, however, that she does not expect her techniques to entirely replace MRIs.

"Optical imaging isn't going to be the next MRI," she said. "MRIs do some things well, but they can't tell you things like how bad the burn on your arm is or whether you have good blood flow in the back of your eye. Our systems can."

*M.Sci., University College London, 1998; Ph.D., University College London, 2002*

*Unlocking the Brain's Secrets*

# ELIZABETH M. C. HILLMAN

Assistant Professor of Biomedical Engineering and of Radiology

## *Reprogramming Cells to Boost Immunity*

# JAMES C. HONE

Associate Professor of
Mechanical Engineering

Nearly four decades after it first emerged, AIDS is still a deadly disease, killing more than 25 million people worldwide. More than 2.5 million people a year are newly infected with HIV (human immunodeficiency virus), a virus that almost always leads to AIDS (acquired immunodeficiency syndrome).

HIV is one of many diseases, like cancer and other viral and bacterial illnesses, that attacks the immune system, the body's defense against infection and disease. Even for healthy people with a normal immune system, improving that system would make an individual healthier.

James Hone and his team want to take some key immune-system cells and genetically modify and immunize them outside of the body. A small percentage of people are born with certain genes that make them immune to HIV. Ideally, scientists would harvest their good HIV genes. Then they would modify other people's genes to look the same way. They would grow a supply of these HIV-resistant genes and put them back into the human body. It's a potential alternative to shots and traditional vaccinations.

Hone's goal is to create the basic tools needed to engineer the immune system outside the body, and then to put it back inside the body.

Hone, whose work focuses on carbon nanotubes (CNTs), nanoelectromechanical systems (NEMS) and nanoscale structures with applications in cellular and molecular biology, solar and fuel cells, electronics, and sensors, teaches Carbon Nanotube Science and Technology to graduate students.

Hone is also working with IBM and Professors Ken Shepard and Tony Heinz—as well as two professors in the Department of Chemistry—on a project funded by the U.S. Department of Defense to develop field-effect transistors using graphene to determine if they are more efficient than III-V and silicon semiconductor technologies. Recent research by Hone and Columbia Engineering professor Jeffrey Kysar has shown that graphene is the strongest material ever measured and holds great promise for the development of nanoscale devices.

In addition, Hone is the co-investigator of a team led by researchers at the Mt. Sinai School of Medicine. The group won six million dollars over five years to look at how cells interact to form tissue in the kidneys.

"The specific thing we're looking at is part of the kidney that acts as a filter," said Hone. "You have cells that come together like interlocking fingers. The question is: What is it that gets cells to do that?"

Hone's lab will build microscopic scaffolds—three-dimensional structures that will allow scientists to artificially control the environment for cells to begin to form these tissues.

*B.S., Yale, 1990; Ph.D., University of California-Berkeley, 1998*

Arrhythmogenic right ventricular cardiomyopathy (ARVC), which affects one in 5,000 people worldwide, is a leading cause of sudden death. With this disorder, fibro-fatty tissue replaces healthy heart muscle, and the heart's beating becomes uncoordinated. As a result, the heart can't pump well.

With ARVC as their inspiration, Hayden Huang and his team are figuring out how heart cells respond to physical stresses. ARVC can be caused by genetic mutations that affect proteins which link cells together. Huang is testing whether changes in these proteins interfere with how cells stick together and send signals, making the heart less able to withstand the stresses associated with constant pumping and ultimately damaging its tissue.

To do so, he looks at factors such as cell stiffness (how hard it is to deform the cell), cell adhesion (how well cells stick to surfaces or to each other), cell structure (what the cell is made of and how the components are arranged), and cell response (how cells react to physical stresses like being stretched).

Once Huang and his team unravel the mystery of how heart cells work and how ARVC progresses, they can help develop a diagnostic test to determine who suffers from the condition, which can be asymptomatic for a long time, and formulate a treatment to repair or prevent changes in the heart muscle. They also want to solve the mystery of why ARVC primarily affects the right heart when the left heart apparently does most of the heavy work. This research will help scientists better understand the differences between the two sides of the heart and heart function in general.

Huang teaches the Tissue and Molecular Engineering Laboratory and Fluid Biomechanics. He came to Columbia from a position as associate biophysicist and instructor of medicine at Brigham and Women's Hospital, Harvard Medical School.

Huang directs the Biomechanics and Mechanotransduction Laboratory, which studies cellular mechanics and mechanotransduction in cells and cell clusters. While the current scope of the projects are focused on the cardiovascular system, the techniques and insight are relevant to any number of cell and tissue systems.

"The current interest of our laboratory is in determining how cell-cell interactions, especially at the junctions where cells make contact, influence cellular mechanical behavior," Huang said. "Several techniques are used for studying cell-cell interactions, including fluorescence microscopy (wide-field and two-photon), time-lapse microscopy, cell stretching, magnetic micromanipulation, and physical micromanipulation (pipette aspiration, for example)."

*B.S., Johns Hopkins University, 1995; S.M., Massachusetts Institute of Technology, 1997; Ph.D., MIT, 2002*

## Understanding How Heart Cells Work

# HAYDEN HUANG

Assistant Professor of Biomedical Engineering

## Cushioning the Blow of Joint Pain

# CLARK T. HUNG

Professor of Biomedical Engineering

For many people, stiff, aching joints are the first sign of age. For more than 20 million Americans, it is also the first sign of osteoarthritis, a disease characterized by loss of the lubricating and load-bearing tissue that lines the joints and that is behind an estimated $128 billion each year in health care costs and lost productivity.

"Since the lifespan of most joint replacements is limited typically to 15 or 20 years, restoring joint function with living tissue is almost always preferred," said Clark Hung.

The trouble is, that this tissue, known as articular cartilage, is made up of a network of chondrocyte cells embedded in a stiff matrix of collagen and other substances that is subjected to daily, repetitive mechanical deformation and a lack of nutrient-rich blood flow. Because of this, damaged tissue does not heal easily and replacement cartilage with natural properties has proved difficult to grow in a lab. Until now.

By growing chondrocytes under mechanical loads that mimic the conditions inside joints, Hung and Gerard Ateshian, professor of mechanical engineering and biomedical engineering, have been able to culture tissue that is almost identical to the body's own. The tissue loading helps transport nutrients to the chondrocytes. As a result, their engineered tissue grows faster, is more durable, and, they anticipate, will provide better restoration of the joint.

Hung has so far succeeded in growing bovine and canine articular cartilage and foresees a near future in which human cartilage will routinely be produced in the lab using his method. Good news for anyone who plans on growing older.

In August of 2010, the American Society of Mechanical Engineers (ASME) named Hung to its most recent class of fellows.

"Becoming a fellow in ASME is particularly fitting," Hung says, "as I came to Columbia to build a research program in cell and tissue engineering that capitalized on the institution's long-standing strengths in the area of biomechanics."

Hung serves on the ASME's executive committee of the bioengineering division and he is an associate editor for its *Journal of Biomechanical Engineering*. The organization has more than 100,000 members. Hung joins the group's select group of fellows, which includes just 3,012 members.

Hung is also a member of Columbia's Bioreactor Core faculty that includes Gordana Vunjak-Novakovic, Elisa Konofagou, Helen Lu, and Jeremy Mao. Their group is funded by the National Institutes of Health to support advanced research into functional tissue engineering, stem cells, and the study of disease.

*Sc.B., Brown, 1990; M.S.E., University of Pennsylvania, 1992; Ph.D., University of Pennsylvania, 1995*

Osteoporosis is a major public health threat for more than half of all Americans. An estimated 10 million already have the disease and another 34 million are at high risk of developing porous bones, shortening lives, and increasing health care costs.

Christopher Jacobs is working to unlock a stem cell mystery that could provide significant advances in the treatment for osteoporosis. He has received a $1 million New York State grant to research stem cell behavior related to the condition.

Osteoporosis occurs when bone marrow stem cells fail to produce bone-forming osteoblasts in sufficient numbers. Very little is known, however, about the cellular mechanism by which bone marrow stem cells sense and respond to changes in their mechanical loading environment.

Jacobs' Cell and Molecular Biomechanics Laboratory will determine whether a novel cellular sensor, the primary cilium, is responsible for the stem cell's ability to sense mechanical loading. His lab was one of the first to show that primary cilia act as mechanical sensors in bone cells. The project will characterize the ability of transplanted stem cells to home in on sites of bone loading and form new bone and then determine whether the stem cells retain this ability if their primary cilia are first disrupted.

"If the hypothesis is proven to be true, it will be a breakthrough in skeletal mechanobiology and suggest approaches for new anti-osteoporosis drugs," Jacobs said. "It will also be a significant advance in relating primary cilia dysfunction to human disease."

Jacobs describes the overall focus of his lab is to understand how cells sense and respond to changes in their mechanical environment.

"Although a wide range of tissues are known to be regulated by physical signals, outside of sensory mechanisms, the cellular apparatus responsible for the initial 'mechanotransduction' event is poorly understood," he said. "Our group is primarily focused on mechanosensitivity of bone cells as it relates to osteoporosis, stress fractures, and disuse bone loss associated with spinal cord injury and space flight."

The group's active projects include Mechanotransduction in Bone via Oscillatory Fluid Flow; Mechanosensitive Primary Cilia in Osteogenic Differentiation of Stem Cells Due to Loading; Primary Cilia as Mechanosensors in Bone; and Primary Cilia Mechanics and Mechanobiology.

Jacobs was an assistant professor in the Department of Orthopaedic Surgery at Pennsylvania State University and an associate professor in the Department of Mechanical Engineering at Stanford University before coming to Columbia.

*B.S., Washington University, 1988; M.S., Stanford, 1989; Ph.D., Stanford, 1994*

*Combating Bone Loss*

# CHRISTOPHER R. JACOBS

Associate Professor of
Biomedical Engineering

# Creating Personalized DNA Chips for Everybody

## JINGYUE JU

Samuel Ruben-Peter G. Viele Professor of
Chemical Engineering

Genes play an important role in nearly every disease—a major reason why scientists spent $1 billion sequencing the entire DNA of one individual for the Human Genome Project. This astronomical cost of decoding the code of life makes mapping the three billion base pairs of DNA in each person seem like a pipe dream. However, advances in science and engineering made by Columbia scientists should make this dream come true in the near future.

Jingyue Ju and his team are developing revolutionary technologies to dramatically reduce the cost of DNA sequencing so that each person's genome can be routinely decoded on a chip the size of a credit card for just $1,000. Ju co-invented the fluorescent labeling technology that made the Human Genome Project possible. The new sequencing technology uses different colors of fluorescent dyes to label the four letters of the genetic alphabet for decoding on a chip.

Such a chip should be possible in a few years, said Ju, who directs the Center for Genome Technology and Biomolecular Engineering at Columbia and who collaborates with a group of interdisciplinary scientists including chemistry professor Nicholas Turro on this research. Working with Nobel Laureate Eric Kandel and Professor Ian Lipkin at the Columbia University Medical Center, Ju and his team are using the new genome technologies to study the genetic networks for long-term memory, and to rapidly and accurately detect pathogens.

In the future, every newborn could get his entire genome sequenced on a tiny chip. With this information, doctors could easily look up each person's genetic predisposition to various diseases and could tailor their medical advice. This technology would help doctors better prevent, diagnose, and treat diseases based on each person's genetic profile. It would also make it easier for pharmaceutical companies to develop personalized drugs for diseases like depression and breast cancer.

Drugs for anti-depression, for example, currently only work in about half the patients. With personalized gene chips, doctors would know in advance which drugs would work (and not work) for each patient.

The National Institutes of Health has supported Ju with a three-year, $1.8 million grant for his proposal, "Single Molecule DNA Sequencing by Fluorescent Nucleotide Terminators." His project aims to sequence a human genome with high accuracy and speed at a low cost, an achievement that would be critical to the emerging field of personalized medicine.

*B.S., Inner Mongolia University, 1985; M.S., Chinese Academy of Sciences, 1988; Ph.D., University of Southern California, 1993*

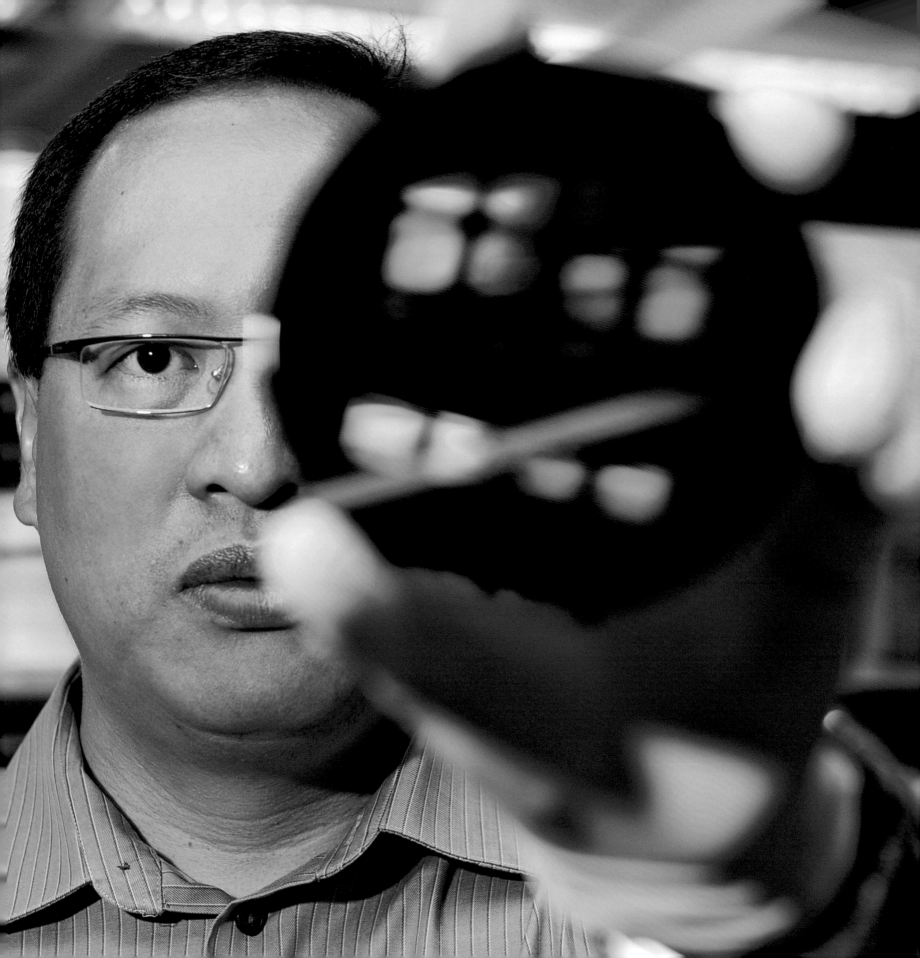

The immune system's ability to detect and counter infectious agents is among the body's most remarkable—and welcome—capabilities. Durable as this response may seem in the face of internal and external invasions, it is extremely intricate, and small disruptions can have large implications to the body's response.

However, the immune system sometimes needs help. Lance Kam seeks to improve immune response by combining cellular and molecular biology with technology adapted from the microelectronics industry. These techniques may one day allow doctors to retrain a patient's immune system to combat cancer, treat autoimmune diseases, and prevent transplant rejection.

Their research has shown that T lymphocytes, key regulators of the body's ability to recognize previous threats and adapt to new ones, respond in specific ways to patterns of proteins and other biomolecules they come in contact with. By recreating these patterns at a scale as fine as tens of nanometers, Kam's group, together with colleagues in an NIH-sponsored Nanomedicine Development Center, has been able to manipulate the activation of T lymphocytes to combat specific threats.

One of the threats of particular interest is cancer. A normally functioning immune system is able to weed out cancer cells that periodically arise in the body. Over time, people appear to lose that ability, making us more susceptible to cancerous mutations as we age. Identifying the patterns that produce cancer-fighting T lymphocytes would allow doctors to produce more of them and effectively retrain a patient's immune system to fight the disease naturally.

Kam directs Columbia University's Microscale Biocomplexity Laboratory, which focuses on understanding proper development, function, and repair of biological systems at scales of the intercellular level (tens of micrometers and hours) reaching down to those of supramolecular assemblies (tens of nanometers and milliseconds).

"Micro- and nano-scale systems have an ever increasing role in biomedical science and engineering," said Kam. "My research group focuses on the use of these systems to understand how cells read and respond to the complex presentation of cues in their extracellular environment.

"We focus particularly on the use of fabrication approaches, which offer a level of control over multiple spatial scales that is not possible through traditional molecular and self-assembly approaches; these are the scales at which cells operate and the realm of an increasing range of biological phenomena."

Kam did postdoctoral research in chemistry at Stanford University prior to coming to Columbia Engineering.

*B.S., Washington University, 1991; M.S., University of Hawaii, 1994; Ph.D., Rensselaer Polytechnic Institute, 1999*

## Engineering the Body's Defenses

# LANCE C. KAM

Assistant Professor of
Biomedical Engineering

## *Delivering Drugs to the Right Place*

# JEFFREY T. KOBERSTEIN

Percy K. and Vida L.W. Hudson
Professor of Chemical Engineering

More than a quarter of U.S. adults live with chronic pain caused by both injuries and a host of diseases. In fact, this physical suffering is the leading complaint of older Americans—and the reason one in five of them takes pain killers. (Back pain leads the list, followed by headaches.) Unfortunately, in 70 percent of cases, medication does not work. As a result, patients miss work and increase health care costs by frequently visiting doctors.

Jeffrey Koberstein and his team are figuring out how to deliver pain relief drugs to the right place. With Richard Ambron from the Columbia University Medical Center, they are creating tiny, easy-to-swallow particles—known as drug-delivery vehicles—that would carry medication to its target. Ordinarily, a mass of nerve cells, called ganglia, shuttles a pain signal to the central nervous system. For them to send this pain signal, they need to create a certain protein. If scientists can stop production of this protein, they can prevent the transmission of pain. They stop production of this protein through a process called RNA interference, which helps control which genes are active and how active they are.

In the future, Koberstein and his team plan to use their "molecular toolbox" to help deliver other drugs. As a result, they should be able to more efficiently and cost effectively treat patients with many conditions and diseases.

Koberstein has also collaborated with colleagues Jingyue Ju and Nicholas Turro on a project that has firmly established the feasibility of using novel fluorescent nucleotides, surface chemistry, and molecular engineering for DNA sequencing on a chip.

"This is a key step to advancing the field of DNA sequencing by synthesis through fluorescence imaging or by single molecule detection," said Ju.

Koberstein's other research interests lie in developing fundamental relationships between molecular structure and properties of polymers and other soft matter, and particularly how polymer surfaces and interfaces can be designed from a molecular perspective. The goal of this work can be generally considered as gaining a molecular design capability to change the chemical composition of a polymer surface through external controls.

Koberstein is a former department chair and is currently co-director of a National Science Foundation IGERT grant on Soft Materials. In 2006, he was awarded the Charles M.A. Stine Award of the American Institute of Chemical Engineers, Division of Materials Science and Engineering, its highest award. He taught at Princeton University and the University of Connecticut before coming to Columbia Engineering in 2000.

*B.S., University of Wisconsin, 1974; Ph.D., University of Massachusetts, 1979*

A study in the *New England Journal of Medicine* showed that two-thirds of adults underwent medical tests in the last few years that exposed them to radiation and, in some cases, a higher risk of cancer. Elisa Konofagou is pioneering new uses for an imaging technology that is radiation free, less expensive than CT scans and MRIs, yet just as effective: ultrasound. Moreover, she is going beyond ultrasound's traditional application as a diagnostic tool, using it to treat diseases like cancer, Alzheimer's, and Parkinson's.

In the area of oncology, Konofagou is developing a tool that could identify and destroy tumors without the need for surgery. Her technology, called harmonic motion imaging, uses ultrasound to probe soft tissue in search of abnormal growths.

"You're basically knocking on different parts of the organ until you detect a different amplitude in one particular location," she said.

She has found that ultrasound can distinguish benign from cancerous tumors and that its beam can be aimed with extreme precision to detect and ablate, or destroy, the abnormality. If proven effective, the technique could be used in inoperable cancers of the brain, prostate, pancreas, and kidneys.

In the area of neurology, Konofagou is deploying ultrasound to temporarily open the blood-brain barrier to help treat patients with diseases like Alzheimer's, Parkinson's, and ALS. Currently, physicians have few good options when it comes to treating these patients. Their choices include direct injection deep into the brain or IV drugs, which flow across the entire brain, not just the diseased areas, causing severe side effects in some cases.

The technique Konofagou has pioneered sends ultrasound waves through a millimeter-specific brain region and the intact skull, causing that part of the blood-brain barrier to open. Medicine would be injected by IV and would reach only its intended target.

Konofagou has also deployed ultrasound in the field of cardiology. Konofagou's myocardial elastography can identify and localize the portions of the heart that trigger atrial fibrillation. Following diagnosis, the same technique can be used to evaluate treatment, such as after using radiation-free ablation to restore the heart's natural rhythm. In the future, she hopes her innovations may allow for an inexpensive, noninvasive screening test for heart disease.

"I believe ultrasound can do anything," she said. Each day, her research is bringing that statement closer and closer to reality.

*B.S., Université de Paris VI (France), 1992; M.S., University of London, 1993; Ph.D., University of Houston, 1999*

## Treating Tumors Without Radiation

# ELISA E. KONOFAGOU

Associate Professor of Biomedical Engineering and of Radiology

# Analyzing 3-D Video Ultrasound of the Heart

# ANDREW F. LAINE

Professor of
Biomedical Engineering
and of Radiology

Heart disease is the nation's leading cause of death. About 80 million Americans suffer from at least one form of cardiovascular disease, and each year about 900,000 people die from it. To understand stages of this disease, Andrew Laine and his team are analyzing real-time video 3-D ultrasounds of the heart. Ultrasound echoes are high-frequency sound waves that bounce off tissues and can be converted into sonograms.

"Recent advances in real-time 3-D ultrasound (RT3-D or 4-D) imaging give us a wealth of dynamic information captured in seconds over the entire cardiac cycle," said Laine. "With the proper analytic tools it can provide a novel and clinically effective 3-D strain-and-torsion measuring tool that will allow cardiologists to routinely measure cardiac wall motion and strain with reliable accuracy."

The modality of real-time 3-D ultrasound imaging has many advantages since it is portable, non-invasive, and doesn't require exposure to X-rays as in CT imaging systems. Cardiac MRIs by contrast are far more expensive and lack real-time processing. By using real-time 3-D ultrasound technology for both screening and treatment of heart disease, we can reduce health care costs while improving the quality of patient outcome.

Ultimately, Laine and his colleagues will develop software that will be able to measure the strain on the muscles of the heart in real-time 3-D and localize infarcted or ischemic tissue that could be salvaged by intervention and thus recognize at an early stage what tissue is damaged or at risk.

"By visualizing and evaluating strain exerted by functioning heart muscle comprising the cardiac wall using 4-D ultrasound," he said, "we hope to detect previously undiscovered cardiac myopathies, as well as more subtle changes over time that will allow us to better quantify cardiac function."

Laine, who received his D.Sc. degree from Washington University in computer science, teaches courses on Medical Image Analysis to graduate students and Wavelet Applications in Medicine to undergraduate students. He serves as vice president of publications for IEEE Engineering in Medicine and Biology Society (EMBS), the largest professional society in the field, and is chair of the Technical Committee on Biomedical Imaging and Image Processing for IEEE EMBS.

Laine holds two patents related to 3-D processing of ultrasound, has authored over 300 peer-reviewed papers, and has graduated over 20 doctoral students in the field of medical image analysis. He is a fellow of the IEEE and fellow of the American Institute of Medical and Biological Engineering.

*B.S., Cornell, 1977; M.S., University of Connecticut, 1980; M.S., Washington University (St. Louis), 1983; D.Sc., Washington University, 1989*

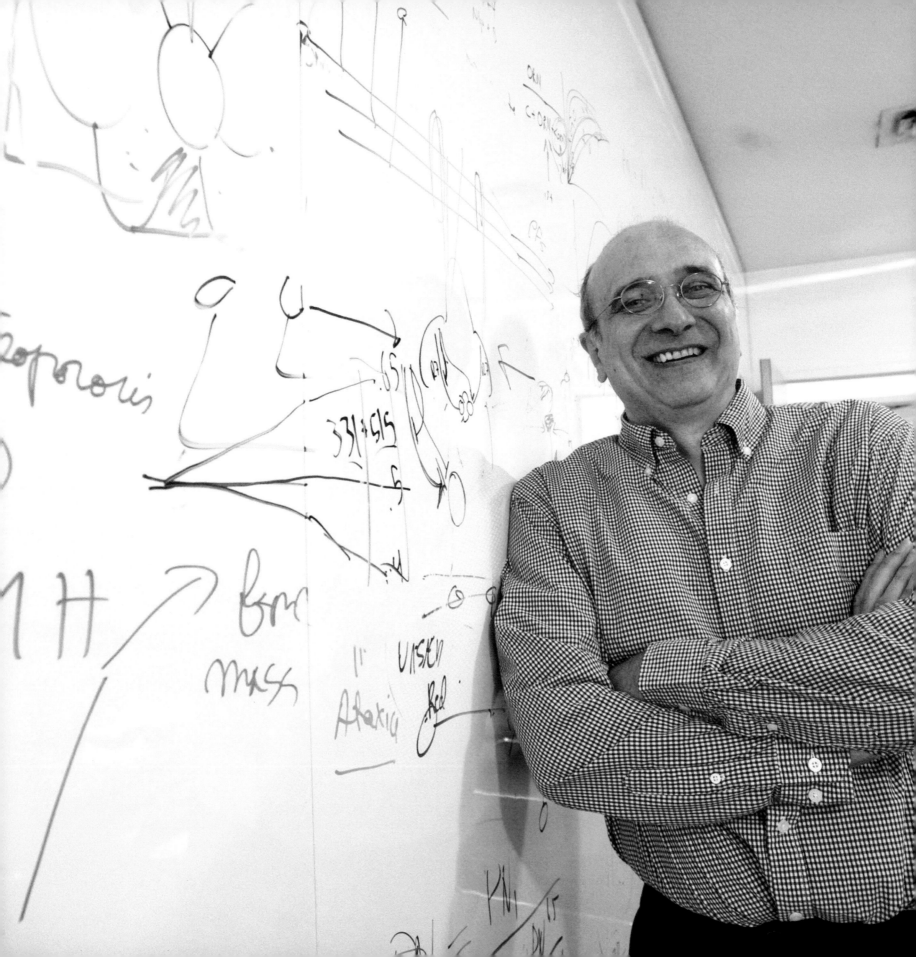

Working with fruit flies, Aurel A. Lazar and his team are trying to understand how insects' brains discriminate one smell from another. The brain gets information as "spike trains"—brief electrical pulses that respond to a stimulus, such as a smell. Lazar is working on how a fruit fly's brain acquires and processes such smells.

Building on a well-developed genetic understanding of the anatomy of its olfactory system, he uses time encoding machines—computer models of olfactory sensory systems—to represent odors as "spike trains." He is investigating the sense of smell as a memory-based, odor-object recognition system.

Lazar is the founder and leader of the Bionet Group of the Department of Electrical Engineering. The group is an interdisciplinary research team bringing together faculty and students from the biological and engineering sciences to address questions that arise in the field of computational neuroscience. The group is an active and integral part of the world class Columbia neuroscience community.

Lazar's team has developed a novel in vivo experimental setup with precise and reproducible delivery of airborne stimuli to fruit flies that has enabled them to map out the process of odor encoding in olfactory sensory neurons. This research is performed in collaboration with Richard Axel, University Professor, in The Axel Laboratory.

In addition, the team is pursuing the implementation of massively parallel models of sensory systems in vision and hearing. The team has demonstrated for the first time the faithful recovery of natural video (movies, animation) and auditory scenes (speech, sounds) encoded with neural circuits. This has the potential to enhance next-generation artificial retinal and cochlear implants.

Lazar describes his research interests as being "at the intersection of computational, theoretical, and systems neuroscience. The computational/theoretical work builds on methods of communications/networking, information theory, machine learning, nonlinear dynamical systems, signal processing, and systems identification. The experimental work employs methods of genetics, neurophysiology, and systems biology."

Lazar teaches Computational Neuroscience: Circuits in the Brain, an advanced undergraduate/graduate introductory-level course, along with follow-up graduate-level courses. He joined Columbia Engineering in 1980.

*B.S., Bucharest Polytechnical Institute, 1971; M.S., Darmstadt Institute of Technology, 1976; Ph.D., Princeton, 1980*

# *Understanding How Flies' Brains Identify Odors*

# AUREL A. LAZAR

Professor of Electrical Engineering

## Developing an Artificial Kidney

# EDWARD F. LEONARD

Professor of Chemical Engineering
and of Biomedical Engineering

Nearly 500,000 Americans depend for their lives on thrice-weekly, in-clinic kidney dialysis to remain alive. The treatment is costly ($23 billion a year or about $46,000 per person), very demanding, and provides only a low quality of life. Some 80,000 Americans are on waiting lists for kidney transplants, with 4,000 dying each year before they get one. A steadily operating, ambulatory blood purification system would decrease patients' burdens and increase quality of life for all of these patients. At present no ambulatory blood processing system exists. Dialysis patients are particularly affected by water accumulation over the typical two-day interval between treatments and thus often experience wide, dangerous, and uncomfortable swings in blood pressure.

Edward Leonard and his team have been working with government and investor support to devise a water extractor for these patients, and also for heart patients who accumulate water. The device, smaller than a lemon, spreads flowing blood into a layer only 100 microns thick. This layer passes between two thin sheets of silicon nitride perforated with many millions of precisely formed nanopores. Cell-free blood plasma is collected from the pores, is processed to extract water, and then is returned along with the cells to the patient. Blood cells move quickly and contact the filter for less than a second. The device, together with the plasma processor, two pumps, and a battery is expected to be about 4 inches square and 1 ½ inches high. It is designed to be worn by the patient at all times, removing water slowly and nearly continuously. This novel blood-cleansing system will not require anticoagulants and will keep treatment costs well within current, federally-mandated cost-containment limits for kidney patients. Testing is underway and first trials on patients are expected in 2013.

Leonard directs Columbia's Artificial Organs Research Laboratory, a component of the Department of Chemical Engineering since 1968. Its mission has grown with the evolution of modern biology and with the increasing sophistication available for the construction of medical devices. Thus, current projects have a wide range: innovations to traditional artificial organs effecting transport (kidney, liver, lung, cardiovascular implants) with special emphasis on the artificial kidney, to regenerative medicine, especially the development and study of methods for introducing stem cells into adult tissue. Leonard, who directs the NSF-sponsored course cluster in Genomic Engineering and is a member of the Columbia Genome Center, is one of the first Columbia Engineering faculty members to engage in bioengineering research. He has worked in the dialysis field for more than 50 years and has been on the Columbia faculty since 1958. His principal medical collaborator is Dr. Stanley Cortell, professor of clinical medicine and chief of nephrology at St. Luke's-Roosevelt Hospital.

*B.S., Massachusetts Institute of Technology, 1953; M.S., University of Pennsylvania, 1955; Ph.D., University of Pennsylvania, 1960*

Nearly three million people in the United States are infected each year with the hepatitis C virus, the major cause of liver cancer. Worldwide, roughly three percent of the population is infected. Jung-Chi Liao is making progress toward the effort to find an effective treatment for the virus. He has focused his research on exploring the DNA helicase—or enzymes—of the hepatitis C virus.

Liao's work is related to the recent discovery of a peptide that inhibits the functioning of the hepatitis C virus enzyme NS3 helicase, providing new insights. Specifically, several hot-spot residues have been identified to convert ATP energy to separate the virus's DNA. Liao is currently conducting comparative studies among different helicases to better understand the variations of coupling mechanisms.

Based on his discovery of dynamical coupling mechanisms and the resulting different conformations, pharmaceutical companies may now be able to identify better drug candidates to inhibit ATP binding sites of hepatitis C virus NS3 helicase. In 2007, Liao was invited by InterMune Inc., one of the major biotechnology companies focusing on drug development for hepatitis C virus infections, to give a seminar presentation of this work.

Liao, who heads Columbia's Liao Research Group, joined Columbia Engineering in 2008 after posts as a research associate in the Department of Bioengineering at Stanford University and as a postdoctoral fellow in molecular and cell biology at the University of California, Berkeley. He says his lab integrates the knowledge of theoretical modeling, molecular and cell biology, and advanced imaging techniques to understand how single molecules play roles in cellular functions as well as the underlying protein structure-function relationship. Their research areas include nanoscale optics, molecular motors and Induced Pluripotent Stem (iPS) Cell Reprogramming.

"Our lab is interested in shedding light on the molecular pathways involved in this process of reprogramming," said Liao. "We hope to identify important transcription factors and signaling pathways crucial to the process to help better understand the specifics of reprogramming and to better control it for clinical use. In an innovative interdisciplinary approach of combining mechanical engineering with biology, we are using high-resolution microscopy to shed light on this event by tracking single molecules."

His research interests are concentrated on how mechanical forces play roles in molecules and cells, using both computational and experimental methods to study molecular motors and related cellular functions. "The focus of my work is to integrate computational modeling and simulation with biological imaging techniques to study dynamics of molecular motors," he said.

*B.S., National Taiwan University, 1993; M.S., Massachusetts Institute of Technology, 1997; Ph.D., MIT, 2001*

*Seeing Proteins at Work*

# JUNG-CHI LIAO

Assistant Professor of
Mechanical Engineering

## Monitoring Glucose Without Pinpricks

# QIAO LIN

Associate Professor of
Mechanical Engineering

More than a million people with type 1 diabetes—an autoimmune disease that is life-threatening unless treated with frequent doses of insulin—will soon be able to check their blood sugar levels without the daily drawing of their own blood.

A team of researchers, led by Qiao Lin, has invented a microfabricated, miniature sensor that can eventually be implanted in a patient's body for long-term, continuous glucose monitoring. It will be part of a closed-loop system that will automatically deliver insulin to diabetic patients based on blood sugar levels.

There are 17.9 million people in the United States of America diagnosed with diabetes, according to the American Diabetes Association.

Lin's glucose sensor consists of a microscopic diaphragm, which vibrates under remote magnetic excitation in a microchamber filled with a glucose-sensitive polymer solution. When glucose enters the chamber through a semipermeable membrane, it binds reversibly with the polymer, changing the viscosity of the solution. As the viscous damping on the diaphragm vibration directly depends on the viscosity, the glucose concentration can be determined by wireless vibration measurements. Depending on the result, insulin can be injected to maintain a normal glucose level.

The reversible binding of glucose to the polymer is key. "It is a physical process and so the glucose is not consumed," said Lin. This is a key difference between his device and current, less reliable, sensors that use an irreversible electrochemical reaction of glucose with an enzyme.

The project has been carried out by an interdisciplinary team including Lin and his mechanical engineering Ph.D. student Xian Huang at Columbia, biopolymer chemists Qian Wang and his Ph.D. student Siqi Li at the University of South Carolina, and Jerome Schultz at University of California, Riverside, an expert in biosensors.

Lin also directs the Columbia BioMEMS Laboratory, which conducts research in microelectromechanical systems (MEMS) as applied to biological sensing and manipulation, with an emphasis on controlling, sensing and characterizing biomolecules and cells by integrating MEMS transducers with microfluidics. The goal of these systems is primarily to facilitate understanding of fundamental biophysical phenomena and to enable practical biomedical applications.

Lin was a postdoctoral scholar in Caltech's electrical engineering department and an assistant professor of mechanical engineering at Carnegie Mellon University prior to joining the Columbia Engineering faculty.

*B.S., Tsinghua University (Beijing), 1985; M.S., Tsinghua University, 1988; Ph.D., California Institute of Technology, 1998*

Many sports-related injuries involve soft tissues such as ligaments, which connect bone with bone, and tendons, which join muscle to bone. Each year, more than 200,000 people suffer damage to their anterior cruciate ligament (ACL), the primary ligament that stabilizes the knee joint. With the rate of ACL tears and other soft tissue injuries increasing in all segments of the population, it is a hopeful sign that Helen H. Lu has developed a new approach to help the body heal after these debilitating soft tissue injuries.

One of the major hurdles preventing healing lies in integrating soft tissue grafts with the body, and Lu's group has focused on engineering the interface that connects soft tissue to bone. While tissue engineering has traditionally involved a single-tissue approach, Lu is growing multiple tissues to build functional organ systems that will integrate with the body.

"With the ACL-bone interface, we see three distinct yet continuous tissue regions—ligament, fibrocartilage, and bone," said Lu. "As we understand how the biological interfaces between these different types of tissues are formed and how to reestablish these distinct tissue-to-tissue boundaries post-injury, we can regenerate the native soft tissue-to-bone interface and promote integration."

Lu has developed a novel "scaffolding" to grow these three different tissue types within one functional system. This interface scaffold is stratified, with each layer differing in architecture, porosity, and composition to best nurture each particular cell type, while integrating seamlessly with the adjacent tissue. Each portion of the scaffold is biocompatible and biodegradable, and will ultimately be replaced by living tissue, thus becoming part of the body.

Lu and her research group are working on the design of an integrative interference screw. The interference screw, used to fix an ACL graft in place, is usually made of titanium alloys, but a tissue-engineered screw has none of the drawbacks of a permanent metallic implant and promotes integrative repair. This new method will move ACL repair from traditional mechanical fixation to biological fixation, resulting in longer-lasting and stronger repair.

Lu's group is extending the interface tissue engineering approach to the repair of another critical soft tissue-to-bone transition area, the rotator cuff. Tears in the rotator cuff are one of the most debilitating and common injuries of the shoulder. In collaboration with Dr. William Levine, a shoulder surgeon at Columbia, Lu is developing special nanofiber-based scaffolds that mimic the native tissue in organization as well as functionality for integrative rotator cuff repair.

*B.S., University of Pennsylvania, 1992; M.S., University of Pennsylvania, 1997; Ph.D., University of Pennsylvania, 1998*

*Repairing Torn Ligaments*

# HELEN H. LU

Associate Professor of Biomedical Engineering and of Dental and Craniofacial Bioengineering

## *Preventing Traumatic Brain Injury*

# BARCLAY MORRISON III

Associate Professor of
Biomedical Engineering

Motor vehicle accidents account for more than half of the 1.5 million traumatic brain injuries (TBIs) that occur each year. Finding ways to prevent, treat, and repair TBIs is the basis for the research of Barclay Morrison and his Neurotrauma and Repair Laboratory team.

At the moment of injury, some brain tissue is instantaneously destroyed and can never be saved by post-injury treatment, so prevention becomes all the more important. Using an atomic force microscope, Morrison is measuring material properties of anatomical structures within the brain that can be used by the National Highway Traffic Safety Administration to set standards for automotive manufacturers.

"We're determining the safe limits of brain deformation, which is the underlying cause of TBI, to learn what the brain can withstand, so safety systems can be designed to minimize the trauma," said Morrison.

Morrison's group is also working with the aftermath of TBIs. One approach investigates the brain's own initial response, which is an attempt to repair the damaged neural connections and replace lost tissue. For reasons yet unknown, this repair process is aborted. If Morrison can find a way to short-circuit this response, it may be possible to harness and control the brain's innate potential for repair. It may even be possible to grow replacement neural tissue from a patient's own stem cells via neural tissue engineering.

In a scenario directly from "The Six Million Dollar Man" or "The Bionic Woman," Morrison sees the possibility of interfacing neurons directly onto silicone circuitry to control a prosthesis. While this technology is now only imagined, he continues to investigate the factors that influence the ability of neurons to form connections with silicone circuitry, hoping for a breakthrough that can immediately impact the lives of thousands.

*WIRED* magazine explored this research in the spring of 2010: "Engineers have now designed silk-based electronics that stick to the surface of the brain, similar to the way a silk dress clings to the hips. The stretchable, ultrathin design would make for better brain-computer interfaces (BCIs), which record brain activity in paralyzed patients and translate thoughts into movements of computer cursors or robotic arms."

"This will significantly improve recording by conforming the electrode array to the surface of the brain," Morrison said in the article. "It will move forward the field of flexible electronics."

Before coming to Columbia Engineering, Morrison was a postdoctoral researcher in TBI at the University of Pennsylvania and later at the University of Southampton, U.K.

*B.S.E., Johns Hopkins University, 1992; M.S.E., University of Pennsylvania, 1994; Ph.D., University of Pennsylvania, 1999*

In recent times, degenerative joint diseases, low back pain, cardiovascular diseases, osteoporosis, and sports injuries have become the focus of biomedical engineering. An overwhelming number of people today suffers from one or more of these clinical problems. As the average age of our population increases, this group of clinical diseases will affect an ever-increasing percentage of the population, worldwide.

The detailed understandings of this group of diseases have been, and are being successfully addressed by bioengineers using advanced engineering methodologies and mathematics. By far the largest subgroup of the family of diseases known as arthritis is degenerative joint disease (osteoarthritis), and it has attracted engineers to study this medical problem. Indeed, engineers have been successful in developing laws that govern the fundamental stress-strain behaviors of articular cartilage (the soft lining covering the bony ends in a joint). This tissue is the major constituent of joints (hip, knee, shoulder, intervertebral disc, meniscus, etc).

"After more than 35 years of concentrated efforts by bioengineers, we now have detailed knowledge on how tissues such as articular cartilage are formed biologically by chondrocytes (cartilage cells), deform under heavy and rapid joint loading, and fail," said Van C. Mow. "Failure of articular cartilage as a bearing material of our joints always leads to osteoarthritis."

Based on this relatively recently gained engineering knowledge, engineers are learning how to influence the cartilage cells to form and shape cartilage within joints, repair the damaged cartilage, and, in general, make the cartilage stronger against the natural wear and tear processes that often result from the activities of daily living, or from extreme loads, such as performing competitive sports.

Currently Mow's lab is developing new models to understand how cartilage cells receive signals (mechanical, electrical, and chemical) to maintain tissue health and to stimulate the cellular repair processes to mend the micro-damages on and in the cartilage that result from excessive and repetitive loading.

Mow, a member of the National Academy of Engineering, the Institute of Medicine of the National Academy of Sciences, Academia Sinica of Taiwan, and the Academy of Sciences for the Developing World, is the founding chair of Columbia Engineering's Department of Biomedical Engineering. He has served as professor of mechanical engineering and orthopedic bioengineering, director of the New York Orthopedic Hospital Research laboratory at Columbia University Medical Center, and is currently director of the Liu Ping Laboratory for Functional Tissue Engineering.

*B.A.E., Rennselaer Polytechnic Institute, 1962; Ph.D., Rennselaer Polytechnic Institute, 1966*

## *Reconstructing Cartilage*

# VAN C. MOW

Stanley Dicker Professor of Biomedical Engineering and of Orthopedic Engineering

# Investigating the Mechanical Behavior of Soft Tissues

# KRISTIN MYERS

Assistant Professor of Mechanical Engineering

Mechanical engineers think about the design, construction, material properties, and operation of mechanical devices that allow functionality. They have responsibility for understanding how engines work, how buildings can be more efficiently built, and how the environment affects bridge architecture. They also apply their knowledge to the workings of the human body.

Consider the structure all humans have their first experience with: the womb. Much more than a structure that protects a growing fetus, the womb is made up of many parts that work together to incubate and then birth the baby. One of those parts is the cervix—the lower end of the uterus—and its strength holds a baby inside the mother while it is developing. To prepare for birth, the cervix must dramatically soften. When the cervix fails as a structure and dilates prematurely, miscarriage or premature birth can be the result. By better understanding the mechanical properties of the cervix, better prenatal diagnostic and screening techniques can be developed to reduce premature births, which is the leading cause of fetal deaths.

Kristin Myers investigates the mechanical behavior of soft tissues in order to understand how their tissue architecture influences constitutive behavior and disease development and to aid in early diagnosis and treatment. One of her main focuses is the characterization of the cervix during normal pregnancy and the pre-term labor condition known as cervical insufficiency. A woman with cervical insufficiency has a softer, weaker, or abnormally short cervix, which may efface and dilate without contractions in the second or early third trimester as the weight of a baby puts increasing pressure on it. Myers works to identify abnormal extra cellular matrix components that lead to the altered mechanical function of the tissue and is developing new instruments that can test the strength of the cervix.

Myers joined Columbia after completing her doctoral work at Massachusetts Institute of Technology and post-doctoral work at Johns Hopkins University. In addition to her cervical research, she also studies glaucoma and examines the strength of the collagen fibers that make up the white part of the eye, or sclera. In this research area she works to determine if corrections to the mechanical structure of the eye can correct glaucoma. She is exploring whether people who are diagnosed with glaucoma have a weaker eye structure, and if so, could there be a way to correct the structure mechanically.

*B.S., University of Michigan, 2002; M.S., Massachusetts Institute of Technology, 2005; Ph.D., MIT, 2008*

Sometimes the building blocks of life—DNA—get knocked askew. The double-helical form that nucleic acids are customarily known for can change and, when it does, the transmission of genetic information is affected. Unfortunately it can be almost impossible to observe, in a laboratory setting, how these different conformations occur.

When experimental attempts fail to capture the details of super-microscopic mechanics like that of DNA, computer simulations on the macromolecular level can deliver valuable insight into what drives assembly in biology. For example, mutations in spectrin proteins are linked to muscular dystrophy and other genetic diseases. These mutations change the way in which the protein unfolds on length-scales that are too small for experimentalists to see. Computer simulation of the process provides atom-by-atom detail about the interactions that occur. This type of research holds promise in providing guidance for the development of better and more efficient biomedical technologies, as well as for innovative disease treatments.

Vanessa Ortiz applies the fundamentals of physics and engineering to understand biological phenomena. She works to describe these phenomena with a multi-scale hierarchical modeling approach, rooted in the use of advanced, state-of-the-art sampling methods, to investigate the behavior of nucleic acids in solution and when in contact with other macromolecules (proteins, nanotubes), surfaces, or assemblies (membranes). Using these models, she is able to predict how a physical system will behave under different conditions, helping scientists draw closer to devising therapies that can treat or even prevent disease.

Her primary research interests are in the development and application of advanced multi-scale computational modeling techniques for the study of biological macromolecules. The goal is to provide insight into the molecular mechanisms that drive assembly in biology, thereby providing guidance for development of better and more efficient biomedical and environmental sensing technologies. In particular, Ortiz concentrates on developing the use of nucleic acids for templating directed organization of nanomaterials, including biomolecules, templating of inorganics, and approaches combining preformed and template materials for use in the areas of nanotechnology and materials.

She has been instrumental in investigating the stability under stress of cytoskeletal proteins and in understanding the stability of diblock copolymer vesicles and worm-like micelles as a function of different design parameters for the development of efficient drug carriers.

*B.S.E., University of Puerto Rico, 2002; Ph.D., University of Pennsylvania, 2007*

*Using Physics and Engineering to Understand Biological Phenomena*

# VANESSA ORTIZ

Assistant Professor of Chemical Engineering

## Figuring Out How Viruses Invade Cells

# BEN O'SHAUGHNESSY

### Professor of Chemical Engineering

Each year as many as one in five Americans get the flu. More than 200,000 end up in the hospital for complications, and 36,000 die from flu-related causes. And those statistics are for only one family of viruses.

Ben O'Shaughnessy and his team are figuring out how viruses invade cells so they can help develop anti-viral drugs to prevent diseases like the flu and AIDS. Like detectives, they're tracking down how viruses break through their own wall-like membranes and those of healthy cells. That is, how do they open up their own barrier and that of the cell they're trying to attack? A virus uses a finger-like protrusion to poke a hole in the cell it is attacking.

The long-term goal of this research is to keep the virus from invading (most likely through preventing the fusion of the virus and healthy cell walls), and then to come up with virus-fighting medications. These drugs are especially important for infections such as AIDS, Ebola hemorrhagic fever, and dengue fever, which have no vaccine.

The research may also help the search for effective anti-viral drugs to treat viral diseases such as flu. While flu vaccines exist, they are imperfect as flu viruses mutate rapidly, which makes it difficult for scientists to decide on the best cocktail to protect against the strains that will appear each November. There is particular urgency to develop anti-viral drugs to protect people from both "regular" flu and from H1N1 or "swine" flu.

The National Institutes of Health awarded O'Shaughnessy a $1.5 million grant in 2010 for a project that takes a closer look at a process essential to all life: cell division. His team is investigating how a muscle-like ring inside the cell is assembled and how it works on a molecular level to complete the closure as the cell physically splits, a process called cytokinesis.

"We are mathematically modeling this machine to establish a quantitative understanding of how it works," he said. The research has potentially far-reaching implications.

"Failed or improper cytokinesis due to improper ring constriction can result in cells with zero or many copies of the genome," O'Shaughnessy added. "Understanding the mechanism of cytokinesis is essential to help combat cancer, neurological disease, and birth defects associated with such failed cytokinesis."

O'Shaughnessy teaches Molecular Phenomena in Chemical Engineering to undergraduates and Statistical Mechanics and Topics in Biology for Physical Scientists and Engineers to graduate students.

*B.Sc., University of Bristol (England), 1977; Ph.D., University of Cambridge (England), 1984*

## Discovering Origins of Diabetes

# ITSIK PE'ER

Associate Professor
of Computer Science

Nearly 50 million people nationwide struggle with type 2 diabetes or high cholesterol, and rates are increasing annually. The clues to why some people are more susceptible than others are being discovered on a small Pacific Island, where Columbia Engineering researchers are discovering new genetic variation and associating it with metabolic disease.

Itsik Pe'er, who leads the Itsik Pe'er Lab of Computational Genetics, is developing analytical methods for analysis of DNA sequence variants. Recent technological breakthroughs now allow high-throughput observation of these genetic alterations along the genome (an individual's collection of genetic material).

Such heritable changes are thought to be responsible for 40 to 90 percent of population risk to a wide variety of health conditions, from diabetes to schizophrenia. The Pe'er group is studying a population from the Pacific Island of Kosrae, in the Federated States of Micronesia, which suffers from increased rates of metabolic disorders, such as obesity, type 2 diabetes, and high cholesterol.

The unique genetic makeup of the islanders, who have been isolated for thousands of years, makes them ideal for genetic studies, but their interrelatedness makes analysis of their DNA extremely complex.

The Pe'er group has developed computational tools to decipher remote family ties between individuals based on identity of genomic segments inherited by descent from a recent unknown ancestor. These analytical methods enabled examination of 500,000 polymorphic sites along the genomes of 3,000 Kosraeans, representing most of the adult population.

The lab was thus able to discover multiple new disease genes for health traits. Based on these disease associations, the researchers were able to sequence the entire genome of representatives of the Kosraean population, resulting in discoveries that have broad implications for anyone with these metabolic diseases.

The unprecedented scope and uniqueness of this recently completed dataset expose the effects of population isolation, and pinpoint severe mutations in individual genomes that are likely associated with disease. The combination of these genome sequences with the precompiled map of segments that are identical by descent delineates large groups of mutation carriers to confirm such associations.

Before joining Columbia, Pe'er was a postdoctoral researcher at several institutions, including the Weizmann Institute of Science and Massachusetts General Hospital. His research group is a home to an interdisciplinary team attracting diverse academic backgrounds, analytical talents, and skill sets to effectively promote computational understanding of human genetics.

*B.S., Tel Aviv University (Israel), 1990; M.S., Tel Aviv University, 1995; Ph.D., Tel Aviv University, 2002*

## Capturing the "Aha!" Moment

# PAUL SAJDA

Associate Professor of
Biomedical Engineering and of Radiology

Countless times a day—often without realizing it—humans make split-second decisions based on what we see and on our subjective knowledge. It might be as simple as clicking a link that catches our interest online, or recognizing a friend from a 50-millisecond glimpse of his or her face across a crowded room. But no matter how effortless the decision-making process may seem, the effort to translate that into an automated system has proved daunting.

"We can build a computer that's good at very constrained decision making, but general purpose, rapid decision making is difficult," said Paul Sajda. "It might be able to detect what is interesting or novel, but it doesn't always know what's interesting or novel to you."

Those two tasks—rapid decision making and identifying subjective interests—are, however, exactly what Sajda and his team are succeeding in building. At the same time, Sajda is attempting to reveal the most basic neural structures in the brain that process visual information. In his Laboratory for Intelligent Imaging and Neural Computing, Sajda connects subjects to an EEG and flashes a series of images on a computer screen to record the neurological equivalent of the "Aha!" moment signaling interest or recognition. Once the "cortically coupled computer vision system" is calibrated to recognize the things that interest an individual, it can present more images that are likely to pique that person's interest.

His work has drawn the attention of the Defense Advanced Research Projects Agency for its potential to help conduct a sort of visual triage by sifting quickly through petabytes (that's a million gigabytes) of satellite imagery or hours of surveillance tapes. He also works with researchers at Columbia University Medical Center on techniques that enhance the brain's ability to make quick decisions. But the question that most fascinates Sajda is what his studies of the brain's visual recognition networks can do to reveal the organ's fundamental ability to process massive amounts of information.

"It's still unclear at what scale the brain processes information," said Sajda. "It could be groups of neurons, it could be the whole brain. We don't know." But he and his research group stand a good chance of finding out.

Growing up on Long Island, Sajda knew he wanted to be an engineer, but was also fascinated by anatomy and physiology. That fascination with living systems continues to infuse his work, at the same time that his engineering perspective is helping redefine what we know about the human brain.

*B.S., Massachusetts Institute of Technology, 1989; M.S., University of Pennsylvania, 1992; Ph.D., University of Pennsylvania, 1994*

**W**elcome to the post-modern biology lab. It's made of silicon, measures 5mm on a side and costs just $20. It can also be deployed to harsh or distant locations and when an experiment is complete, it can be discarded. Welcome to Ken Shepard's lab—or at least one of the many he is designing. This new research combines expertise in chemistry, biology, and integrated circuit design in a manner that gives Columbia unique, high-impact capabilities. While most of the semiconductor industry is focused on continuing to try to scale integrated circuit technology according to Moore's Law, Shepard's lab is focused on "more than Moore" applications of IC technology.

Shepard and his team at the Bioelectronics Systems Lab employ the integrated circuits technology to build their own micrometer-scale arrays of sensors that can detect biological molecules or select strands of DNA. "There are definitely other techniques for doing these things, but they're difficult, time-consuming, and expensive," said Shepard. "The goal here is to come up with something that's as sensitive as the most sensitive instruments, if not more, and reduce everything else about it."

Very often, in order to detect a particular molecule, they have to first be labeled—physically attached to something such as a fluorescent dye that permits detection. Shepard and graduate student Matthew Johnston aim to circumvent this laborious process by directly detecting the weight of individual molecules.

When target protein molecules bond to the surface of one of their chips, it causes the frequency of a vibrating piezoelectric crystal to change. The magnitude of the change quickly confirms the presence of their target.

In their first test of the lab-on-a-chip, Shepard and Johnston are using a sensor designed to search dust samples for common airborne allergens that have been linked to high childhood asthma rates in urban areas. Shepard also envisions a day when his chip-based labs could be used to quickly and easily detect blood-borne cancer proteins.

Shepard's "more than Moore" activities have been funded by corporate sources (Semiconductor Research Corporation) and state and federal grants (New York State Foundation for Science, Technology, and Innovation; National Science Foundation; National Institutes of Health; and the Defense Advanced Research Agency). He is also a principal investigator on a large NSF Ph.D. training grant in the area of bioimaging technologies.

Shepard was given a Faculty Development Award in 2006 by the New York State Office of Science Technology and Academic Research. In 2008, he was named a finalist for the Blavatnik Award for young faculty by the New York Academy of Sciences. He is a fellow of the Institute of Eletrical and Electronics Engineers.

*B.S.E., Princeton, 1987; M.S.E.E., Stanford, 1988; Ph.D., Stanford, 1992*

## *Integrating Biology in a Chip*

# KENNETH L. SHEPARD

Professor of Electrical Engineering and of Biomedical Engineering

# *Streamlining Blood Testing*

# SAMUEL K. SIA

Associate Professor of
Biomedical Engineering

Doctors in developing countries will soon be able to use handheld devices to collect and analyze blood tests at a patient's bedside to diagnose infectious and other diseases, thanks to research by Samuel K. Sia.

The devices, now undergoing field tests in Rwanda, require only a finger prick of blood and provide quantitative results in less than 20 minutes. The aim of the new technology is to significantly reduce the time between testing patients and treating them, without increasing costs or regulatory burdens.

"Nowhere is the need for new diagnostic technologies greater than in developing countries, where people suffer disproportionately from infectious disease compared to the U.S. and Europe," said Sia.

The "lab-on-a-chip" technology uses microfluidics—the manipulation of small amounts of fluids—to miniaturize and automate routine laboratory tests onto a hand-held microchip. The devices are being developed in a collaboration between Sia's lab and Claros Diagnostics Inc.—a venture capital-backed startup company that Sia co-founded in 2004—as well as with the Mailman School of Public Health at Columbia University. Sia's work also focuses on developing new high-resolution tools to control the extracellular environments around cells, in order to study how they interact to form human tissues and organs. His lab uses techniques from a number of different fields, including biochemistry, molecular biology, microfabrication, microfluidics, materials chemistry, and cell and tissue biology.

His device, known as mChip (mobile microfluidic chip), significantly reduces the time between testing patients and treating them and provides medical workers in the field results that are much easier to read at a much lower cost. The microchip inside the device is formed through injection molding and holds miniature forms of test tubes and chemicals; the cost of the chip is about $1 and the entire instrument about $100. Sia's research has recently been featured in *Popular Science* and *Nature Medicine*.

In August of 2010, MIT's *Technology Review* magazine named Sia to its prestigious listing of the World's Top Young Innovators for 2010 for his groundbreaking work in biotechnology and medicine.

Sia received a CAREER Award from the National Science Foundation that supports his work in developing biocompatible microelectromechanical systems and implantable medical devices, such as glucose sensors. A recipient of the Walter H. Coulter Early Career Award in 2008, Sia participated in the National Academy of Engineering's U.S. Frontiers of Engineering symposium for the nation's brightest young engineers in 2007.

*B.Sc., University of Alberta (Canada), 1997; Ph.D., Harvard, 2002*

Childhood vaccines are one of the great success stories of medicine. With timely vaccination, many childhood illnesses have been nearly eradicated. Yet this battle against common childhood epidemics requires constant vigilance and planning. In particular, a steady supply of vaccines needs to be made available to children. This task is especially difficult because the supply of vaccines is inherently fragile. Just in the last decade, the United States has experienced six major protracted disruptions of its vaccine supply. The Centers for Disease Control plans for such emergencies by maintaining a national stockpile. An important decision is how to set stockpile levels in order to minimize cost and the risk of a shortage in a dynamic and uncertain environment.

Such uncertainties exist in many real systems. To make a system more efficient requires an understanding of how to effectively account for uncontrollable random factors. Industrial engineers build mathematical models to capture the behavior of these systems, with the goal of simulating system behavior and optimizing system performance under economic and technological constraints.

Van-Anh Truong studies decision problems that arise in many health care systems and supply chains. Her work has application in the management of pediatric vaccine stockpiles, the allocation of operating room capacity to emergency and elective surgeries, the structuring and pricing of health care services, the tactical purchase of equipment for semiconductor fabrication facilities, and the strategic use of inventory in retailing. She develops scientific theory to design smarter systems, and to help deploy machines, staff, and materials more efficiently. By drawing on mathematics and engineering analysis and design, she develops representative models of real systems, how they interact over time, and how they are affected by random events in the environment. Her analysis of these mathematical models yields insights and algorithms for finding decisions that optimize system performance.

Truong's theoretical interests include separation methods for stochastic dynamic programming, approximation algorithms, and learning-based optimization. Prior to teaching at Columbia University, Truong was a quantitative associate at Credit Suisse and a quantitative researcher at Google. She is a member of the Institute for Operations Research and the Management Sciences (INFORMS).

*B.S., University of Waterloo (Canada), 2002; Ph.D., Cornell, 2007*

*Strategies for a Smarter Health Care System*

# VAN-ANH TRUONG

Assistant Professor of Industrial Engineering and Operations Research

## Fixing Bones and Hearts

# GORDANA VUNJAK-NOVAKOVIC

The Mikati Foundation Professor
of Biomedical Engineering

Approximately 35 million men and women in the United States suffer from TMJ problems, and as many as one in four people experience symptoms of TMJ disorders, including pain in the chewing muscles, jaw stiffness, clicking, popping or grating, or the pain of arthritis. The temporomandibular joint, or TMJ, is the jaw joint that lies in front of each ear, connecting the mandible (lower jaw) to the skull, providing the mobility necessary for biting, chewing, swallowing food, speaking, and making facial expressions.

Gordana Vunjak-Novakovic and her research team have been able to grow bone grafts that will match a patient's original jaw bone for facial reconstruction surgery to repair injuries, disease, or birth defects. This spectacular advancement in bone tissue engineering provides all the advantages of the body's original jaw bone. The team used real bone as a scaffold to grow the new TMJ graft. Taking the knee joints of calves, they stripped them of all their living cells and carved them into cubic centimeter-size parts of a human jaw joint. Using mesenchymal stem cells, which can differentiate into many cell types, to seed the scaffolding, they fed them with streams of nutrients, growth factors, and oxygen in a bioreactor. The next step will be to determine the best way to grow blood vessels in the bone grafts to continue their viability.

In another research area, Vunjak-Novakovic is engineering thick, vascularized, and electromechanically functional cardiac tissue, by culturing stem cells, the actual "tissue engineers," on a channeled elastomer scaffold perfused with culture medium containing oxygen carriers, to mimic blood flow. This research may lead to a heart patch that could be laid over injured heart tissue to restore normal function in someone who has suffered a heart attack. "As a biomedical engineer actively involved in this field, I look forward to unlocking the full regenerative potential of human stem cells, so we can cure disease and live longer than our failing organs," she said.

Her lab hosts the Bioreactor Core of the National Institutes of Health (NIH) Tissue Engineering Resource Center. "This sophisticated bioreactor and imaging instrumentation has moved stem cell research from the 'flat biology' of petri dishes to controllable models of high biological fidelity, which can be studied in real time to observe the interacting factors mediating self-renewal and differentiation of stem cells," said Vunjak-Novakovic. "We now have the capacity to develop entirely new research paradigms and approaches to engineering human tissues."

In 2002, Vunjak-Novakovic was elected a fellow of the American Institute for Medical and Biological Engineering. In 2007, she gave the Director's lecture at the NIH, as the first woman engineer to receive this distinction. She was inducted into the Women in Technology International Hall of Fame in 2008, elected to the New York Academy of Sciences in 2009, and, in 2010, received the Clemson Award of the Biomaterials Society for contribution to literature.

*B.S., University of Belgrade (Serbia), 1972; S.M., University of Belgrade, 1975; University of Belgrade, Ph.D., 1980*

The key to unlocking complex problems like the biological cause of cancer—the second-leading cause of all deaths—may be found in the fundamental building blocks of life. How genes control each other—and how to predict that activity—is a research focus of Chris Wiggins. He is working to develop models that predict how genes behave to explain how some cells become cancerous.

"The relationship between biology and mathematics has completely changed in the last decade," said Wiggins. "New technologies have transformed biology into a data-rich science, and advances in algorithms have made possible data-driven predictive modeling in biology. At the same time, the World Wide Web made it possible for any biologists to share their data with the entire mathematical community with the click of a mouse."

Wiggins and his collaborators have shown how one can use these data, along with the appropriate math, to learn which genes are controlling which other genes and why.

"The problem is a bit like watching stocks go up and down, and trying to predict which stocks are driving each other," he said. "In this case, our models are also constrained and guided by the hard work of decades of bench biologists and medical scientists."

While the architecture of the underlying genetic network is a basic biological topic, Wiggins said, "it is at the root of numerous biological diseases, including cancer, and we are now on the threshold of finding more of those genetic links."

Wiggins, who was a National Science Foundation postdoctoral research fellow in biomathematics at the Courant Institute, was profiled in *Scientific American* in 2008. In recent months, numerous publications have explored his work trying to lure the school's top math students to tech startups instead of joining Wall Street banks.

The influx of new talent would expand the city's technology sector, the brain drain of math and engineering students to West Coast schools and companies would ebb, and New York City's intellectual environment would be enriched. "I want young people to realize the creative things they can do with math," he said.

Wiggins received the Janette and Armen Avanessians Diversity Award in 2007. The award was established to recognize outstanding performance of engineering faculty in enhancing diversity in departmental, school, and university programs at Columbia. The award winner receives a cash prize of $1,000 and a plaque. Nominations are evaluated on the basis of excellence in advancing diversity at Columbia Engineering.

*B.A., Columbia, 1993; Ph.D., Princeton, 1998*

HEALTH

## "Turning Off" Cancer Genes

# CHRIS H. WIGGINS

Associate Professor of Applied Physics and Applied Mathematics

EXCELLENTIA ✿ COLUMBIA | ENGINEERING   85

## Detecting "Dirty Bomb" Radiation

# Y. LAWRENCE YAO

Professor of Mechanical Engineering

In the realm of national preparedness, few scenarios are as scary as the possibility of a "dirty bomb." The National Institutes of Health (NIH) is funding a $25 million grant to find new technologies that will provide rapid mass-screening of radiation exposure.

Y. Lawrence Yao, together with researchers from Columbia University Medical Center and department colleagues, is part of a multi-institute consortium that, among other tasks, is charged with developing a high-throughput "biodosimetry" device capable of rapidly testing a large swath of the population in the event that an RDD (radioactive dispersal device), commonly called a "dirty bomb," is detonated in a major metropolitan area. This group is collaborating on an effort to design the most effective and quickest technologies that involve advanced imaging, lasers, and robotics.

Radiation affects cell division. When cells divide under normal conditions, the break is clean, with no extraneous cellular material. After radiation exposure, however, pieces of damaged chromosomes, micronuclei, appear along with divided cells and can be tested for DNA breaks.

The advances in these technologies being pioneered by Yao and his colleagues will accelerate the screening process based on blood from a finger stick. With the help of a highly automated, efficient, and eventually portable device—a prototype of which is already whirring in Mudd's basement—doctors can quickly determine the scope of radiation exposure and whether medical treatment is needed by processing tens of thousands of samples per day, instead of only a few hundred.

Yao and his colleagues, and the NIH, are confident that this device can operate at high volume and full throttle, with the hope that it is never needed.

Yao, who also directs Columbia's Manufacturing Research Laboratory (MRL), engages in multidisciplinary research that includes nontraditional manufacturing, laser materials processing, laser assisted material removal, shaping, and surface modification, laser applications in industry and art restoration, and robotics in industry and health care.

In 2009, he received the Janette and Armen Avanessians Diversity Award, established to recognize outstanding performance of engineering faculty in enhancing diversity in departmental, school, and university programs at Columbia. The award winner receives a cash prize of $1,000 and a plaque. Nominations are evaluated on the basis of excellence in advancing diversity at Columbia Engineering.

Before joining Columbia in 1994, Yao served as a senior lecturer in the School of Mechanical and Manufacturing Engineering at the University of New South Wales, Sydney, Australia.

*B.E., Shanghai Jiao Tong University (China), 1982; M.S., University of Wisconsin-Madison, 1984; Ph.D., University of Wisconsin-Madison, 1988*

The Columbia School of Mines was established in 1864, at a time when we were anxious to learn ways that Earth could yield its resources for our use. Today, many of our faculty, especially those in the successor Department of Earth and Environmental Engineering, are finding new ways to help our planet endure—working on issues of water, climate, and energy that have impact around the globe.

# SUSTAINABILITY

## *Putting a New Spin On the Science of Electronics*

# WILLIAM E. BAILEY

Associate Professor of Materials Science and of Applied Physics and Applied Mathematics

It is often said that there is nothing new under the sun. However, looking more deeply into what is commonly understood can result in surprising new knowledge. Consider the electron, the negatively charged particle on the outer layer of the atom. The electron's charge is responsible for electricity and makes it possible to process data. The electron's spin underlies magnetism and makes it possible to store data. The entire electronics industry has been built on the known utility of this most basic particle.

The electronics industry is now undergoing rapid change, being pushed by a worldwide consumer desire for smaller and more efficient appliances that have increased data processing and storage capability. To meet this demand, engineers are working to lay the stepping stones to new technological breakthroughs in computer, audio, and video storage as well as sensor technology by using the spin as well as the charge of the electron, and by discovering how to transport electrical charge and magnetic spin through single atoms or nanoparticles. This science is leading to the development of magnetic thin films—single atomic layers of magnetic film, layered one upon the other and tested for their response to frequency, electrical resistivity, and their agility in signal processing.

This science could mean a new era defined by increased data processing speed, decreased power consumption and more affordable technology. Imagine an MP3 player that could store hundreds of thousands of songs; a laptop computer that could run on a single battery for weeks; or a cell phone that could store and protect data from degradation for decades. It's all possible, once breakthroughs are made in understanding how to best manipulate the electron's spin via electric and magnetic fields.

William Bailey studies the deposition and properties of magnetic ultrathin films. His research interests include nanoscale magnetic films and heterostructures, materials issues in spin polarized transport, and materials engineering of magnetic dynamics. He investigates novel magnetic properties for application in the emerging field of spintronics, and is particularly interested in designing magnetic materials with reduced energy loss for application in computing.

Prior to joining Columbia Engineering, Bailey held a National Research Council Postdoctoral Fellowship at the National Institute of Standards and Technology (NIST) in Boulder, Colorado. Honors for his research include the National Science Foundation CAREER and Army Research Office Young Investigator awards.

*Sc.B., Brown, 1993; M.S., Stanford, 1995; Ph.D., Stanford, 1999*

Assessing potential damage to aging infrastructure is an ever more critical issue every day. One of the areas in which Raimondo Betti, chair of the Department of Civil Engineering and Engineering Mechanics, specializes is damage detection for bridges using data correlation analysis. He and his team are leading the effort to develop a state-of-the-art corrosion monitoring system to be used in main cables of suspension bridges. His research is aimed at finding ways to safely extend the life of existing suspension bridges, focusing on those in New York City.

"New York City has among the oldest suspension bridges in the world," said Betti. "Many have been in service for over 100 years, in a harsh environment. They have deteriorated and will continue to, if nothing is done. Main cables are the most critical structural element in a cable suspension bridge. If a cable fails, the entire bridge fails and so special attention must be given to such elements." Replacing a bridge would be prohibitively expensive in a densely populated area as New York City. It is estimated that the failure of one of the city's suspension bridges could cost billions of dollars.

Over the past five years, Betti has been conducting a unique experiment on the development of a corrosion monitoring system to be applied in main cables of suspension bridges. To test such a system, a mock-up of a bridge cable, 20 feet long, 20 inches in diameter, and made up of nearly 10,000 galvanized bridge wires, has been built inside an environmental chamber and subjected to a one-year cyclic corrosion test.

The cable—one of the largest ever built in the world and the only one subjected to a tensile axial force of 1,200 kips—has been enclosed in an environmental chamber to accelerate deterioration, simulating decades of wear, such as that endured by New York's Williamsburg, Manhattan, and Brooklyn Bridges. Buried in the cable mock-up are 76 miniature sensors that are measuring corrosion rates, temperature, humidity, acidity, and chlorine content.

Betti and his team are now analyzing the results in order to provide meaningful methods to assess, in real time, the actual conditions of the cable. The answers he finds should help insure a longer life for suspension bridges around the world.

This project—the first systematic study ever done on monitoring the corrosion of suspension cables—is also the first in a series focused on damage assessment in main cables of suspension bridges and is part of a National Center on Aging Infrastructure in Urban Environments created by the Department of Civil Engineering and Engineering Mechanics.

*B.S., University of Rome La Sapienza (Italy), 1985; M.S., University of Southern California, 1988; Ph.D., University of Southern California, 1991*

*Assessing Damage in Aging Infrastructure*

# RAIMONDO BETTI

Professor of Civil Engineering and Engineering Mechanics

## *Short-Circuiting Blackouts*

# DANIEL BIENSTOCK

Professor of Industrial Engineering
and Operations Research and of
Applied Physics and Applied Mathematics

On August 14, 2003, an unusual combination of events shut down electrical power for 55 million people in the United States and Canada. The event was what statisticians call a black swan, something so rare that no one plans for it.

Yet major blackouts also occurred—with significant consequences—in 1965 and 1977. Daniel Bienstock believes that by studying these black swans, he can help utilities prepare for and even prevent the next major blackout.

"We're borrowing ideas from other engineering disciplines," said Bienstock. "If you design an aircraft wing, you test it by strapping it to a fixture and vibrating it to see what breaks. We do the same thing by using our model of the grid. Our objective is to stress the grid and see where it breaks."

The 2003 crisis involved a number of unusual events that occurred in different parts of the Eastern United States grid. These included human errors, control room computer bugs, and a plant shutdown. These events put too much strain on several major power lines, causing them to overheat and eventually shut down. This started a process that snowballed until it knocked down much of the Eastern grid.

"One or two things like this can happen frequently and the grid can handle it," said Bienstock. "But here, the particular combination proved catastrophic. After gathering momentum for several hours, the snowball caused hundreds of lines to fail within 15 minutes."

His goal is to create software that will let utilities analyze cascading events and react to them before the grid comes down. First, though, he needs to anticipate what combination of events could trigger a blackout. "The traditional way is to enumerate every possible combination of individual lines coming down and determine the consequences," he said. "There are not enough computers in the world to do this."

Instead, Bienstock created a mathematical model of the grid and stresses it in different ways. "We can use the model to show us where the grid will break. Then we see what we can do to address those vulnerabilities," he said.

He also runs what-if scenarios. "It's a chess game. We look at cascading events and test different strategies to find the best way to react. These become templates that can guide utility responses before these events turn into a major outage," Bienstock said.

"Imagine," he concluded. "We would have had at least one hour to do our computations in 2003. We could have calculated the right moves to prevent a blackout."

*B.S., Brandeis Unversity, 1982; Ph.D., Massachusetts Institute of Technology, 1985*

The solid oxide fuel cell, which runs on hydrogen and oxygen to produce water as exhaust, is seen as a promising technology of the future for transportation. These fuel cells are now used on an experimental basis to power some city buses. But the fuel cells have proved unreliable because the nanoparticles of platinum that serve as a catalyst for the chemical reaction sometimes do not function optimally.

"Scientists want to exploit the nanoparticle in the device but still don't know that particle's basic properties," said Simon Billinge. "Sometimes it works, and sometimes it doesn't."

These catalysts, nanoparticles of platinum, are balls one-millionth of a millimeter in diameter. The properties of the metal change when they are so small and scientists have yet to fully characterize them. By determining the nanoparticle's structure and properties—its electrical conductivity, thermal conductivity, melting point, and stiffness—scientists will be better able to predict a fuel cell's performance, based on what particular nanoparticle is used as the catalyst.

To help provide a solution, Billinge is developing new methods to characterize the structure of nanoparticles, figuring out the arrangements of atoms in particles that are made up of a few hundred to a few thousand atoms. He uses intense x-ray and neutron source technology, carrying out his research using particle accelerators at the Brookhaven National Laboratory in Long Island, N.Y., the Los Alamos National Laboratory in New Mexico, and the Argonne National Laboratory in Illinois.

In these accelerators, electrons circle at high energy, emitting intense x-ray beams that impinge on the nanoparticles. The scattered x-rays interfere with each other to produce "diffraction" patterns of intensity. Billinge has made important breakthroughs by developing novel Fourier transform methods to analyze the data.

He also has worked on measuring the surface energy of the platinum catalyst. The surface atoms, like those on the meniscus of a water droplet, have higher energy than those inside of the particle. And it's the surface area of the nanoparticles that provides the reactivity for the hydrogen and oxygen that come together to produce the energy that propels the vehicle.

Earlier this year, Billinge won the J.D. Hanawalt Award for his contribution to the field of powder diffraction. The International Center for Diffraction Data gives the award every three years. Awardees are chosen by the Hanawalt Award Selection Committee, which is comprised of past recipients.

*B.A., University of Oxford (England), 1986; Ph.D., University of Pennsylvania, 1992*

## *Characterizing Nanoparticles for Fuel Cells*

# SIMON BILLINGE

Professor of Materials Science and of Applied Physics and Applied Mathematics

## *Shaping Magnetic Fusion*

# ALLEN BOOZER

Professor of Applied Physics and Applied
Mathematics

Magnetic fusion, a potential long-term source of electricity, occurs when isotopes of hydrogen, deuterium, and tritium combine at temperatures of about 200 million degrees C. At such temperatures, the electrons and the ions separate and form an electrically conducting gas called a plasma, which can be confined by magnetic fields in a chamber, shaped like an inner tube, called a torus. In a symmetrical torus, the electric current that creates the magnetic field runs both through external coils surrounding the chamber, and through the plasma. Helical shaping of the torus allows the confining magnetic field to be produced entirely by currents in the coils.

This shaping in effect forms a cage around the plasma making it more robustly stable as well as eliminating the difficulty of driving currents in the plasma. However, the helical shaping greatly complicates the issue of obtaining adequate plasma confinement. Major issues are the reduction of the power required to sustain the plasma so that power can be supplied by the deuterium-tritium reactions, and the achievement of plasma conditions consistent with engineering requirements, such as robust plasma stability.

Allen Boozer has developed the design principles by which the magnetic field strength in a helically shaped torus could be made consistent with adequate particle confinement. These ideas have been tested in the Helically Shaped Experiment (HSX) at the University of Wisconsin and will be tested in the $1 billion W7-X experiment under construction in Germany.

Boozer has played a critical role in the understanding of how the detrimental effects on confinement of an asymmetry as small as $10^{-4}$ can be controlled. He was a co-inventor of a method of driving currents in plasmas, electron cyclotron current drive, which allows the current to be driven in the precise spatial location it is needed. He also showed that thermodynamics implies the power required to drive the current in an axisymmetric torus is sufficiently large to place strong constraints on the plasma performance. Boozer has developed theoretical techniques that are used to enhance the performance of axisymmetric plasmas through feedback.

Boozer was one of two recipients who received the 2010 Hannes Alfvén Prize—the best-known European award in plasma physics. Boozer and his colleague, Jürgen Nührenberg, from the Max Planck Institute for Plasma Physics (Greifswald, Germany) were honored at the June 2010 conference of the Plasma Physics Division of the European Physical Society, which established the award in 2000. The Society cited them for "outstanding work in the formulation of criteria allowing stellarators to improve fast particle and neoclassical energy confinement." The result of their work is considered important for magnetic fusion energy, in which isotopes of hydrogen (deuterium and tritium) fuse to release energy while confined in a magnetic field at a high temperature.

*B.A., University of Virginia, 1966; Ph.D., Cornell, 1970*

In 1985, Mark Cane and his student, Steve Zebiak, published the results of a model they developed to predict the movement of warm water across the tropical Pacific Ocean in a cyclical phenomenon known as the El Niño Southern Oscillation, or ENSO. When it forms, El Niño's meteorological reach spans the globe, causing a well-known pattern of extreme weather events.

The 2009 El Niño, for example, resulted in deep droughts in India and the Philippines and deadly rains in Uganda. Aside from the regular progression of the seasons, no other phenomenon influences Earth's short-term climate as profoundly as ENSO.

Despite its impact, in the early 1980s there was still no accepted theory for how it worked. "If you're predicting the weather you get to verify your models every three or four days," said Cane. "For El Niño, you have to wait four years to find out if you're right."

The Zebiak-Cane model showed a moderate El Niño developing in late 1986. People in Peru, Australia and elsewhere still had vivid memories of the devastating effects of the powerful El Niño that formed in 1982 and 1983, so many scientists opposed publishing forecasts they didn't yet understand. "People said, 'What if you're wrong?,'" said Cane. "I said, 'What if we're right and we don't tell anyone?'"

Cane and Zebiak published their forecast in *Nature* in June of that year, which gave anyone who cared to listen time to prepare. Despite a delay in its formation early in the forecast window, by the autumn of 1986, the predicted El Niño developed, bringing its associated weather patterns to much of the globe.

Most of Cane's work since that time relates to the impacts of human-induced climate change and natural climate variability on people around the world, such as a seminal paper studying the implications of El Niño on maize yields in Zimbabwe. He has also created a highly successful master's degree program in Climate and Society that prepares students to understand and cope with the impacts of climate variability and climate change on society and the environment.

"Science should be more than just an academic exercise," said Cane. "We're not just predicting this thing in the Pacific, we're trying to predict all these consequences around the world that people care about."

*B.A., Harvard, 1965; M.A., Harvard, 1966; Ph.D., Massachusetts Institute of Technology, 1975*

## *Predicting El Niño*

# MARK CANE

Professor of Applied Physics and Applied Mathematics and
G. Unger Vetlesen Professor of Earth and Climate Sciences

## *Recycling Carbon Dioxide for Energy*

# MARCO CASTALDI

Assistant Professor of
Earth and Environmental Engineering

Marco Castaldi, head of the Combustion and Catalysis Laboratory, focuses his research on understanding catalytic and non-catalytic reactions that occur when carbon dioxide is introduced into thermal conversion processes such as the gasification of coal. He recently developed and tested a simple method for converting biomass to fuel in which he added carbon dioxide to the process. When he did, he found that he produced significantly more fuel and less waste.

Humans currently produce nearly 30 billion tons of carbon dioxide each year, almost all of which ends up in the atmosphere. Most strategies to combat global warming focus on reducing the amount of carbon dioxide being emitted or on ways to remove the gas from the atmosphere. Castaldi's aim is to redirect a portion of those emissions to a useful purpose.

Producing energy from biomass is generally done in one of two ways: by burning the material and using the heat to spin a turbine or by extracting the carbon and hydrogen in plant material and using it to produce a hydrocarbon fuel. Of the two, the latter is more efficient and much less harmful to the environment. Synthesis gas, or syngas, is produced by heating biomass in a reaction vessel and injecting steam. It can be used as a stand-alone fuel or, as its name implies, to synthesize other chemicals and fuels. The reaction is an energy- and water-intensive process that can also leave behind large amounts of carbon in the form of unprocessed lignin.

Five years ago, Castaldi began investigating what would happen if he reused some of the carbon dioxide generated during syngas production by pumping it back into the reaction chamber. When he did, he discovered that the carbon dioxide reacted with the biomass resulting in higher efficiency. He also found that replacing about 30 percent of the steam with carbon dioxide reduced water usage and converted all of the biomass to syngas, leaving behind only a carbonless char.

Castaldi estimates that if the biomass were used to replace 20 percent of existing demand for transportation fuels, 1.4 billion tons of carbon dioxide would be kept from the atmosphere. Incorporating carbon dioxide into the fuel-making process would increase this to more than 1.8 billion tons—the same as removing 308 million vehicles from the roads.

"This is what engineering does best," said Castaldi. "Developing processes that can extract value from unwanted materials—to help make the world a better place."

*B.S., Manhattan College, 1992; M.S., University of California-Los Angeles, 1994; Ph.D., UCLA, 1997*

Polycrystalline materials are ubiquitous in all engineering structures and devices. Any two misaligned grains in these materials form a planar defect called a grain boundary. Boundaries can trap electrons in certain devices and can also demonstrate novel properties depending on the particular geometric misalignment, such as in superconducting oxides in regard to electrical transport. But that geometric misalignment is not the same between any two grains, even of the same material, making grain boundaries and interfaces among the least understood in materials science.

Identifying boundary types that have similar electrical responses has important relevance for next-generation technology like high temperature superconducting quantum interference devices (squids) for magnetic cardiograms and rare mineral explorations. Also, identifying chemical additions that can improve certain properties at boundaries has important implications; consider how adding manganese to steel in order to abate its brittleness could have changed the story of the Titanic. Already special boundary engineering has enabled zinc oxide varistors as surge protectors; positive temperature coefficient materials for temperature-activated switches; and new thin film transistors.

Siu-Wai Chan has focused on a systematic study of grain boundaries and interfaces relating their geometric structure, chemistry, and energetics with their electrical properties. Her research activities include the study of grain boundaries and interfaces in metals and oxides, particularly the fast ionic conductors and YBCO, a high-temperature oxide superconductor. She has placed emphasis on isolating and examining particular boundaries and their structures via high-resolution transmission electron microscopy (TEM) and measuring electrical properties via scanning squid microscopy. She has also developed methods to increase twin boundary density in superconducting oxide wires pinning magnetic flux lines and increase their super-current capacity.

Current research involves oxide crystallites with special metal additions as catalysts. Many researchers propose that the boundaries and interfaces exist in these catalysts play special roles in stabilizing the nanostructure and promoting reactions. Her early work on grain rotations explains accelerated grain growth in nanoparticles and thus reduced effectiveness as catalysts. These nanocrystals prepared in a single size and shape will be used to investigate optimization of catalytic reactions with crystallites of special shape and size. She investigates certain surfaces as active catalysts using scanning tunneling microscopy and spectroscopy and is exploring new techniques such as in-situ TEM applied to crystallites to look at their reduction and oxidation as they occur to lend insight into catalysis mechanism. She has five U.S. patents.

*B.S., Columbia, 1980; Sc.D., Massachusetts Institute of Technology, 1985*

*Investigating the Magical Properties of Grain Boundaries and Interfaces*

# SIU-WAI CHAN

Professor of Materials Science and of Applied Physics and Applied Mathematics

## Repairing the Microbial Nitrogen Cycle

# KARTIK CHANDRAN

Associate Professor of Earth and Environmental Engineering

Not everyone can lay claim to having helped found a new field of study or to having a unit of measurement named after them. Kartik Chandran can, but he tends not to. In fact, he'd prefer not to talk about either, except that the subject is very important these days.

Chandran focuses on the influence of nitrogen on global climate and the biosphere. As $N_2$, nitrogen is a largely non-reactive, but crucial, part of Earth's atmosphere. As nitrous oxide ($N_2O$), it is one of the strongest greenhouse gases. As nitric oxide (NO), it plays a role in ozone depletion and, at the molecular scale, in promoting resistance to anti-microbial products. Both can be formed in the process of wastewater treatment.

"We'd ideally like to convert everything to di-nitrogen gas," said Chandran. "But if we don't engineer bioreactors well, we'll just end up impairing air quality and possibly creating robust microorganisms."

Ideally, household and industrial wastewater is treated to convert nitrogen-containing compounds to $N_2$. However, the U.S. Environmental Protection Agency estimates that improper treatment methods lead to the accidental release of 24,000 tons of nitrous oxide in the U.S. alone each year. Because the gas is more than 300 times more effective at trapping heat in the atmosphere, the combined effect is equivalent to having more than one million extra cars on the road.

Nitric oxide is a byproduct of faulty or improper wastewater treatment. In the atmosphere, it converts to nitrogen dioxide, a major component of ground-level smog in cities. It also has the surprising property of helping microorganisms "learn" to become resistant to the human immune system and, potentially, to antibiotics such as tetracycline.

The obvious need for continued treatment of wastewater coupled with increasing concerns over the impacts of improper treatment have led to efforts by Chandran and others to launch the new field of azotomics, which examines the microbial structure and function of the global nitrogen cycle. In addition, Chandran's work has resulted in a new unit of measure, the Chandran number, which describes the propensity of microbes to produce nitrous oxide.

"We are going to be dealing with wastewater treatment and nitrogen pollution for a long time," said Chandran. "By improving understanding of the molecular mechanisms of the microbial nitrogen pathways and coupling that with new engineering tools, we can tackle these issues in a better fashion than we have been thus far."

*B.S., Indian Institute of Technology (Roorkee), 1995; Ph.D., University of Connecticut, 1999*

Every day around the world, an enormous amount of energy is wasted during power generation. The efficiency of fossil fuel power plants is about 40 percent and that of solar panels 25 percent, with the majority of the chemical and solar energies lost as low-grade heat. While scientists work on producing low-cost, efficient "clean" energy, 70 percent of the United States still relies on traditional carbon-based power and it is clear that, over the next few decades, we will still have to live with these traditional energy sources.

One researcher who may have found a way to harvest some of this lost energy through nanomechanics is Xi Chen. He is working with nanoporous materials, including nanoporous carbon, silica, and zeolite, materials that are readily available and low-cost, to convert ambient thermal or mechanical energy to electricity. The ultra-large specific pore surface area provides an ideal platform for energy conversion that yields unprecedented performance.

Chen has coupled nanoporous solids and functional liquids to create a multifunctional nanocomposite. "Depending on the combination of the solid matrix and liquid filler, the thermomechanical and electrochemical processes amplified by the large surface area may enable high efficiency energy conversion among mechanical, thermal, and electrical energies," he said.

The nanocomposite can simultaneously harvest electricity from the ambient low-grade heat and/or mechanical motions. Significant power output—many times higher than other energy-harvesting materials—has already been successfully demonstrated by his group. Chen envisions that the integration of such a system into existing power plants would be relatively simple, requiring no major change, and the nanocomposite would generate "recovered" power as inexpensively as several cents per watt. He is currently in talking stages with several companies for implementing this technique.

Chen is also looking ahead, "not so far into the future," he said, to multifunctional nanocomposite materials that could have broad, almost mind-boggling impacts: things like self-powered liquid armor that not only protects soldiers but also alleviates their battery needs, impact/blast-resistant skin for vehicles or aircraft whose shape will also morph to perform optimized functions, self- and wirelessly-powered sensors, among others. With these wide potential applications in aerospace, military, national security, and consumer areas, Chen is at the frontier of generating building blocks of intelligent materials for a smarter and more sustainable planet.

*B.E., Xi'an Jiaotong University (P.R. China), 1994; M.E., Tsinghua University (P.R. China), 1997; S.M., Harvard, 1998; Ph.D., Harvard, 2001*

## Harvesting Energy Via Nanomechanics

# XI CHEN

Associate Professor of
Earth and Environmental Engineering

SUSTAINABILITY

## Greening Infrastructure

# PATRICIA CULLIGAN

Professor of Civil Engineering
and Engineering Mechanics

In 2009, the American Society of Civil Engineers gave the country's water and sewage treatment, energy, and transportation backbone a barely passing grade of D, citing long-overdue maintenance and lack of much-needed upgrades. Patricia Culligan believes she can begin to address some of these inadequacies by changing the way engineers design infrastructure. At the same time, her work may help improve conditions for millions around the world living in rapidly growing urban slums who lack basic services.

Culligan would replace or augment these with smaller, more decentralized systems and facilities that can either meet the needs of a fast-growing population or help take the strain off an existing, aging network. One way is studying the role of small-scale infrastructure projects by examining the effectiveness of green roofs—flat roofs covered in a thin layer of vegetation—to cool buildings and reduce or mitigate storm runoff that flows from buildings into overburdened water treatment facilities.

Despite their growing popularity, Culligan has found that many arguments in favor of green roofs are lacking. "A lot of the claims being made are simply not proven," she said. "If this is going to work, there needs to be a scientific rationale behind it."

Culligan began her career studying the transport of chemical and radioactive contaminants through porous media such as soil, fractured rock, and ocean sediments, and later focused on mitigating contaminated groundwater. Since green roofs contain a thin layer of porous media through which water passes before being taken up by the plants or released, it was a natural segue to quantifying the technology's function and effect.

Old wastewater treatment systems in places such as New York City are routinely overwhelmed by street and building runoff, resulting in millions of gallons of raw sewage being dumped in local waterways each year. Green roofs may help absorb some of the runoff.

Columbia has seven green roofs, many of which Culligan and her colleagues have instrumented to study heat and fluid flows through the system. But the heart of the local green roof movement is the South Bronx, where many neighborhoods, finding themselves politically isolated, have begun to look for their own community-based solutions to such socially complex problems as environmental pollution. For this reason, Culligan has made community partnerships and interdisciplinary research the core of her approach.

"Our work is about giving people a better life," said Culligan. "It's about helping society prosper."

*B.Sc., University of Leeds (England), 1982; M.Phil., University of Cambridge (England), 1985; Ph.D., University of Cambridge, 1989*

Gautam Dasgupta has been working on a wide range of basic engineering problems that span from analytical formulation and mathematical modeling to practical applications. His work in classical civil engineering focuses on analyses of safe but economical design-analysis, such as the dynamic response of nuclear power plants in conjunction with the outwardly radiating waves generated at the soil interface under the action of earthquake excitation, and the effects of acoustic vibrations created by ocean waves on submerged or floating structures, initiating excessive material degradation and damage. He has also worked with spacecraft engineers, dentists, anthropologists, and historic preservationists. The common thread of his research is to relate the force and deformation of real-world systems. His personal interests are reflected in his research applications in computer music and computer-aided graphics.

Dasgupta focuses on research in engineering mechanics. The major objective is to relate the forces (causes) and changes of shapes and sizes (effects) in the real world of uncertainty. Thus his stochastic (models based on probability and statistics) were used by the NASA Glenn Research Center in Cleveland, Ohio, (then NASA Lewis Research Center) in the 1980s to analyze the damage in the main engine turbine blades of the space shuttles. His high-accuracy finite element formulations have been used since the 1990s to analyze the changes in facial bones, including the shape of teeth, as clinicians perform corrective surgery on patients.

Basic engineering mechanics also focus on material properties that change with time under sustained static loading or dynamic impact. The subsequent shape and size changes, which are studied under viscoelasticity and plasticity, have been adapted to computer simulations. Dasgupta derived important theorems for such changes that can vary with frequency and are different in different directions of deforming bodies. In conjunction with his defect-free (finite element) numerical models (of extremely low error), he proposed very large-scale simulations of crash tests for super computers. In order to minimize computing time, a large part of the calculation is carried out algebraically. This led to Dasgupta's development of symbolic computer programs to derive equations and generate conceptual (elegant) codes for numerical execution in a parallel computing environment.

Dasgupta is working on 3D analyses and computer code generation of incompressible fluids and solid mechanics modeling of complex surfaces and solid objects with zones of mechanical failure to be applied in a wide class of applications ranging from blood flow to the cooling mechanism of wind turbines.

*B.Engr., University of Calcutta (India), 1967; M.Engr., University of Calcutta, 1969; Ph.D., University of California-Berkeley, 1974*

## *Relating Forces to Real-World Systems*

# GAUTAM DASGUPTA

Professor of Civil Engineering and Engineering Mechanics

SUSTAINABILITY

# *Quantifying Uncertainty in Infrastructure Studies*

# GEORGE DEODATIS

Santiago and Robertina Calatrava Family
Professor of Civil Engineering

D o you ever wonder, as you drive across a suspension bridge, whether anyone really ever checks the bridge's cables? Or what might happen if you are in a building when the ground beneath it starts to tremble during an earthquake? George Deodatis has made numerous contributions in the general field of probabilistic mechanics: the reliability and safety analysis of structures, risk assessment, and risk management of civil infrastructure systems, earthquake engineering, and hazards analysis.

One of his current research projects deals with the monitoring and prediction of the safety of aging suspension bridge cables, with New York City's Williamsburg Bridge as one of his models. He is using stochastic field theory to deal with the various uncertainties involved in the problem of estimating the strength of the thousands of wires (several of which can be broken) contained within a suspension cable. His results are already helping to assess the current safety and future reliability of suspension bridges around the world.

Deodatis is also studying the effect of climate change on the civil infrastructure. "This is a problem of truly major societal significance," he said. "For example, how is sea-level rise—in combination with hurricanes—going to affect densely built coastal megacities?" He is working on this challenging problem, which involves a wide range of difficult-to-quantify uncertainties, with the ultimate objective of estimating the consequences of climate change and suggesting a wide range of mitigation measures.

Another important application of stochastic field theory that Deodatis is working on has to do with soil liquefaction, a destructive phenomenon that occurs during earthquakes, causing major structural damage, and with bearing capacity of soils, another phenomenon with major impact for the behavior of a wide range of structures on relatively weaker soils. "We are hoping to account for the inherent uncertainty of the soil mass," said Deodatis. "Learning more about these phenomena should lead eventually to improved mitigation strategies."

Deodatis is currently finalizing a book with Cambridge University Press about "Simulation of Stochastic Processes and Fields" in which he develops the theoretical foundations as well as the corresponding simulation formulas for a broad array of stochastic processes and fields. There are numerous applications of these theories in various fields of engineering and applied science, including earthquake engineering, wind engineering, micro- and nano-mechanics, offshore engineering, environmental engineering, materials science, atmospheric science, oceanography, finance, and many others.

*B.S., National Technical University of Athens (Greece), 1982; M.S., Columbia, 1984; Ph.D., Columbia, 1987*

Mining and mineral processing have occurred since the earliest times, producing materials for the manufacture of all types of useful objects, devices, shelter, and infrastructure. Half a century ago, it became paramount to mine and process minerals while protecting the environment and insuring the sustainability of Earth's resources.

Today, the multinational extraction and processing industry is making another step toward sustainability by refining present technologies that often result in waste. This waste can be commercially costly and environmentally hazardous when released into the air, ground, and water; in addition, significant amounts of minerals or metals can be lost to waste. The industry's goal is now to devise new reprocessing, recycling, and protection methods that comply with demands for responsible and sustainable business practice which could also turn hazardous waste into a profit generator.

Paul F. Duby is a prominent researcher in the areas of applying electrochemical principles and technologies to improve and design new mineral processing protocols. Examples of his and his students' work include a patent on fuel-assisted electrolytic metal extraction that lowers energy consumption and carbon dioxide emissions; a process to remove heavy metals and other contaminants like arsenic from sediments or from wastewaters; a recycling method that uses electrolysis on industrial waste to recover heavy metals and solar cell material; and a chemistry modification that improves hydrometallurgical processes.

His contributions to the reduction of energy consumption include the use of more efficient anodes for the production of metals in aqueous solutions and the electrolysis of mixtures of molten chlorides for the production of heavy metals or rare earths. The modeling of a hybrid system consisting of a high-temperature fuel cell and gas turbines that converts about 75 percent of the low heating value of natural gas to electric energy is an example of improvement of the efficiency of a power plant.

Corrosion and the resulting degradation of materials properties are natural processes that affect sustainability. Professor Duby has contributed to a better understanding of corrosion typically found on super alloys used on plane engines and steels for non-traditional power plants, and was part of the consulting faculty engineering team that designed and supervised the testing of and development of a rehabilitation and maintenance program for the Williamsburg Bridge in New York City.

*Ingénieur Civil Mécanicien et Electricien, Free University of Brussels (Belgium), 1956; Ingénieur Commercial, Free University of Brussels, 1958; Eng.Sc.D., Columbia, 1962*

## Driving Efficiency and Sustainability into Materials Processing and Energy

# PAUL F. DUBY

Professor of Earth and Environmental Engineering

# *Mathematically Modeling the Behavior of the Ocean*

## VINCENT DUCHÊNE

Ju Tang Chu and Wu Ping Chu
Foundation Assistant Professor of
Applied Mathematics

The ocean is a vast frontier that has fascinated mankind for centuries. But as much as we think we know about it, much more is mysterious. Consider the phenomena of internal waves. When two or more layers of ocean water—like fresh and salt water, or warm and cold water—rest one on top of the other without mixing, waves form between the two layers. This wave energy forms and dissipates, affecting everything from ships and submarines, drilling rigs and undersea cables, and the ecosystem of the ocean.

Studying waves on the surface of the ocean—where their formation and dissipation can be easily observed—is one thing. Trying to understand what happens below depths at the interfaces of water layers is almost impossible because measurement techniques are limited and available data are sparse.

By developing mathematical models to study the propagation of internal waves, scientists can numerically compute and study the behavior of hidden waves in relation to different parameters like depth and fluids densities. By applying that knowledge to oceanic fluid mechanics, new models can be constructed to improve our understanding of the effects of these waves and the energy they generate.

With that understanding, the design of marine structures and ships can be improved and the results of how pollutants mix and percolate to the depths of the ocean can be better monitored.

Vincent Duchêne develops mathematical models that seek to explain oceanographic challenges, especially those regarding the behavior of density-stratified flows constituted of two immiscible fluids influenced by gravity. He has been successful in producing and rigorously justifying models related to the dead water phenomena by reproducing the phenomena's key aspects which include generation of transverse internal waves at the rear of a body while moving at the surface of stratified flows and the positive drag on a body when an internal elevation wave is located at its stern. These models allow scientists to study the behavior of internal waves in relation to different parameters like the depth of the layers, densities of the fluids, and velocity of a ship.

Duchêne's other research interests include understanding problems related to the propagation of light through photonic crystals and partial differential equations with particular emphasis on hyperbolic equations.

*Ancien élève, École Normale Supérieure de Lyon (France), 2007; M.S.C., Université Bordeaux 1 (France), 2008; Ph.D., Université Pierre et Marie Curie (Paris VI), 2011*

Clean drinking water is something most of us take for granted. But many people around the world do not have access to clean water and the problem is only going to get worse in coming years, as populations increase and the water supply becomes more scarce. Researchers, including Christopher J. Durning, are working on improving the decontamination of water, in particular on developing ways—at lower cost and using less energy—to safely use wastewater and to desalinate sea and brackish water.

A current project Durning is working on is developing better filtration membranes for both the reuse of wastewater and the efficient desalination of sea and brackish water. In a project funded by the Pall Corporation, a leading manufacturer of water purification systems, Durning and his team are modifying the surfaces of ultra-filtration membranes with ultra-thin polymer/nanoparticle coatings to enable nanofiltration (NF) and/or reverse osmosis (RO) performance. "This surface modification method we use, layer-by-layer deposition, is a directed self-assembly process, and provides outstanding control of the surface layer architecture and chemistry," said Durning, adding that the resulting new NF and RO membranes will expand the range and capability of membranes useful for production of potable water via wastewater treatment and desalination. "Our aim," he said, "is to contribute relevant technology for the impending 'water crisis'."

Durning's research focuses on exploiting "soft" materials in a variety of new applications through their manipulation at the nanoscale. This requires an understanding of the key factors that control their structure and dynamics. He studies transport and diffusion, surface and interfacial behavior in polymeric systems, and self-assembly processes in soft matter systems. He is particularly interested in nanostructured materials, which he says offer unique advantages in many applications, such as high-capacity magnetic storage media, ultra-small photonic and electronic devices, graded layers and films for super-mirrors and notch filters, and "labs-on-a-chip."

He and his team are currently working to develop new ways to generate nanostructures, such as well-ordered arrays of nanoparticles and nanorods, via supra-molecular chemistry and self-assembly. They are also working to exploit established self-assembly methods, to provide new materials, such as nanocomposites, nanoporous solids, and structured surface coatings, that help address compelling technological problems, such as natural gas refining, fuel cell development, water purification, and toxin detection.

"It's very satisfying to see what starts as an esoteric basic finding develop into a practical solution for an important technological problem," said Durning. "It is especially exciting that our work in membrane science could help supply one of the world's most basic needs—clean drinking water."

*B.S., Columbia, 1978; M.A., Princeton, 1979; Ph.D., Princeton, 1982*

# Using Nanomaterials to Filter Clean Drinking Water

# CHRISTOPHER J. DURNING

Professor of Chemical Engineering

## Predicting Droughts and Floods

# PIERRE GENTINE

Assistant Professor of Earth and
Environmental Engineering

Climate change has brought increased concern over the rise of extreme weather events around the globe. Water resources are fundamentally impacted by climate change with more regions of the world affected by extreme weather, such as droughts. Incidents of heavy rain leading to flooding have increased as well.

Such events can have far-reaching effects on human health, the environment, and our society. The growing prevalence of drought conditions increases the risk of water shortages and wild fires as well as water- and food-borne diseases. Heavy precipitation affects the quality of surface and groundwater, can contaminate the water supply, and cause substantial disruption to settlements, commerce, and the infrastructure that sustains these communities.

Pierre Gentine studies the relationship between hydrology and atmospheric science, and its impact on climate change. His research began in Morocco from 2002 to 2004 as an engineer with the French space agency. There, he studied hydrology in a semi-arid region—a transition between the desert and a vegetated region.

Based on the data collected during those years, he has developed simple models to understand the hydrological cycle and the link between water resources and climate change. While other scientists are analyzing huge data sets in supercomputers, Gentine's models are simplified, to explain what's happening in the global climate in broad terms.

Gentine's research focuses on land and atmosphere interactions and the inherent feedback between the two systems. The overall motivation of his work is to improve the estimation of evaporation over land, which in turn improves water resources management, weather, and climatic forecasts.

"The Sahara desert was once green, some centuries ago, and is now totally dry," Gentine said. "We expect these semi-arid regions to evolve in the same way."

His scenarios predict more extreme weather—drier in places now experiencing drought, and wetter in regions beset with floods. In dry regions, increasing temperatures will make the soil even drier, which will stress vegetation, and result in less transpiration into the atmosphere. That, in turn, will lead to less rainfall. "With this feedback loop, the phenomena become worse," he said.

It's just the opposite in areas now experiencing higher than normal rainfalls, which has led to extensive flooding. Warm temperatures will increase humidity, and water from the soil will evaporate, putting more water into the atmosphere, creating the likelihood of even more precipitation.

*B.S.c., SupAéro (France), 2002; M.S., Massachusetts Institute of Technology, 2006; Ph.D., MIT, 2009*

The amount of energy from the sun that falls to the earth far, far exceeds our demand for energy. Sunlight would surely be of broad use in today's world if we could capture and convert it into electricity sufficiently, efficiently, and economically. The conversion of light to electricity is carried out in photovoltaic devices or, as they are known more commonly, solar cells.

These devices are typically made from silicon. Silicon, the basis for electronic circuits, is in many ways an excellent material. However, the basic properties of electrons in silicon imply that more than two-thirds of the incident energy will necessarily end up as heat rather than as electricity. Is there a way to avoid this energy loss and increase the efficiency of photovoltaic devices?

Tony Heinz is working to revolutionize our understanding of energy-conversion processes and the practical production of electricity from sunlight. He is exploring a new energy-conversion process, in which a single absorbed photon creates two or more electronic excitations. This process, Multiple Exciton Generation (MEG), is weak in conventional semiconducting materials, but Heinz is convinced that it will work with the right materials—novel nanoscale materials.

Heinz and his collaborators are making such structures—individual nanoscale photovoltaic devices based on carbon nanotubes and other tailored nanoscale materials—in which these ideas can be rigorously tested. He said that both the electrical and optical measurements require experimental advances. The program builds on recent progress in extracting photogenerated charges from individual carbon nanotubes and indirectly measuring the amount of light absorbed by such tiny structures through the use of new laser-based techniques.

"This is a very exciting fundamental scientific issue that goes to the core of understanding how light interacts with electrons in solids," said Heinz. "At the same time, it is a problem with the potential to have an important impact on addressing the world's needs for sustainable energy.

"As part of the Energy Frontier Research Center recently established at Columbia University with the support of the U. S. Department of Energy, we have the good fortune of being able to pursue these fascinating questions," he said. "At Columbia, we also benefit from an excellent collaborative research environment. This allows us to bring together the diverse expertise in science and engineering disciplines that is indispensible for progress in attacking these demanding problems."

*B.S., Stanford, 1978; Ph.D., University of California-Berkeley, 1982*

# Collecting Solar Energy with Nanomaterials

# TONY HEINZ

David M. Rickey Professor of Optical Communications and Professor of Physics

# *Tuning Nanomaterials for a Better World*

# IRVING HERMAN

Professor of Applied Physics and Applied Mathematics

Nanomaterials are viewed as a key part of 21st century manufacturing, with tiny particles whose properties change, depending on their size and shape, and how they are manipulated during the manufacturing process. Applications have already been seen in electronics, pharmaccuticals, and food products. Nano-sized structures can be built in different ways, with pre-selected properties.

For example, nanocrystals, which are intermediate in size between molecules and bulk crystals, emit more blue light when they are successively smaller, due to quantum mechanical effects. Creating such effects becomes more complex when working with assemblies of various nanocomponents

Irving Herman's research focuses on the fundamental aspects of matter and nanoscience. His work involves the assembly of nanomaterials from nanocomponents, as well as the investigation of the optical and mechanical properties of new materials composed of semiconductor and metal-oxide nanocrystals. His work has potential applications in harvesting light for solar cells, improving electrical and optical communications, and manufacturing products containing nanomaterials.

In one project, Herman synthesizes nanocrystals made of cadmium selenide or iron oxide, and assembles them with electrical fields to create materials that have properties in the nanomaterial intermediate-size range. This technique allows scientists to "tune" the materials to have different properties, based on their size, such as optical properties or magnetic properties. In other projects, Herman assembles three-dimensional arrays of nanocrystals, called supercrystals, which are comprised of many layers of ordered nanocrystals. He also assembles hybrid materials composed of nanocrystals and carbon nanotubes.

Herman's research also looks at the optical properties of these materials—how they absorb light or emit light after it is absorbed, which is called photoluminescence. He uses a process known as Raman scattering, in which the wavelength or frequency of light after it hits matter is discerned, to better understand the nanomaterial's properties. This has allowed scientists to couple nanocrystals and other nanocomponents to form nanomaterials. He has used Raman scattering to investigate strain and mechanical properties of nanocrystal films, which helps determine the integrity of products containing nanomaterials.

In addition, Herman teaches a course to Columbia undergraduates, "Physics of the Human Body," which looks at human physiology through the lens of engineering and the physical sciences. His textbook on this subject explains the mechanics of the static body and the body in motion. It also describes the body's materials properties, circulation, breathing, the acoustics of speech, as well as the body's electrical properties.

*B.S., Massachusetts Institute of Technology, 1972; Ph.D., MIT, 1977*

The battery has long been the energy storage device of choice, but limitations persist in life span, storage capacity, and weight. A growing number of researchers—including Sanat Kumar, chair of the Department of Chemical Engineering—are working to make high-energy capacitors (energy storage devices) become a viable replacement in electronics, hybrid cars, and electric power systems.

"Electrical energy is stored by a difference in charge between two metal surfaces, but unlike a battery, capacitors are designed to release their energy very quickly," he said. Kumar said the objective is to design high-energy capacitors, which would have big impact in industry and the military.

"Such an improvement in the state-of-the-art would have a substantial impact on the Department of Defense, making the move to electrified systems much more practical, for example, for aircraft launchers on ships," added Kumar. "Further, since we want to use plastics to make these capacitors, it will provide considerable savings in weight, which is highly desirable from a fuel consumption point of view."

Technological advancements would have an impact on transportation, as well.

"Advanced low-voltage capacitors are needed to facilitate more power-efficient and compact, portable electronic devices for communications, medical applications, and high-power electronics," he said. Applications include implantable defibrillators and power electronics for power conversion and distribution in hybrid electric propulsion systems."

The present and future needs do not stop there.

"Advanced high-voltage capacitors are needed for reactive compensation of electric power systems, energy storage, and distribution related to the interfacing of renewable energy sources to the power grid," said Kumar, "and for energy storage for pulsed power applications such as electromagnetic-based pulse power systems."

To meet the present and future demand, substantial advances beyond the present state-of-the-art in dielectric materials and capacitor technology are required. At the same time, new technologies will be developed for fabricating compact, high-voltage, high-current, high-repetition-rate capacitors that deliver energy in sub-microseconds.

"We will help to model the behavior of new materials that the group will propose as new capacitors," he said. "The goal is to design better capacitors from the ground up."

*B. Tech., Indian Institute of Technology, 1981; S.M., Massachusetts Institute of Technology, 1984; Ph.D., MIT, 1987*

## Storing Energy More Efficiently

# SANAT KUMAR

Professor of Chemical Engineering

SUSTAINABILITY

## *Producing Organic Photovoltaics*

# IOANNIS (JOHN) KYMISSIS

Associate Professor of Electrical Engineering

Long before the Gulf oil spill and President Obama's call for new efforts to reduce U.S. dependence on oil, Columbia researchers were working to reduce our dependence on the world's rapidly dwindling supply of fossil fuels. Ioannis (John) Kymissis and his team are working on producing organic photovoltaics that are easier and cheaper to manufacture than solar cells currently on the market.

Photovoltaics, which convert energy from the sun into electricity, have been around for more than 50 years. They are currently used in a variety of applications, such as roadside emergency telephones and traffic signs, and recharging batteries in remotely deployed electronics. Such installations potentially present a number of grid-level advantages in both advanced and developing economies. Distributed power generation through photovoltaics can reduce the load on strained distribution systems and provide power to remote locations where it may be cost-prohibitive or environmentally problematic to run power lines.

The rate of photovoltaic production has been increasing rapidly—more than 50 percent per year—but photovoltaics are still dwarfed by other sources of energy. Kymissis notes that photovoltaics produced only 0.02 percent of the total energy used in the United States last year; a new approach to photovoltaics is required to meet global energy needs.

Kymissis' team is involved in improving the performance and processability of photovoltaics using organic thin-film semiconductor materials that are elementally abundant, inexpensive to synthesize, and straightforward to deposit in large installations. The team is working on how to improve efficiency, reduce processing costs, improve storage lifetime, and increase the operating lifetime of organic photovoltaic devices.

Kymissis believes that thin-film semiconductors, with their ability to scale to large sizes, can solve a variety of sensing and power conversion problems. His group can fabricate systems that integrate a variety of thin-film devices, including photovoltaics and organic photodetectors, organic field effect transistors, piezoelectric polymer sensors, and organic light-emitting diodes. These integrated devices can be applied to applications in which electronics need to interface with large objects in the real world, such as sensors that can measure sound and airflow over an airplane wing.

"Our children will see the end of petroleum and our grandchildren will see the end of coal," said Kymissis. "It's essential that we start working today to reduce our dependence on finite energy resources to insure a better standard of living for future generations than we have today."

*M.Eng., Massachusetts Institute of Technology, 1999; Ph.D., MIT, 2003*

Engineering and science rely on the ability to make accurate predictions of material behavior in order to create innovative and transforming technological advances. Most properties of materials—such as electric, magnetic, thermal, and optical properties—are sufficiently well understood so that scientists can make meaningful predictions from fundamental principles of physics. Important exceptions to that rule are the mechanical properties of a material. Certain mechanical properties such as stiffness and thermal expansion can be calculated with great accuracy. However, others such as strength, plastic hardening, fatigue limit, ductile-to-brittle transition temperature, and fracture toughness cannot yet be calculated from fundamental principles. Therefore, engineers must rely predominantly on experiments to determine properties when designing new materials for life-critical applications such as those for the aerospace and automotive industries.

The defects of a material determine its interesting mechanical properties. Different types of defects can be idealized as being points, lines, areas, or volumes within a material, and the defect sizes can range from the atomic-length scale to the millimeter-length scale. Further, initial defects in a material create new defects, all of which subsequently move about within the solid and interact with each other in complex and different ways. The conceptual and computational challenges that must be overcome in order to predict the resulting mechanical behavior are daunting. One of the researchers at the forefront of this work to make meaningful predictions of mechanical behavior is Jeffrey W. Kysar.

Kysar's current research is focused on the mechanics and mechanical behavior of materials at multiple scales and under extreme conditions. A second focus is to create new materials that have mechanical properties which interact with other properties, such as optical or electrical, that can be used to make microscale sensors, actuators, and power generation devices.

Kysar was part of the Columbia Engineering team that completed the first strength tests on graphene in 2008, proving it to be the strongest material ever measured. The specimens used in those experiments were sufficiently small so that no defects were present in the material, which is the reason why graphene is so strong. According to Kysar, "The mechanical properties of graphene will enable its use in many new applications that require materials with excellent strength." More practical applications of graphene include use as a transistor that can take the strains of faster microprocessing in computers or as a durable, mechanically operated electrical switch for communications devices, including cell phones and advanced radar.

*B.S., Kansas State University, 1987; M.S., Kansas State University, 1992; S.M., Harvard, 1993; Ph.D., Harvard, 1998*

## Analyzing Materials Under Extreme Conditions

# JEFFREY W. KYSAR

Professor of Mechanical Engineering

## Creating Artificial Trees

# KLAUS LACKNER

Maurice Ewing and T. Lamar Worzel
Professor of Geophysics

There are people who think outside the box. Then there are people like Klaus Lackner who throw the box away entirely when they think. While others argue over new ways to reduce greenhouse gas emissions, Lackner has methods process that will, as he puts it, "close the carbon loop" altogether.

"Stabilizing the concentration of carbon dioxide in the air requires reducing carbon dioxide emissions to nearly zero," Lackner said to a congressional subcommittee recently.

"Think of pouring water into a cup. As long as you pour water into the cup, the water level in the cup goes up. It does not matter whether the maximum level is one inch below the rim or one and a half inches below the rim. In either case, you will eventually have to stop pouring."

To truly control carbon emissions, we would have to remove carbon dioxide directly from the air. The wind, he calculated, was vastly more efficient at transporting carbon dioxide to a collection device than it is as a means of generating electricity. By capturing the greenhouse gas from the air and locking it away permanently underground as carbonate minerals, it may be possible to fully neutralize the impact of large, concentrated sources of greenhouse gases.

Now Lackner has taken his ideas one step further and is working with Global Research Technologies to create artificial trees that will pull carbon dioxide from the air, just as real trees do. His air capture machines are like giant filters that trap the carbon dioxide that will be later freed and converted into a liquid, such as syngas, synthetic gas that can be used as a fuelstock. Alternatively, it could be disposed of through geologic and mineral sequestration.

Our reliance on liquid hydrocarbon fuels for transportation has led Lackner to search for affordable low-carbon production methods. He and his colleagues at Columbia's Lenfest Center for Sustainable Energy are looking for ways to apply the benefits of mass production to energy and fuels to drive down costs. In addition, he is taking a serious look at solar power as a way to eliminate carbon emissions from fuel production entirely and bring us closer to achieving a carbon-neutral society.

"Imagine if we decided to solve our garbage problem by putting houses on stilts and raising them a little every year," said Lackner. "That's what a lot of geoengineering amounts to, and that's not a solution to the problem. A real solution will only come by completely rethinking the way we use carbon."

*B.S., Heidelberg University (Germany), 1974; M.S., Heidelberg, 1976; Ph.D., Heidelberg, 1978*

The *Journal of International Affairs* might seem like an odd place for an engineer to publish, as Upmanu Lall recently did, but this engineering professor is used to addressing big questions with broad reach. Foremost in his mind these days: Will we run out of fresh water in the 21st century?

Since the 1980s, Lall has been focused on how society and water intersect. His interest began when he moved to Texas from his native India in order to study systems analysis and very quickly got involved in one of the most complex systems in the American West: water use. As part of his doctoral thesis, Lall examined the state's future energy and water demands, treating both as parts of one vast, interconnected system with often conflicting parts.

Today, Lall sees a looming global water crisis. In fact, the water crisis, as he sees it, is actually three separate crises—one of access, one of pollution, and one of scarcity—that do not lend themselves to simple solutions. Moreover, each is inexorably linked to the others and to additionally intractable problems like climate change and population growth.

Lall helped found the Columbia Water Center in order to address climate risk management across a range of temporal and spatial scales. "The possibility that North India may run out of groundwater in a decade leading to a collapse of agriculture in India is not viewed as a global problem," Lall and his co-authors wrote in the *Journal of International Affairs*. "In essence, the global crisis is viewed as a collection of local crises—whether they are related to access, pollution, or scarcity—for which there is a global policy imperative. We rarely address the global elements of these individual problems."

A key player in the looming water crisis is agriculture, which accounts for 70 percent of global water use on average and more than 90 percent in arid regions. Lall thinks that it should be possible to dramatically reduce regional water use while maintaining food security by improving irrigation systems, irrigation scheduling, and when and where different crops are grown. He also sees room for improving water use by improving food processing, storage, and delivery.

With one-third of the developing world expected to confront severe water shortages in this century, Lall sees a problem that is particularly suited to an engineer's mindset. "The goal of engineering to develop solutions to societal problems," said Lall, "fits into the domain of engineering better than anything else."

*B. Tech., Indian Institute of Technology (Kampur), 1976; M.S., University of Texas, 1980; Ph.D., University of Texas, 1981*

*Solving the Global Water Crisis*

# UPMANU LALL

Alan and Carol Silberstein Professor of Earth and Environmental Engineering and Professor of Civil Engineering and Engineering Mechanics

## *Stabilizing the Slippery Slope*

# HOE LING

Professor of Civil Engineering and
Engineering Mechanics

Sometimes the ground beneath your feet isn't as solid as it might seem. For many people living on hillsides and in flood plains or seismically active regions, this can be a deadly fact of life. Hoe Ling literally wants to reengineer the ground to make disasters like the one he surveyed in Taiwan recently a thing of the past.

In 2009 during Typhoon Morakot, more than 450 people died when Hsia-Lin Village in southern Taiwan was wiped off the map by a massive landslide that occurred when rain-weakened hillsides above the village let go.

"When you go to the site of a landslide, you really feel you should do something to help people," said Ling. "There are just too many slope failures."

Every year, nearly 100,000 people around the world die because the ground they are living on or the ground somewhere above them fails. The most common causes are earthquakes and heavy rainfall. In the United States, landslides account for as much as $2 billion in damages annually.

Ling is pursuing two lines of inquiry in order to address the problem. First, he is simulating the effect of heavy rain on soils using the department's geotechnical centrifuge to help model and predict soil and slope failure. Ling has used the instrument, which is one of the largest in the country and can generate a force 200 times that of gravity, to study such things as the failure of New Orleans' levees after Hurricane Katrina.

The other approach Ling takes is to develop geosynthetic materials that help reinforce areas potentially prone to fail. The polymer sheets he has developed are installed between layers of compacted soil to create walls and slopes that stand up to heavy loads and severe shocks such as earthquakes better than soil alone. Because geosynthetic materials don't rot or corrode like wood and metal, they are also more suitable as permanent reinforcing materials.

By combining his work to understand how and under what conditions a particular slope might slip with the application of new materials and techniques, Ling hopes engineers will eventually be able to quickly identify and reinforce high-risk areas. Then perhaps he and millions of others around the world will be able to sleep better knowing that the ground is safe.

Ling received the Career Award from the National Science Foundation in 2001. He has published more than 170 journal and conference papers in the fields of geomechanics and geotechnical engineering.

*B.S., Kyoto University (Japan), 1988; M.S., University of Tokyo (Japan), 1990; Ph.D., University of Tokyo, 1993*

P redicting the behavior of materials challenges scientists and engineers intent on developing new sources of alternative energy and applications for new materials, such as graphene, the one-atom layer of carbon that researchers say holds promise in a wide variety of applications. The materials used in battery storage are a key part of strategies to exploit renewable resources.

Understanding the behavior of material used in nuclear power and nuclear weaponry is also crucial to their safe storage. Plutonium, an active ingredient in nuclear weapons, has proved particularly challenging. With the international test ban treaty prohibiting experiments, scientists now predict how the materials react with many-body quantum theory, using supercomputers to determine how the electrons within these materials will behave.

"The plutonium in the weapons ages, and we have to be able to predict the properties of plutonium under a variety of conditions," Chris Marianetti said. "You need the material to be stable and work like you think it will work, and it turns out that it's difficult to predict."

Marianetti came to Columbia in 2008. He earned his Ph.D. in computational materials science and engineering at the Massachusetts Institute of Technology, focusing on applying first-principles methods, such as Density Functional Theory (DFT) and Dynamical Mean-Field Theory (DMFT), to energy storage materials.

Marianetti continued on to a postdoctoral position in condensed matter physics at Rutgers University. There, he continued developing/applying DFT and DMFT to strongly correlated electron systems. Following Rutgers, Marianetti moved on to a second post doctoral position at Lawrence Livermore National Laboratory (LLNL) where he utilized LLNL's world-class supercomputers to apply DFT and DMFT to plutonium.

With an element like plutonium, it can take several weeks to carry out his computations on one of the world's largest supercomputers. He has made numerous pioneering predictions, including the most accurate computation of the temperature dependence of plutonium's magnetic properties.

His research has also played a role in understanding the behavior of graphene, the single-atomic layer of carbon whose honeycomb lattice structure is among the strongest ever measured. Graphene, seen as a next-generation material, has many potential uses, from nanoribbons used in integrated circuit connections to transistors that could one day replace silicon, to construction of a tether winding its way through the atmosphere to outer space.

Marianetti's computations have determined how and why graphene fractures under tension, an important step in determining the limits of the material's future use.

*B.S., Ohio State University, 1997; M.S., Ohio State University, 1998; Ph.D., Massachusetts Institute of Technology, 2004*

*Predicting Behavior of Materials*

# CHRIS MARIANETTI

Assistant Professor of Applied Physics and Applied Mathematics

## Containing Hot Plasma for Fusion

# MICHAEL MAUEL

Professor of Applied Physics and
Applied Mathematics

Strong magnetic force fields confine high-temperature ionized gas, called "plasma," throughout the universe. At the surface of our sun, magnetized tubes of hot plasma, several millions of degrees, are launched with tremendous energy through the solar system. Around the earth, the strong magnetic field that we measure with a compass extends tens of thousands of kilometers into space and forms a protective atmosphere of ionized matter called the "magnetosphere."

"Scientists have been studying how strong magnetic fields confine high-temperature matter since the dawn of the Space Age," said Michael Mauel. "Today, a grand challenge of applied physics is to use our know-how of plasma physics to achieve one of the world's most important technical goals: a source of energy that is clean, safe, and available for thousands of years."

Fusion energy is the most promising source of energy meeting these requirements. Fusion uses the heavy isotope of hydrogen, called deuterium, to form helium and release huge amounts of energy. Every bottle of water contains enough deuterium to generate the equivalent of a barrel of oil when used in a fusion power source. But a major challenge remains: deuterium must first be heated to the temperature of the stars before fusion energy can be released.

Mauel is building experiments that test whether or not the magnetic fields used to confine high-temperature plasma at the surfaces of stars or in planetary magnetospheres can be used in the laboratory to produce the conditions that will make fusion energy work.

Together with colleagues at Massachusetts Institute of Technology and Professor Gerald Navratil at Columbia Engineering, Mauel builds and operates fusion experiments. These experiments, which have achieved temperatures of more than 100 million degrees, have pioneered numerous techniques for magnetic confinement.

Using these experiments, students and scientists explore how the shape of the magnetic force fields allows the hot plasma to be confined and heated; how the plasma mixes and swirls within the containment vessels; and how sophisticated high-speed control systems maintain the perfect symmetry required to maximize fusion power output.

Mauel has been awarded the Rose Prize for Fusion Engineering and received commendations of appreciation from the United States Department of Energy and Department of State. During the 2006-07 academic year, Mauel was the recipient of a Jefferson Science Fellowship from the National Academies. While at the Department of State, he served in the Office of International Energy and Commodity Policy assisting U.S. diplomatic efforts to promote energy security.

*B.S., Massachusetts Institute of Technology, 1978; M.S., MIT, 1979; Sc.D., MIT, 1983*

As an undergraduate at the California Institute of Technology, Faye McNeill studied the atmosphere for a very personal reason. "The air pollution there was bad," she said. "I have asthma, so I'm always a little more aware of atmospheric composition just because of the way I feel."

McNeill is particularly interested in how aerosols affect global climate. Because they are so small, gravity has little effect on aerosol particles and they can remain airborne for several days. Aerosols such as the sulfur compounds and ash emitted by Mount Pinatubo in the Phillipines pushed down global average temperatures for two to three years after it erupted in 1991.

Other aerosols can absorb incoming solar radiation or long-wave radiation reflected from Earth's surface, resulting in a warming effect on climate. The range of direct and indirect, compounding and conflicting effects makes aerosols one of the biggest unsolved problems facing climate scientists.

Aerosols can also have a wide range of chemical compositions, which reflect their diverse origins. Recently, McNeill and her team have focused on understanding the sources and properties of light-absorbing organic material, or brown carbon, in atmospheric aerosols. Often a byproduct of the burning of biomass, it turns out that brown carbon can also form through complex reactions in airborne atmospheric particles.

Brown carbon also interacts very differently with the atmosphere and environment than its inorganic cousin black carbon, and its roles in atmospheric chemistry and climate are just beginning to be understood. For one thing, black carbon tends to absorb radiation across the visible spectrum, but brown carbon preferentially absorbs shorter wavelengths of light and thus can influence the formation of ground-level ozone—the "bad" kind that leads to McNeill's asthma attacks.

McNeill is focused on the basic chemistry and physics behind the cloud-forming and light-absorbing characteristics of organic aerosols in the lab. She also works with other groups to integrate their piece of the climate puzzle into the big picture, including climate modelers who write the massive, computer-based simulations that attempt to predict how individual parts of the environment interact to govern Earth's climate.

"A big part of what we do is to communicate the results of our work to modelers," said McNeill. "The fundamental information we get in the lab will eventually find its way into better climate models." And that is something that can help us all breathe a little easier.

*B.S., California Institute of Technology, 1999; M.S., Massachusetts Institute of Technology, 2001; Ph.D., MIT, 2005*

## *Understanding Brown Carbon*

# V. FAYE McNEILL
Assistant Professor of Chemical Engineering

## Making Concrete "Green"

# CHRISTIAN MEYER

Professor of Civil Engineering and
Engineering Mechanics

One of the world's most important building materials, concrete, leaves a huge environmental footprint. The production of Portland cement, a basic ingredient of concrete, is estimated to cause the release of one ton of $CO_2$ into the atmosphere annually. The cement industry alone generates about seven percent of this greenhouse gas across the globe.

But Christian Meyer claims that concrete can be an environmentally friendly material—if, as he puts it, "you use as much concrete with as little Portland cement as possible." Meyer is at the forefront of the "greening of the concrete industry," from basic science to commercial production.

He has had great success using recycled materials in concrete, most notably, glass. Early attempts to use post-consumer glass failed because of the alkali-silica reaction, damaging the concrete. Meyer uses various cementitious admixtures as partial substitute of Portland cement, and has shown how colored glass can be incorporated for stunning architectural and decorative concrete applications, including tiles and countertops.

He has added shredded Styrofoam to make lightweight concrete, which has strong insulating and acoustic qualities and is cheaper to transport. He is currently exploring using recycled concrete as aggregate, noting that the United States generates about 150 million tons of construction waste annually and that concrete debris is more than 50 percent of that amount.

Meyer said that a key challenge is to identify special properties intrinsic to recycled materials that can be exploited and thereby generate added value, as in the glass tiles his team has made. He added that the use of recycled materials in concrete is governed by economic factors. "The profit motive is key," said Meyer. "If people don't think they can earn a reasonable profit doing something, they won't do it." But rather than simply using any waste materials as ingredients of concrete, Meyer prefers to explore how to add value to the various waste stream components and find ways to make better, more useful products while conserving natural resources.

Meyer is also using his expertise in concrete technology to explore ways to safeguard oil wells drilled deep into the ocean floor. He is hoping to develop novel materials that will reinforce the cement slurry with fibers to improve the fracture behavior and energy absorption. A specially developed device to measure the properties of slurries that hydrate under simulated downhole conditions has undergone the first successful tests in the Carleton Laboratory of the Civil Engineering Department.

*Vordiplom, Technical University Berlin, 1965; M.S., University of California-Berkeley, 1966; Ph.D., UC Berkeley, 1970*

Vijay Modi is an engineer in search of problems. That is, he has changed the way he approaches engineering, and in the process, is helping address some seemingly minor challenges that, on further investigation, are extremely complex and can change the lives of a large portion of the world's poor.

"Instead of starting with a particular narrow skill I had and trying to apply it, I'm trying to figure out what the interesting problems are and then seeing how we can bring engineering to bear on them," said Modi. "Sometimes it can be something as simple as creating a solar-powered lighting system that enables people in rural villages to do things after sunset like study or run a small shop."

By taking this bottom-up approach, Modi has discovered that he can categorize the problems he encounters into three groups: those he can make little immediate impact on, those that can have impact but require decades of research to solve, and those he might be able to solve with the help from the right people. It's that last group of problems that has attracted his attention of late.

It wasn't always that way. When Modi arrived at Columbia in 1986, he focused on questions involving fluid flow and heat transfer. Exposure to fellow Columbia Engineering professor Nicholas Themelis, and the Earth Engineering Center soon re-focused his priorities on problems that have fallen through the cracks of the academic community and private sector alike.

"Engineering research carried out in academia has started to lose connection with the profession of engineering, which is about solving problems," said Modi. "What historically separated science and engineering was that science was curiosity driven and engineering was problem driven." But many engineering problems today are inherently multi-disciplinary and require "system" integration.

The key, he believes, lies in assembling people with the diverse skills needed and a desire to apply them. In recent work to understand the problem of electricity access for the two billion who do not have it, Modi's team recognized the importance of allowing a "pay as you go" model for providing electricity from a "system" that did not require long wires from a central power station. The team included engineers who can design low-wattage meters, programmers writing communication, control and payment gateway software, and field practitioners who understand rural needs and capabilities.

Modi has helped design and test solutions to such developing-world problems as the need for a cleaner and more efficient cook stove, and robust IT systems that allow one to access information from remote villages. "These are projects that are not typically driven by large amounts of funding, but they occur in places that are in need of innovation," said Modi. "The key is to figure out how to make innovation happen in a low-tech, low-cost market."

*B. Tech., Indian Institute of Technology (Bombay), 1978; Ph.D., Cornell, 1984*

*Engineering in the Developing World*

# VIJAY MODI

Professor of Mechanical Engineering

## *Tailoring Thermal Transport*

# ARVIND NARAYANASWAMY

Assistant Professor of
Mechanical Engineering

Everyone knows that electronic devices can overheat and fail. This is becoming more of an issue as the devices used in our daily lives, from cell phones to laptops, get smaller—the influence of the size-scale effect becomes increasingly important. The ability to extract heat rapidly and efficiently is critical for electronic and optoelectronic devices. Arvind Narayanaswamy is one of the leading researchers studying energy transport in nanoscale structures and devices.

Shrinking a device's size greatly impacts its ability to transport energy, due to classical as well as quantum size effects. Fourier's law of heat conduction, which describes heat transfer well at macroscopic scales, breaks down at nanoscales. So does Planck's theory of radiation, when objects get much closer than a few microns. Recently, researchers, including Narayanaswamy, have discovered that the enhancement in thermal radiative transfer at nanoscale gaps can be utilized to increase the power density of thermo-photovoltaic energy conversion devices.

Narayanaswamy's team is addressing two broad areas of thermal transport: nanoscale effects on thermal radiative transfer and thermal transport in nanoscale polymeric materials. His work in radiative transfer focuses on understanding photon transport between nanostructures, and he has shown that by choosing appropriate materials, it is possible to overcome the limit on radiative transfer imposed by Planck's law by a significant amount. While this phenomenon may seem esoteric—most often, heat transfer in nanoscale devices is by thermal conduction—it could have an important impact on hard-disk drive technologies. Narayanaswamy is working with industrial collaborators to ensure that nanoscale thermal radiation does not have a deleterious effect on the performance of magnetic recording devices.

While nanoscale effects on thermal transport in solid-state materials have been well investigated, their influence in polymeric materials is less clear. Polymers are used everywhere, from credit cards and plastic bottles to organic optoelectronic materials. Thermal transport in polymers becomes especially important since they are poor conductors of heat; any means of improving heat conduction through polymers will improve device performance. Narayanaswamy's work focuses on understanding thermal transport in polymeric nanowires synthesized in his lab by different techniques. An important component of his research is technique development to enable measurement of heat transport through single nanowires.

"Our work on nanoscale thermal radiation is very exciting," said Narayanaswamy. "While it will be some time before we can translate our research into applications, the tools we've already developed are helping us start examining thermal transport in polymers. Our discoveries will have immediate engineering implications, especially in electronics cooling."

*B. Tech., Indian Institute of Technology (Madras), 1997; M.S. University of Delaware, 1999; Ph.D., Massachusetts Institute of Technology, 2007*

Gerald Navratil is among the world's leading researchers in the field of fusion energy. His findings have been incorporated in the design of ITER, the $12 billion international experimental fusion reactor project now under construction in France, which is expected to generate up to 500 MW of fusion power after completion of construction by 2018.

"It's a carbon-free way to provide energy, where the fuel sources are unlimited, and there's minimal long-term radioactive waste," said Navratil. "It could be an important part of our energy profile by the turn of the next century."

He conducts his experiments at three tokamaks—a donut-shaped machine that confines the super-hot plasma with magnetic fields. Ideas for experiments on his major projects are generated out of small-scale HBT-EP experiment in Columbia's Plasma Physics Laboratory. He then collaborates with teams of fusion researchers at larger tokamaks, like the DIII-D National Tokamak Facility in San Diego, Calif. and the National Spherical Torus Experiment in Princeton, N.J.

In 2010, his Columbia team on DIII-D was awarded $1.1 million and his team on HBT-EP was awarded $3.3 million to continue their work on these projects for three more years. Both projects are supported by grants from the United States Department of Energy.

A crucial issue in fusion energy research involves creating magnetic fields to contain the plasma at high pressure and at temperatures hotter than the interior of the sun. If the confined plasma become unstable, it comes in contact with the cold tokamak walls, loses its energy, and the fusion plasma is extinguished.

Navratil's experiments have focused on understanding the pressure limits of fusion systems. His team has created ways to increase the pressure—and the production of energy in future fusion power plant designs—while keeping the plasma stably contained. His team on DIII-D has been able to double the pressure in fusion systems, which quadruples the fusion-energy output. That's done by rapidly rotating the magnetically confined plasma. This important result was recognized in 2007 with the award to Navratil and his colleagues of the John Dawson Award for Excellence in Plasma Physics Research by the American Physical Society.

Another strategy for extending plasma pressure limits involves developing advanced forms of active feedback-control of the instabilities. That technique was pioneered on the HBT-EP experiment at Columbia, and is now being used in demonstration projects at the DIII-D tokamak in San Diego. Ultimately it will be employed in the operation of ITER in the next decade.

*B.S., California Institute of Technology, 1973; M.S., University of Wisconsin, 1974; Ph.D., University of Wisconsin, 1976*

## Stabilizing Plasma for Fusion Energy

# GERALD NAVRATIL

Thomas Alva Edison Professor of Applied Physics and Applied Mathematics

## *Looking at Light*

# RICHARD OSGOOD

Higgins Professor of Electrical Engineering
and Professor of Applied Physics and
Applied Mathematics

Sometimes, to solve big problems, you have to think small. Richard Osgood thinks very small. One of the biggest energy questions today is how to make solar cells more efficient and more affordable. This is particularly important for the billion or so people who live in poverty and, in most cases, entirely off the grid.

Osgood and the other members of the Surface Group in his Research Laboratory for Fundamental and Applied Science study the basic processes that allow some materials to convert light to electricity. It is a phenomenon that makes photovoltaic cells and fuel cells possible and that lays at the foundation of many hopes for a more sustainable future. But for all its promise, the process is surprisingly not well understood.

"This is a very basic question we're trying to address," said Osgood. "We need to know more about the fundamentals that limit the efficiency of charge transfer."

He and his team use ultra-short bursts of laser light to watch individual molecules of titanium dioxide accept or reject electrons. They also have made some of the first studies of titanium dioxide nanoparticles using the atomic-level resolution of a scanning tunneling microscope (STM) to understand how these novel structures can be used to improve solar cells.

Titanium dioxide is of particular interest because it is used in Graetzel cells, a type of low-cost photovoltaic cell that is easy to manufacture from readily available materials. Most low-cost cells are sensitive to only a narrow band of sunlight. The Graetzel cell, however, contains a layer of organic dye that produces free electrons from a wide spectrum of sunlight, much like chlorophyll does in plants.

The trouble is, Graetzel cells are only about seven to 10 percent efficient, meaning that, at best, only one out of 10 free electrons produces a current. Osgood and others would like to improve on this, but the reasons why one electron is captured and another is not remain elusive. Observing short bursts of laser light at a titanium dioxide crystal with an STM, Osgood and his team are nearing the ability to observe individual electrons being taken up or rejected by the crystal matrix.

Osgood hopes that, by focusing on the small stuff, answers to the big questions are not far off. "The world is changing in the way things are done," he said. "The number of people doing interdisciplinary work is growing every day. It's an exciting time."

*B.S., U.S. Military Academy, 1965; M.S., Ohio State University, 1968; Ph.D., Massachusetts Institute of Technology, 1973*

Ah-Hyung (Alissa) Park has been called the "Carbon Lady" for good reason. She is one of the leading experts in the many forms that carbon takes as humans transform the environment, and her path-breaking work may help pave the way to a future in which society obtains energy and materials from a wide range of sustainable sources and deals with its excess carbon in surprising ways.

"The future of humanity depends on our ability to use energy and materials with an eye towards environmental sustainability," said Park, who is also the associate director of the Lenfest Center for Sustainable Energy. "This will inevitably have to include efficient extraction of energy and materials from fossil resources, biomass, and municipal solid wastes."

Park studies the ways that carbon circulates through industrial and environmental processes. "The reason we take so much carbon out of the ground is because of our needs for energy and materials," said Park. "If we can find a way to keep the carbon circulating above ground while providing energy and materials, we won't have to take so much out of the ground."

More than seven billion tons of carbon produced by human activity around the world ends up in the atmosphere each year, primarily in the form of the greenhouse gas, carbon dioxide. Being able to manage our role in the global carbon cycle is an important step in the future of our society. Park is investigating novel ways to integrate carbon capture and storage (CCS) technologies with those that synthesize hydrogen and liquid fuels from coal, biomass and municipal solid wastes including non-recyclable plastics.

Today, Park is also working to advance efforts to capture carbon dioxide from emissions and lock it away permanently and economically. To do this, she is exploring the use of nanoparticle organic hybrid materials (NOHMs), a new class of organic-inorganic hybrid materials that consist of a hard nanoparticle core surrounded by functionalized corona. NOHMs are essentially solvent-free, particle-based fluids that provide a large number of capture sites for $CO_2$. By imposing frustration onto the corona structure, $CO_2$ capture can be enhanced via not only enthalpic but also entropic effects.

Park is also looking for ways to safely and permanently dispose of the captured carbon dioxide as mineral carbonates or to convert it to other useful materials such as paper or plastic fillers. The key to achieving sustainability is to take a more holistic view of the systems that process carbon.

"In the past, engineering has mainly focused on optimizing the individual unit of a process," said Park. "Today, we need to look at the big picture and add environmental sustainability to our equations."

*B.S., University of British Columbia (Canada), 1998; M.S., University of British Columbia, 2000; Ph.D., Ohio State University, 2005*

*Capturing Carbon for Sustainable Energy*

# AH-HYUNG (ALISSA) PARK

Lenfest Junior Professor in Applied Climate Science

# *Re-evaluating the Ozone Layer*

# LORENZO POLVANI

## Professor of Applied Physics and Applied Mathematics

**W**e don't hear much about the hole in Earth's ozone hole these days, and for good reason. Collective international action has been successful in reversing a decades-long deterioration of the protective layer in the stratosphere. The hole, which grows and shrinks seasonally over Antarctica, is expected to close by sometime mid-century.

Now, however, models and observations of Earth's atmosphere are showing that the ozone hole might have an effect on global climate patterns that may be masking the full impact of global warming. "The ozone hole has been ignored for the past decade as a solved problem," said Lorenzo Polvani. "But we're finding it has caused a great deal of the climate change that's been observed."

Polvani, who also holds an appointment in the Department of Earth and Environmental Sciences, has studied atmospheric dynamics from the surface to the upper stratosphere and from both poles to the equator. In the last few years, he has focused on understanding the effects that ozone depletion, and its eventual recovery, have on Earth's climate.

Ozone—a molecule made up of three atoms of oxygen—absorbs much of the sun's UV-B radiation. In the mid-1980s, it was discovered that chlorofluorocarbons, a chemical used as aerosol propellants, were breaking down the planet's ozone. In 1987, world governments signed the Montreal Protocol to ban chlorofluorocarbons.

Ozone warms the stratosphere when it absorbs UV radiation. Its relative absence over Antarctica for the past 40 years has had a cooling effect on the upper atmosphere over the South Pole that is as much as 10 times as strong as the warming effect associated with increasing carbon dioxide concentrations.

The effects of this cooling already appear to be affecting the location of the Southern Hemisphere's mid-latitude jet stream. Cooling of the upper troposphere—the highest part of the lower atmosphere—has been connected to a shift of the southern jet stream towards the south by a few degrees.

This shift has resulted in precipitation patterns moving south as well, and in the tropical dry zones expanding. Polvani's next task is to find out what will happen as the ozone hole closes and the full brunt of global warming is felt throughout the atmosphere.

"These next couple of decades are going to be interesting times," said Polvani. "We're going to see these climate changes play out in our lifetimes."

*B.Sc., McGill University (Canada), 1981; M.Sc., McGill University, 1982; Ph.D., Massachusetts Institute of Technology, 1988*

Any one of Peter Schlosser's three jobs could be a full-time undertaking. First, he studies Earth's hydrosphere as Vinton Professor of Earth and Environmental Engineering and professor of earth and environmental sciences. Second, as senior staff scientist at Lamont-Doherty Earth Observatory, he is involved in an array of large scientific programs. Finally, he is the associate director and director of research at the Earth Institute.

Rather than keeping them separate in his mind, he tackles all three together. "They all retain some distinct character," said Schlosser. "But in my daily life, they are all intertwined." Not only are they intertwined, but they also speak to the way Schlosser has always approached his work.

As an undergraduate student in his native Germany, he chose to study physics at a university with a long tradition and broadly-based research and teaching, because, he said, he wanted to see science as a holistic part of the entire university. Physics, he felt, gave him the opportunity to acquire a set of skills that would be useful for studying a wide range of scientific problems with societal relevance.

He eventually ended up in environmental physics, in part because of a natural curiosity in the world around him. Since arriving at Columbia in 1989, Schlosser has continued to feed his omnivorous curiosity about his surroundings by fostering connections with faculty members from departments across campus.

That broad perspective has helped him become a key part of efforts to establish and expand the Earth Institute. Schlosser has been integral in guiding the Institute's research agenda, which focuses on developing practical solutions to the problems that humankind faces in designing a sustainable future. At the same time, he recently founded the Columbia Climate Center, a part of the Earth Institute that specifically addresses society's needs for strategies to mitigate and adapt to climate change.

"Whether we can turn the world from a non-sustainable to a sustainable path has been on my mind a lot," said Schlosser. "I don't think we have a real answer yet, but the important thing is that we can see a path forward that is supported by technological innovation."

Schlosser emphasizes the need for communicating the messages of science clearly and accurately to a public that is often charged with deciding how to allocate resources to achieve a sustainable future. Exactly how to do that is a difficult question, but he feels it is possible with involvement from many different fields across campus.

"That, to me, is enough motivation to continue working and to look for solutions," he said.

*B.S., Heidelberg University (Germany), 1981; M.S., Heidelberg University, 1981; Ph.D., Heidelberg University, 1985*

## *Sustaining the Environment*

# PETER SCHLOSSER

Vinton Professor of Earth and Environmental Engineering and Professor of Earth and Environmental Sciences

# Harnessing Fusion: The Ultimate Green Energy

## AMIYA SEN

Professor of Electrical Engineering
and of Applied Physics and Applied
Mathematics

World demand for more efficient energy production is colliding with the need for environmental responsibility. Finding and harnessing a sustainable energy source is a paramount universal goal. If the nuclear fusion which occurs naturally in the sun can be replicated by science here on Earth, it will be possible to turn the heavy hydrogen that is available in abundance in seawater into a powerful, nearly inexhaustible source of energy.

However, while thermonuclear fusion has great potential as an efficient and environmentally friendly energy source, harnessing that power is hampered by fusion plasma's instabilities, fluctuations, and turbulence. The large variety of instabilities and fluctuations drain energy out of their core and vitiate the success of fusion devices.

An important tool in identifying and studying these instabilities is the Columbia Linear Machine. It was developed, repeatedly redesigned, and appropriately tailored with striking ingenuity for the physics requirements of each instability by Amiya Sen. His efforts, extending over many years, led to the very first production, identification and detailed parametric studies of trapped particle, ion, and electron gradient instabilities and their transport consequences.

With his sustained pioneering theoretical and experimental efforts in the relatively new field of feedback control of plasma instabilities, Sen has established himself as a leader in this critically important area. These efforts include the Lyapunov stability of plasmas, the observability, controllability, and feedback suppression of most plasma instabilities.

Recently, Sen has pioneered a new paradigm for plasma transport, which challenges the 50-year-old gold standard of Bohm/gyro-Bohm scaling. This finding promises to have a great impact on the quest for fusion.

By far the most prestigious archival journal in physics and applied physics is *Physical Review Letters*. Sen and his students have published 17 papers in this, and in numerous other publications.

Sen has been a consultant and advisor to the Lawrence Livermore National Laboratory, the Princeton Plasma Physics Laboratory, the United States Department of Energy, and the National Science Foundation. He is a fellow of the American Physical Society and the Institute of Electrical and Electronics Engineers, and is a member of Sigma Xi and the American Geophysical Union.

*Dipl., Indian Institute of Science, 1952; M.S., Massachusetts Institute of Technology, 1958; Ph.D., Columbia, 1963*

Adam Sobel once bought a plane ticket to the city of Darwin in Australia's tropical north based on a colleague's weather prediction. That in itself is nothing new—people do it all the time. But the prediction he followed was for the start of the monsoon rains three weeks hence, a prediction that was virtually unheard of just a decade earlier for the length of its foresight. When he got off the plane, no one was happier to see the sky open up and the rain begin right on schedule.

"We had half a meter of rain in 10 days," said Sobel. "It was exciting."

For more than one billion people, the seasonal monsoons are both a life-giving annual event and a potential disaster. Although much is known about how the monsoons occur, very little is understood about how they vary.

Monsoons are an atmospheric circulation pattern that develops in the tropics at fairly well-defined times of year. The sun warming the surface of the earth draws moisture from ocean waters and forms the iconic, seasonal rains of South and Southeast Asia or sub-tropical Africa and South America. The people who live in these regions, particularly the rural poor, rely on the monsoon rains to water crops and recharge aquifers.

When the monsoons are weak, drought and famine can result; if they come with too much gusto, flooding and disease occur. The fine line between life and death makes monsoon forecasting one of the most important topics within climate modeling these days. Sobel is trying to develop models to predict the variations within a monsoon season, known as "active" and "break" cycles, which have so far been beyond the ability of climate modeling. Recently, he helped demonstrate the central importance of heat stored in the oceans on the formation of active and break cycles.

The atmospheric patterns that drive the monsoon are also responsible for spawning tropical storms in distant ocean basins and may influence the formation of El Niño and La Niña cycles in the western Pacific. As a result, Sobel's work may one day have an impact on people who live well beyond the reach of the monsoon rains.

"We need a central theory that can be stated simply that explains the variations we see," said Sobel. "Weather prediction can look two weeks in the future, max. Climate models can give us the probability for a strong or weak monsoon a year in advance. This is in between. It's kind of the Holy Grail right now."

*B.A., Wesleyan University, 1989; Ph.D., Massachusetts Institute of Technology, 1998*

## *Modeling Monsoons*
# ADAM SOBEL

Professor of Applied Physics and Applied Mathematics and Professor of Earth and Environmental Sciences

## Fostering New Ways to "Green"

# PONISSERIL SOMASUNDARAN

LaVon Duddleson Krumb
Professor of Mineral Engineering

Ask Ponisseril Somasundaran to say something in Hindi and he will jokingly beg ignorance aside from "a few common bad words." Ask him what he thinks "sustainability" means, though, and he will quote the Hindu tenet of *nishkam karma*, or selfless action, that entails making sacrifices today for the sake of the future.

A world leader in surfactant science, Somasundaran has used his expertise to take on problems as wide-ranging as the enrichment of scarce minerals from ultra-lean ores, to the impact of cigarette smoke on lungs, to the behavior of nanoparticles. His current mantra, however, is sustainability.

"Sustainability has several different meanings," said Somasundaran. "It is like the four blind men describing an elephant." In that Sufi tale, four blind men each disagree about the true nature of an elephant because each feels a different part of the animal. Like those men, but with his eyes wide open, Somasundaran is approaching sustainability from several perspectives.

"There is a fundamental disconnect in the sustainability movement when it comes to consumer products," he said. "An increasing number of people are choosing products based on third-party green certification, but many of these labeling programs give little weight to the full scope of a product's lifecycle, from manufacture and shipping, to use and disposal."

An example is liquid soaps and detergents, which contain large amounts of water. Somasundaran's approach has been to reduce the amount of water in these products to lower the amount of packaging they require and the amount of fuel needed to ship them. He has applied a similar water-saving approach to mineral processing and mine tailing treatment by developing chemicals that require less water consumption.

More recently, Somasundaran has begun to focus on agriculture, which is notorious for its enormous demand for water. Even modest savings in agricultural water use could translate to huge gains globally. Using cellulose nanoparticles, which naturally curl to trap droplets of water, he is trying to develop a targeted release mechanism to water just the roots of crops and only when the soil is too dry or when high temperatures threaten crops.

His next target may be the carbon footprint. Somasundaran is convinced that focusing solely on carbon is far too narrow. "We need to broaden our notion of what is sustainable," he said. Then, perhaps, we will all be able to see the entire elephant.

*B.Sc., University of Kerala (India), 1958; B.E., Indian Institute of Science, 1961; M.S., University of California-Berkeley, 1962; Ph.D., UC Berkeley, 1964*

# MARC SPIEGELMAN

Professor of Applied Physics and
Applied Mathematics and Professor of Earth
and Environmental Sciences

Growing up, Marc Spiegelman dreamed of one day being the next Jacques Cousteau. The only problem was he enjoyed hiking more than diving and he excelled at math and physics rather than oceanography. Two summers spent working as a ranger for the United States Forest Service and the discovery that the planet often reveals its secret inner workings through calculus sealed his future.

Spiegelman now studies the interior of the planet using the tools of a computational physicist to understand how Earth's crust and mantle behave in tectonically active regions of the world. More recently, he has begun considering a problem that has traditionally attracted scientists with a more airy focus: what to do with all the carbon dioxide in the atmosphere.

Spiegelman's principle expertise involves applying theories that describe the migration of magma and fluids in the solid earth, and the behavior of solid materials under the immense heat and stress of the deep earth. His efforts are helping create a more general understanding of the interactions between solids and fluids in the mantle and crust. This work has applications to understanding the behavior and output of volcanoes around the globe like Eyjafjallajökull, the volcano in Iceland that erupted in early 2010 and shut down air travel over much of Europe for nearly one month. His work also provides insights into such problems as the interactions between reactive fluids and a variety of minerals found in the earth.

His expertise is attracting attention from new circles because it turns out that one of the more promising ideas for dealing with excess carbon emissions involves the solid earth. Geological carbon sequestration, a problem that Spiegelman's colleagues at the Lamont-Doherty Earth Observatory are actively investigating, entails injecting carbon dioxide into certain mineral formations found in many places around the world.

Spiegelman's ability to work between the worlds of observation and modeling may one day prove crucial in understanding what happens when carbon dioxide under immense pressure reacts with mineral formations containing magnesium. Such reactions produce extreme heat, which cracks the rock, and form solid magnesium carbonate, locking the carbon dioxide away safely and permanently.

It is this ability to model unobservable interactions between solids, fluids and heat deep underground that gives him a leg up on his old hero, Jacques Cousteau. Instead of a view into the depths of the ocean, Spiegelman has been able to see through his equations and models into the deepest recesses of the upper Earth.

*B.A., Harvard, 1985; Ph.D., University of Cambridge (England), 1989*

## Keeping Wind Turbines Turning

# ELON J. TERRELL

Assistant Professor of Mechanical Engineering

Around the world, communities are increasingly utilizing wind power because it is a clean, sustainable source of renewable energy, is fast to deploy, creates jobs, uses very little water, and is economically competitive. In fact, wind power is the fastest-growing source of energy production, having grown from zero production in the early 1980s to more than 120,000 megawatts worldwide as of 2008. But as wind turbines are increasingly being installed, their power systems are being challenged by a number of issues, especially exposure to harsh operational and environmental conditions, as well as the effects of contamination from the environment.

Elon J. Terrell is an expert in tribology, the science of friction, lubrication, and wear within sliding and contacting interfaces. He uses analytical, numerical, and experimental techniques to analyze the interfacial interactions and the wear between sliding surfaces in either dry sliding or lubricated contact. Since friction and wear are challenges for devices that contain moving components, his research interests include power generation, energy conversion, energy harvesting, microelectromechanical systems (MEMS), and health sciences.

One of Terrell's current projects is focused on the multiphysics analysis of contaminated cyclic rolling-sliding contacts to gain a better physical understanding of the behavior of an interface between two lubricated surfaces. His primary testbed involves particulate contaminants in a lubricated gearbox system, such as those used in wind turbines. A vital aspect of his research is the combined modeling of the various physical interactions that take place within this interface, including lubricant fluid flow, particle motion, particle-surface contact, and the resultant abrasive wear experienced by both surfaces.

To better understand the lubrication of contaminated gear trains, Terrell's group is using mesh-free particle methods, wherein the lubricant flow, the contacting surfaces, and the particles are all represented by virtual particles that interact with one another and move dynamically with time. Although studies have involved the use of these methods for fluid mechanics and solid mechanics, Terrell's group is seeking to be the first to use them to integrally connect fluid mechanics, solid mechanics, and particle dynamics into a single predictive simulation.

His other research interests include the study of crack initiation, propagation, and agglomeration under low-amplitude cyclic loading, work that will help to better explain why the bases of gas turbine blades fail after a given amount of use. Terrell is also exploring the possibility of applying electrokinetics to thin film lubrication, a project that is mostly applicable to devices such as MEMS and magnetic data storage devices.

*B.S., University of Texas (Austin), 2002; M.S., University of Texas, 2004; Ph.D., Carnegie Mellon University, 2007*

Aging infrastructure is of great concern to all of us on the planet—no one wants to drive over a bridge that may collapse or live or work in a building whose structure is failing, but oftentimes it is difficult to predict catastrophe. Rene Testa is an expert in structural mechanics and materials, and has focused his research on the deterioration and failure of materials and structures of all kinds, especially buildings and bridges.

Testa, who is also the director of research for the Carleton Laboratory at Columbia Engineering, has extensive experience in infrastructure assessment and rehabilitation, including work on New York City's Whitestone, George Washington, Brooklyn, and Triborough bridges. He has also done testing on the Manhattan, Walt Whitman, Verrazano Narrows and Throgs Neck Bridges, as well as on high- and low-rise buildings. He has formulated an optimal maintenance and repair strategy for management of a system of bridges like the one developed for, and used by, the city. His current research focuses on the use of vibration monitoring to detect damage in structures, the characterization of damage in materials, and the management of bridge maintenance.

Many of Testa's projects dealing with material and structural performance are conducted in the Carleton Lab. Research on sustainability of aging urban infrastructure is being greatly advanced by the development of a new accelerated-aging test facility in the lab. Testa notes that "this will provide far greater capability for research relating to aging infrastructure by both senior and junior members of the civil engineering faculty."

Testa's research has also included the analysis of failed structures, mechanical systems, and components of metallic and cementitious materials. He has worked on composite materials, the inelastic response of concrete, and modeling of the mechanical response of structural fabrics for which he holds a patent for a stress transducer.

"Much of my work over the years has involved real structures, especially when there is a failure—its cause must be determined to provide an opportunity for learning," said Testa.

"In fact, a failure is only a total failure if nothing is learned from it. While research that focuses purely on fundamental theory of structures and continuum mechanics is elegant and valuable in propagating knowledge and gives me much satisfaction, it is the research that is driven by actual application that is the most gratifying."

*B.E., McGill University (Canada), 1959; M.S., Columbia, 1960; Eng.Sc.D., Columbia, 1963*

*Maintaining Aging Urban Infrastructure*

# RENE B. TESTA

Professor of Civil Engineering and Engineering Mechanics

# *Building Single-Molecule Circuits*

# LATHA VENKATARAMAN

Associate Professor of Applied Physics
and Applied Mathematics

As electronic devices become ever smaller, and the demand for ever tinier components grows, understanding how current flows through these materials at the nanometer (billionth of a meter) scale is becoming increasingly important. Latha Venkataraman conducts research on the molecular level, where she focuses on probing, manipulation, and control of single molecules as active elements in electrical circuits. "I am working to understand the interplay of physics, chemistry, and engineering at the nanometer scale," she said.

By probing and understanding electronic structure and properties at this scale, her research findings will not only influence the design of molecules as active electronic components; they will also enhance the understanding of charge transport across metal-organic interfaces, with impact on the fields of organic electronics, photovoltaics, catalysis, and biological processes, including respiration and photosynthesis. "These experiments provide a deeper understanding of the fundamental physics of electron transport, while laying the groundwork for technological advances at the nanometer scale," she said.

To fabricate circuits with a single molecule, a physical connection has to be made between the single molecule at the nanoscale and the metal electrodes, in microscale. Building such circuits with atomic precision is beyond the capabilities of top-down approaches; indeed, one of the main challenges has been to figure out how to measure the resistance of electronic components that consist of a single molecule. Although there are a number of techniques that have been used, the large variations in the experimental results produced by these techniques had made it difficult to predict how individual molecules will behave as electronic devices.

Venkataraman's pioneering research has made possible these measurements by using a bottom-up approach to form single-molecule circuits where a molecule self-assembles into a gap between two metal electrodes. The ability to create devices with known structure is then controlled by the chemistry at the metal-molecule interface, which can be tuned.

In her lab, these device fabrications and their characterizations are carried out using state-of-the-art scanned-probe microscopes, which are built inhouse to have sensitivity to small currents and forces, as well as to have the required mechanical stability. In her group, these instruments are then used, for example, to measure electronic conduction or single bond breaking forces. They show that these properties relate not only to the molecular structure, but also to the metal contacts and linking bonds.

"A single-molecule circuit is the ultimate limit one can achieve," says Venkataraman. "Understanding how to control and transfer charges on this scale allows us to push the frontier."

*B.S., Massachusetts Institute of Technology, 1993; M.S., Harvard, 1997; Ph.D., Harvard, 1999*

# HAIM WAISMAN

Assistant Professor of Civil Engineering
and Engineering Mechanics

The I-35 bridge collapse in Minneapolis, Minn. in 2007 killed 13 people and resulted in untold economic disruption for the Upper Midwest. It also brought to stark relief a problem with the nation's infrastructure: it is old and getting older every day.

Haim Waisman is developing computational techniques to help understand how and why things fall apart, and how this may be predicted and prevented. "Fractures govern our lives," he said. "Everything is connected by fractures."

Waisman is refining computational methods known as extended finite elements and multiscale modeling to design high-strength, nanocomposite materials that might one day shore up aging structures, such as pipes and bridges, in corrosive environments. He also has developed a non-invasive method of detecting fractures in things such as an airplane wing using measurements from only a few common stress sensors.

In particular, he has been using his methods to study how suspension bridge cables age. The main cables are made of thousands of wires clamped and wound together. When a wire breaks, the loads it carries are redistributed to neighboring wires. Understanding and predicting the fracture response of the entire cable considers as many as 50,000 wires wound into a tightly compressed bundle more than two miles long, and requires a supercomputer.

He has found that, when a wire breaks, friction between the remaining wires can effectively transfer the strain throughout the cable bundle without compromising the entire bridge. That's a relief for the millions of people who daily cross the graceful, but aging, bridges that lead into and out of Manhattan.

Fractures also play a role in nature and Waisman has recently turned his attention to a dramatic example—the collapse of ice shelves in Greenland and Antarctica. As the climate warms, water from melting ice seeps to the bottom of glaciers, allowing them to slide more easily over bedrock and forming networks of cracks in ice shelves.

In 2002, 1,250 square miles of the Larsen B ice shelf in West Antarctica shattered, sending icebergs into southern shipping lanes. Since then, several other shelves have collapsed, threatening sea-level rise around the world. Understanding how things like ice shelves and bridges break and fail is a necessary first step to understanding the inevitable changes going on all around us all the time.

*B.S., Technion Israel Institute of Technology, 1999; M.S., Technion Israel Institute of Technology, 2002; Ph.D., Rennselaer Polytechnic Institute, 2005*

# Using Optoelectronics for Chemical and Environmental Sensing

# WEN WANG

Thayer Lindsley Professor of Electrical Engineering and Professor of Applied Physics and Applied Mathematics

The human body naturally emits trace amounts of about 500 chemicals. Likewise, the atmosphere contains hundreds of chemicals that, in trace amounts, do not adversely affect our breathing or health. When these chemicals become out of balance—such as from illness, chemical weapons, or hazardous waste—often only complex chemical testing can diagnose their presence.

Because every molecule has a unique absorption signature, optoelectronic devices hold the promise of providing effective identification of chemicals, by analyzing a molecule's absorption. For example, light from a semiconductor laser could pass though the molecules in a person's breath, the absorption could be measured and determination made—within minutes—about what chemicals are present and in what amounts. By providing fast and effective trace gas detection, this technology has application in environmental sensing (measuring the atmosphere for pollutants), industrial process control (chemicals and food products) and medical diagnostics.

Wen Wang is an eminent researcher in optoelectronic materials, devices, and molecular beam epitaxy. He focuses his research on creating knowledge that can be applied to real-world problems. His current projects include nano and heterostructure material properties, optoelectronic devices, infrared lasers, detectors, and photovoltaics.

He has contributed some 250 papers and published extensively in this area, e.g. Type-II InAs/GaSb superlattices for mid- and long-wavelength applications (Quantum Structure Infrared Photodetectors International Conference, 2010, Istanbul, Turkey); High detectivity InGaAsSb photodetectors with cutoff wavelength up to 2.6 um (J. Crystal Growth, 2009); Interface and optical properties of InGaAsNSb quantum wells (very low threshold 1.3 um lasers, J. Vac. Sci. Tech. 2007); Mid-infrared InGaAsSb quantum well lasers with digitally grown tensile-strained AlGaAsSb barriers (J. Vac. Sci. Tech. 2007); Strain-compensated InGaAsSb quantum well lasers emitting at 2.43 um (environmental and glucose sensing, IEEE PTL, 2005); Invention of a new quinternary dilute nitride InGaAsSbN for mid-infrared optoelectronic devices (JAP 2003 and APL 2001).

Wang is a fellow of the Institute of Electrical and Electronics Engineers, the American Physical Society, John Simon Guggenheim Foundation, and is an Electron Device Society distinguished lecturer.

*B.S., National Taiwan University, 1975; M.E.E., Cornell, 1979; Ph.D., Cornell, 1981*

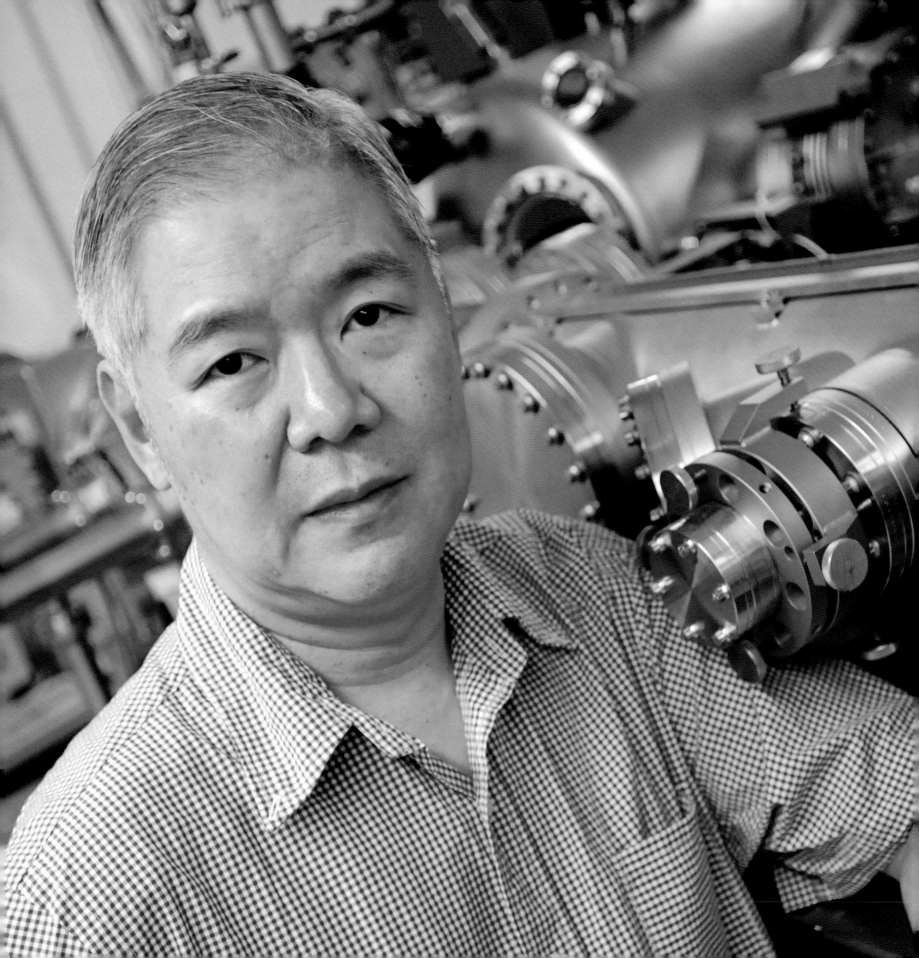

Imagine genetically engineering a microbe to produce a biofuel by growing on ambient carbon dioxide from the atmosphere and ammonia from wastewater or generated electrochemically. This carbon-neutral bio-electrochemical process is being developed to produce butanol, a biofuel compatible with today's vehicles, and is just one of many projects that Alan West is working on with his colleagues.

West's research focuses on a large number of problems that he says are often characterized as belonging to "electrochemical engineering." He and his team have studied applications of electrochemistry to the production of advanced electronic devices. For example, the "wiring" used to make integrated circuits in logic and memory chips used in personal computers is made through the process of electroplating.

West works on electrochemical application for energy storage (i.e., batteries) and conversion (fuel cells). Working closely with Scott Banta of the Department of Chemical Engineering and Lt. Col. Robert Bozic from the USMA, he has also developed bio-electrochemical sensors that can be employed in a range of applications, including environmental monitoring of potential toxins in groundwater and assessing the safety of drinking water.

West notes that electrochemical technologies will play a key role in sustainable energy, and he and his colleagues have increasingly turned their attention to studies of batteries that can be economically scaled for use in conjunction with large-scale renewable energy production and with a smarter electrical grid. Energy storage such as that provided by batteries accommodates variations in energy production by renewables. For some applications, it may be better to store excess electrical energy in the form of a fuel by using electrolysis (think of a fuel cell running in reverse). In such a technology, a fuel cell is used to oxidize the fuel to produce electricity. West has also been collaborating with Klaus Lackner of the Department of Earth and Environmental Engineering on developing these electrochemical conversion systems.

"We continue to be fascinated by our studies of electrochemical systems because we collaborate with colleagues from a wide variety of disciplines," said West. "It is very gratifying that our work is directly applicable to industrial interests, while addressing long-term environmental and energy needs. We particularly enjoy working with industrial colleagues, in part to keep our ideas grounded in reality and also to provide job opportunities for our students."

*B.S., Case Western Reserve University, 1985; Ph.D., University of California-Berkeley, 1989*

## Applying Electrochemical Technologies for Sustainable Energy

# ALAN C. WEST

Samuel Ruben-Peter G. Viele Professor of Electrochemistry

## *Controlling Light with Nanostructures*

# CHEE WEI WONG

Associate Professor of
Mechanical Engineering

Quantum physics has come a long way, and the advent of nanostructures has enabled researchers to observe experiments once relegated to textbooks. Chee Wei Wong is at the forefront of examining the control of light with nanostructures, with interesting results.

"When you can trap light in a confined space and bounce it back-and-forth for a time equivalent to one million optical cycles, its intensity gets really strong," said Wong. This intensity, when tuned to resonances, such as atomic transitions or mechanical radio-frequency vibrations, can speed up or cool down the other process. An exciting subset is laser cooling of nanomechanical beams to its fundamental quantum mechanical ground state, "the coolest state of its eigenmodes," he said. With the discovery of nanostructures and coherent lasers, researchers can now explore mechanics of quantized structures, "where it's mind-boggling that so many atoms can act in such a coherent way."

Wong focuses on the physics and engineering of nanoscale optics, e.g. optical interconnects and ultrafast lasers for infrastructures, and photovoltaics for sustainability. His team can not only trap light in a small box, but also use nanostructures to slow light down, forcing increased interactions with its surroundings. Wong is compressing light pulses at 100-femtosecond timescales and generating new frequencies for next-generation optical networks.

Wong notes that even the single photon has many properties not yet fully understood. It can encode much information in its many degrees-of-freedom (vortices, timing, polarization, etc.). It can interact with a single quantum dot for new computational ways. It can interact with, or generate, another photon in non-classical distributions. It can interact with a phonon for metrology purposes. Trapped in a confined nano-space for one million cycles, many of these effects are enhanced. These have fundamental security implications because, Wong observed, "with the newly discovered ability to artificially engineer materials for negative refraction, people are fantasizing that one day we can cloak objects, hiding objects from the enemy's electromagnetic radar."

Understanding photon-material interactions has implications for next-generation photovoltaics. "The sun is our most abundant energy source and in an hour floods our planet with sufficient energy for one year, if we know how to collect it efficiently," said Wong. "We used to think each photon gives one electron (or less), and hence there is a glass ceiling on the performance and cost effectiveness of photovoltaics. It turns out that, with new materials and a better understanding of the dynamical processes, we can develop photovoltaics that are better and cheaper, trapping light longer for more electricity. This is our challenge."

*B.S., University of California-Berkeley, 1999; M.S., Massachusetts Institute of Technology, 2001; Ph.D., MIT, 2003*

"Extreme" is perhaps the last thing that comes to mind when talking to Tuncel Yegulalp. "Orderly" and "soft-spoken" seem more appropriate. Nevertheless Yegulalp was the last student of Columbia Professor E.J. Gumbel, who helped found the field of extreme value statistics.

Today, Yegulalp is a leading expert in the field, which is used to analyze and predict statistical outliers of common events, such as large earthquakes and severe floods, as well as the failure strength of rocks. In addition, his career has recently come full circle, returning him to the fields of mining and geology, only this time he's trying to figure out how to put something into the ground—namely, carbon dioxide—rather than remove it.

Yegulalp arrived at Columbia in 1963 to continue his studies of uranium mining. It was during that time he discovered "there was more to the world than just uranium," he said. That world included a graduate course in extreme value statistics—a class for which students had to be interviewed and handpicked by Gumbel. Yegulalp tried to use extreme value analysis to develop a statistical model of large earthquakes, but gaps in the seismic record made it impossible to create accurate forecasts.

Yegulalp eventually devised a new method to allow for the data gaps, but it wasn't until 1999 that he was able to verify his work. While on vacation in Turkey, he experienced the magnitude 7.6 Izmit earthquake. The quake fit squarely into the range of what might be expected, given its magnitude and the time since the region's last large event.

These days, Yegulalp is teaching extreme value methods to an entirely new group of students who are interested in understanding and predicting extremes of climate that might arise in the wake of global warming. At the same time, he is applying his expertise in geology and mining to projects focusing on geologic sequestration of carbon dioxide. The idea is that pumping carbon dioxide into minerals that contain magnesium will form magnesium carbonate, a stable solid that will keep the greenhouse gas out of the atmosphere permanently.

The only problem, he said, is the sheer volume of the carbon dioxide we will eventually have to sequester and the large amount of magnesium carbonate rock that it will result. "If we want to maintain coal as a major contributor of energy, we will have to mine at least six billion tons of rock per year and learn to dispose of an even greater weight and volume of magnesium carbonate," said Yegulalp. Spoken like someone with a mind for extremes.

*M.S., Istanbul Technical University (Turkey), 1961; Eng.Sc.D., Columbia, 1968*

# TUNCEL YEGULALP

Professor of of Earth and Environmental Engineering

SUSTAINABILITY

# *Raising the Roof*

# HUIMING YIN

Assistant Professor of Civil Engineering
and Engineering Mechanics

If Huiming Yin has his way, solar panels will one day all but disappear from view on rooftops—and from a builder's bottom line. Yin is working on a prototype for an inexpensive photovoltaic (pv) cell that produces both electricity and hot water. He is also attempting to integrate his new design into roofing materials, perhaps one day eliminating the need for both solar panels and roofing shingles.

Sunlight spans a wide range of the electromagnetic spectrum—from nearly 120 to 20,000 nanometers, but the typical pv cell can only convert a narrow sliver of this to electricity. The rest is wasted or converted to heat—the enemy of many pv cells. In particular, the most inexpensive silicone-based cells virtually stop producing a current above 85 degrees Celsius, but rooftop solar cells often reach temperatures exceeding 100 degrees Celsius, making them all but useless in most parts of the world.

"As civil engineers, we want to produce something that really changes peoples' lives," said Yin. His design incorporates a functionally graded material (FGM), a relatively new type of material made up of two components that, instead of meeting in an abrupt transition, change gradually in composition from one to the other. This allows designers to take advantage of the physical properties of both components without having to create a physical bond between them—often the weakest point in any composite.

The FGM that Yin uses in his solar panels helps both draw heat from the base of the photovoltaic cell and insulate the roof. Water-filled tubes embedded in the thin FGM layer carry that heat away to be used in the building. By cooling the cell, Yin is aiming to improve the efficiency of existing silicone pv cells.

His earlier research focused on improving the wear and durability of roads using FGMs to prevent buckling and heat stress. The shingled roof, which is essentially another asphalt-covered surface, seemed like the next obvious focus of Yin's attention—particularly when that surface is forced into double duty as both a shelter and an energy producer. Installing solar panels on an existing roof, he says, is a quintessential civil engineering problem, one that involves structural dynamics, wind loading, and heat dissipation.

The next step is to fashion his cells into durable roofing elements that can take the place of shingles. Yin envisions a day when any building will be able to convert sunlight to electricity and hot water for less than the cost of a conventional roof. Until that time, he will continue trying to change the world, one rooftop at a time.

*B.S., Hohai University (China), 1995; M.S., Peking University (China), 1998; Ph.D., University of Iowa, 2004*

Columbia Engineering can claim that the information era began when Herman Hollerith, an 1879 graduate of the Columbia School of Mines, founded the company that was to become IBM. Today, computers, microcomputers, computerized machinery, robots, fiber optics, and all manner of digital technologies provide a research area in which many of our faculty are engaged, by advancing digital frontiers and cybersecurity to keep our information safe.

# INFORMATION

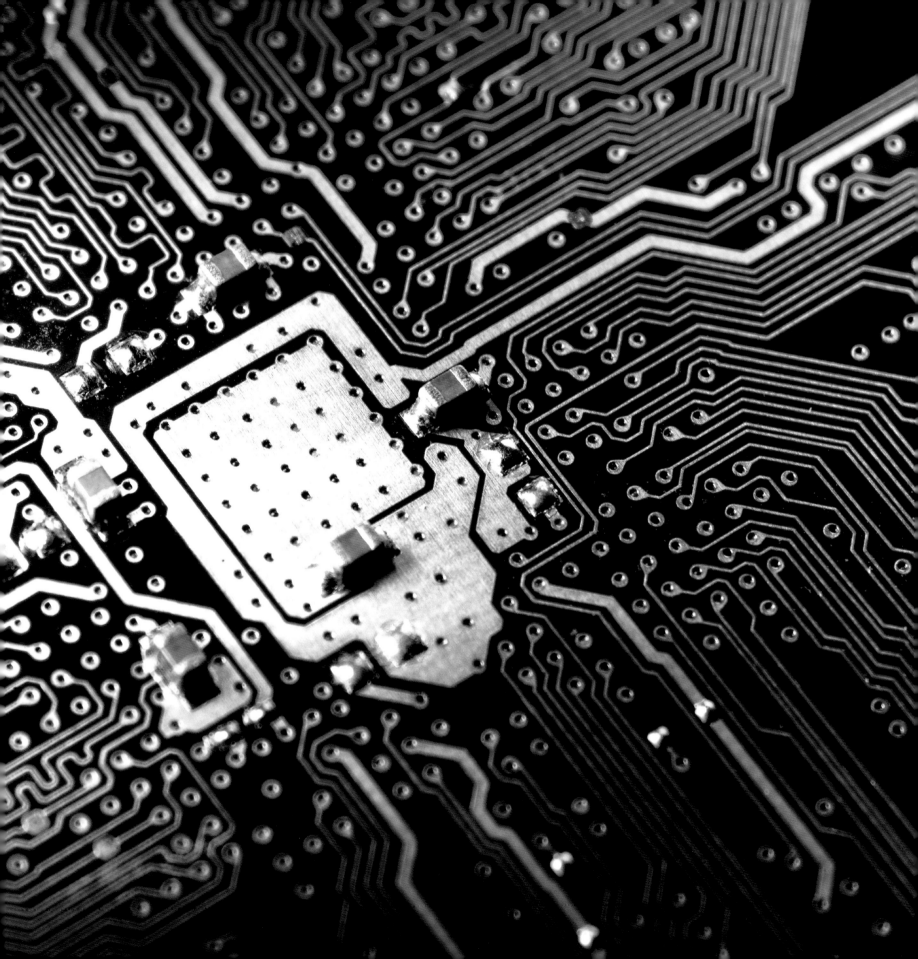

# Creating Reliable Programs from Unreliable Programmers

# ALFRED V. AHO

Lawrence Gussman Professor of
Computer Science

For Alfred Aho, the question is simple: "How can we get reliable software from unreliable programmers?" The issue is more than academic. Aho can point to such high-profile fiascos as a $1 billion write-off for failed flight control software and hundreds of millions of dollars spent fixing an airport's automated baggage handling system.

In fact, a 2002 National Institute of Standards and Technology (NIST) study found that software defects cost the economy $60 billion annually and account for 80 percent of software development costs. Even then, Aho estimates that most commercial software has 1,000 to 10,000 defects per million lines of code.

"If you're developing a computer game, that doesn't matter much. But if you're programming a pacemaker, it's a matter of life and death," he said.

Aho's goal is to create a system that automatically tags potential problems. He hopes to do this by using the technology behind compilers, programs that translate easy-to-use programming languages like C into instructions a computer processor can understand.

When a compiler translates a program, it captures details about how it was built. Aho wants to compare this actual implementation with the program's technical specifications, which define such things as naming conventions, allowable operations, associations, data sets, and order of functions. This is similar to inspecting a building's structure, wiring, and plumbing against schematics and code.

Software, however, is more complex. "Let's say the source program has one million lines of code, and you want to look for all examples of addition," Aho explained. "It's written by several different people. Some may not have consulted the specification. They might use their own names for variables. Instead of writing 'add,' they might write it as 'plus.'"

Those subtle changes make it incredibly difficult to track errors. A plus function might use different data types than an add function, and produce unequal results. Or a programmer may discover a problem involving add functions, but fail to look for plus functions to see if the same problem exists.

"All large programs have a specification document that itemizes how the program should be written. I would like to specify a property from this document and test for its properties in the software. We already know how to create tools that do some of this in compilers. Now we want to extend these tools to software development," Aho said. "This is a long-term project, but if we can make a small dent in software development and maintenance costs, we can save billions of dollars."

*B.A.Sc., University of Toronto (Canada), 1963; M.A., Princeton, 1965; Ph.D., Princeton, 1967*

Metallic films are critical to many modern technologies such as integrated circuits, information storage systems, displays, sensors, and coatings. In semiconductor chips, these metallic films interconnect the transistors that amplify and switch electronic signals. As the dimensions of metallic films shrink into the nanoscale regime, their structure, morphology, and arrangement of the boundaries between the grains that the material is made of change. When these changes happen, there is a profound impact on their properties and on the performance and reliability of the engineered systems they are made for.

When a complete understanding is gained about how these metallic materials form, evolve, and change, new or improved materials for engineered systems like computer hardware and advanced permanent magnets that underlie the operation of generators, alternators, and motors can be developed.

Katayun Barmak works to discover, characterize, and develop materials for engineered systems; to develop theories and models for phase transitions, structure and morphology evolution in metallic materials; and to understand the relationship between structure and property. Her aim is to quantify and to understand the differences in materials structure at the macro-, micro-, and nano-scales and to investigate the impact of these differences on the properties exhibited by the material. Her studies of materials structure immerse her in the exhilarating and powerful world of electron microscopy.

Her research interests include thin-film phase transformations and microstructures, high throughput electron diffraction-based metrology of nanocrystalline materials, identification of a next generation metal to replace copper in semiconductor interconnects, the discovery and development of rare-earth-free advanced permanent magnets, and quantitative kinetic experiments and models of alloys for extremely high-density magnetic recording media. She is also working collaboratively with colleagues in applied mathematics on the development of theories for evolution of materials structure and morphology.

Barmak is a member of the Institute of Electrical and Electronics Engineers; Materials Research Society; American Physical Society; The Minerals, Metals & Materials Society; ASM International; Microscopy Society of America; and Microbeam Analysis Society.

*B.A., University of Cambridge (England), 1983; M.A., University of Cambridge, 1987; S.M., Massachusetts Institute of Technology, 1985; Ph.D., MIT, 1989*

*Helping to Rapidly Transform Materials for Engineered Systems*

# KATAYUN BARMAK

Philips Electronics Professor of Applied Physics and Applied Mathematics

# Turning a New Leaf on Face Recognition

# PETER N. BELHUMEUR

Professor of Computer Science

Could centuries-old techniques used to classify species hold the key to computerized face recognition? Peter Belhumeur certainly thinks so. Face recognition has many potential uses, from verifying financial transactions to recognizing criminals. Today's systems work by superimposing a subject's face over images in a database. If they align, the computer samples pixels from each image to see if they match.

The process is not very reliable. "Recognition algorithms make mistakes that they should never make, like confusing men with women, or one ethnicity with another," Belhumeur said. Belhumeur was working on improving those algorithms when Smithsonian Institution taxonomists asked for help developing software to classify plant species from photos of their leaves.

Instead of superimposing images or matching pixels, Belhumeur drew on the wisdom of taxonomists dating back centuries. They classified plants by asking a series of questions whose yes-or-no answers narrowed the choices until they came to the right plant.

To this end, Belhumeur has developed LeafSnap, a new mobile application available on the iPhone and iPad. The free app allows users to photograph a leaf, upload it, and see a list of possible matches within seconds. LeafSnap's database covers New York City's Central Park trees and the 160 species in Washington, D.C.'s Rock Creek. Belhumeur, who co-developed the software with colleagues at the University of Maryland and the Smithsonian, hopes to eventually map species across the United States and give users the ability to add their own images to the database.

The way this technology works "is exactly the opposite of how computerized object recognition is done," said Belhumeur. "Instead of pixels, we are comparing visual attributes."

Belhumeur wondered if he could use a similar strategy to recognize faces. "Could we develop software that made qualitative decisions about each image? Is it a male or female? Young or old? Broad or pointy nose? … If we could build reliable classifiers to answer these questions, " he said, "we could search for pictures based on their attributes."

Belhumeur's system uses roughly 100 labels, ranging from eye and nose shape to hair color and gender. In tests that compare a photo to a known image, like an identity card, it outperforms pixel-based technologies.

It also makes it possible to search for pictures with words that describe visual attributes. "We could search through a database based on a victim's description of an assailant, or use it to search one's seemingly endless collection of digital photos," he concluded.

*B.S., Brown, 1985; M.S., Harvard, 1991; Ph.D., Harvard, 1993*

A sk Steven Bellovin about computer privacy and he might start by discussing aviation. "The technology is so good, there are no single causes of airplane crashes any more. But when complicated systems interact in complicated ways, you have unexpected failures," he said.

Bellovin has seen that complexity emerge on the Internet. Thirty years ago, he helped create USENET, a precursor of today's Internet forums. He wrote the first book on Internet security, and is now creating software to simplify network security. He remains an important voice in public discussions about privacy.

"Computers interact with the world around them," Bellovin said. "We cannot be only scientists or engineers. We have to bring our knowledge to the debate. We have no more right to a policy opinion than anyone else, but no less right either."

He sees the Internet's interconnected technologies eroding personal privacy. For example, nearly all commercial websites collect information about users. While some keep that information private, others do not. Anyone can cross-check for-sale databases to unearth personal information.

"In 1994, Congress mandated that telecommunications switches include technology to make it easier to tap phones," said Bellovin. "We could tell this would be abused. Sure enough, someone tapped 100 people in Greece, including the prime minister. When we see proposals like this, it is our obligation as specialists to say something."

Some privacy mechanisms fail because large Websites actually consist of many different services. Not all of them share the same privacy policies. Facebook, for example, stored pictures on servers that did not enforce privacy rules. Hackers could scrape supposedly private data by entering through those servers.

A third area of concern is anonymization, a process that wipes identifying data from database records. Yet many companies can use anonymized data to build detailed records of individuals. Google, for example, captures queries, offers check-out services that record purchases, and owns Double-Click, which tracks clicks for advertisers.

This could enable it to create detailed profiles. "Some people want to see ads about things they like. Others find it creepy that somewhere there's a repository of all your information," Bellovin said.

"Part of the solution is educational," he continued. "We can teach people to protect their privacy. But it's also a technology issue."

His group is looking at better ways to preserve privacy. This includes creating unlinkable aliases, improving the privacy of database searches, and encrypting advertising clicks so merchants cannot access private information.

*B.A., Columbia, 1972; M.S., University of North Carolina (Chapel Hill), 1977; Ph.D., University of North Carolina, 1982*

*Protecting Privacy in Complex Systems*

# STEVEN BELLOVIN

Professor of Computer Science

INFORMATION

## *Battling Internet Gridlock with Light*

# KEREN BERGMAN

Charles Batchelor Professor of Electrical Engineering

Gridlock doesn't just happen on highways. Interlocking congestion that prevents movement is also a threat to the Internet. As more people exchange more information on a more frequent basis, the Internet's traffic management system (routers) is forced to use more energy to forward and receive data between computer networks. As routers lose ground against traffic demands, performance bottlenecks occur.

Photonics, the science and technology of generating and controlling photons, could ease up electronic traffic jams by providing the solution to Internet gridlock. Through photonics, the potential exists to achieve advanced information traffic management performance along with energy efficiency by symbiotically merging the computation-communications infrastructure. Optical routers would transmit data as light, avoiding unnecessary electronic processing. In addition, they would use less power consumption while manipulating gargantuan amounts of data with complete format transparency in a smaller device footprint.

Keren Bergman leads the Lightwave Research Laboratory at Columbia University. She investigates the realization of dynamic optical data routing in transparent optical interconnection networks. Through this work, she is developing potentially disruptive technology solutions with ultra-high throughput, minimal access latencies, and low-power dissipation that remain independent of data capacity. These solutions will ultimately capitalize on the enormous bandwidth advantage enabled by dense wavelength division multiplexing.

Her work on large-scale optical networks focuses on embedding real-time substrate measurements for cross-layer communications. As envisioned by the community, this suite will support a wide range of network science and engineering experiments such as new protocols and data dissemination techniques running over a substantial fiber optic infrastructure with next-generation optical switches, novel high-speed routers, city-wide experimental urban radio networks, high-end computational clusters, and sensor grids.

Bergman's research in large-scale optical switching fabrics includes cross-layer optimized optical substrate and embedded real-time measurements. Her work in optical interconnection networks for high-performance computing systems includes data vortex optical packet switching fabric, optical network interface card and scalable optical packet buffers. Her work in integrable interconnection network systems and subsystems includes parametric optical processes and systems and nanophotonic optical broadband switches. Her work in inter- and intra-chip multi-processor interconnection networks includes on- and off-chip photonics communications for multi-processor systems and silicon photonic devices for networks-on-chip.

*B.S., Bucknell University, 1988; M.S., Massachusetts Institute of Technology, 1991; Ph.D., MIT, 1994*

In early 2008, few investors saw the whirlwind coming. The financial crisis was what economists call a black swan, an earthshaking event so unlikely, no one anticipates or plans for it. Jose Blanchet would like to rectify this situation.

"I study black swan events by using probabilistic methods. That doesn't mean I predict them. Instead, I use computers to understand how they evolve," Blanchet said. His goal is to help investors see the warning signs of extreme events before they occur, while they still have time to respond.

Blanchet does this by building realistic computer models of portfolios. As they evolve, he shocks them with random events, such as bond defaults and bankruptcies. Ordinarily, the portfolio absorbs the hits. Rarely, very rarely, a combination of random shocks sends values crashing, just as cascading events did to real portfolios in 2008.

The shocks, Blanchet explained, must be truly random. "If you try to model a crisis that simulates these events, you could get it wrong and it will not reflect reality," he said.

"For example, suppose this is 2006 and you want to see what happens if lots of people default on their mortgages. Rather than start with a bankruptcy, we want to start with the events that cascade to create the bankruptcy. We let the probability model capture the events that occur naturally, even if they are rare."

"We look at extreme events in such contexts as queueing networks and risk management of financial and insurance portfolios. We want to understand what happens when there are huge backlogs or when companies post enormous losses. What are the consequences of that? What is the likelihood?"

Ordinarily, it would take a week or two to run enough simulations to generate a single black swan. That is far too slow to build a large enough database to study these events for similarities and differences.

To get around this problem, Blanchet devised algorithms that generate black swans rapidly. He then runs hundreds of simulations using a variety of portfolio models to see how they behave.

"We have a family of models that capture the features we want to study, and a computational tool that lets us observe these events as they unfold," said Blanchet. "It's like watching a crack in a dam. Most of the time, nothing happens. But sometimes it propagates and then the dam goes."

*B.S., Instituto Tecnológico Autónomo de México, 2000; Ph.D., Stanford, 2004*

*Understanding How Black Swans Evolve*

# JOSE BLANCHET

Assistant Professor of Industrial Engineering and Operations Research

INFORMATION

# *Networking Chips*

# LUCA CARLONI

Associate Professor of Computer Science

As microprocessors grow more powerful and complex, engineers dream of putting an entire computer system on a single chip. Such chips would be smaller, faster, and more energy efficient than today's designs. To get there, though, we will need to reinvent how we design chips, Luca Carloni argues.

Today, engineers create microprocessors using tools that help them build circuits from libraries of proven designs. Yet new technologies pose many problems for traditional tools. In the past, for example, chips synchronized all operations with a single clock. "Compared to the times needed for computation, on-chip communication was basically instantaneous," Carloni explained. "Today, local calculations run so fast, it takes several clock cycles for remote signals to arrive. This is a physical issue we need to address."

Carloni ticks off other problems. New chips have multiple processors, or cores, whose parallel operations create new challenges in programmability. Billions of transistors create new levels of complexity and generate lots of heat that is hard to remove. Resolving these issues has extended the amount of time and design iterations needed to create new chips.

Those same emerging technologies also offer new opportunities. Instead of trying to develop a system-on-chip with old tools, Carloni proposes reinventing chip architectures and the tools used to design them. "We need to create communication infrastructures that make it easier to integrate new components into our designs," he said.

His solution is a network on a chip. "Our vision is to create an on-chip communication and control infrastructure," he added. "When we have a network that touches every component on a chip, we can dynamically configure the processor to optimize speed or efficiency. We don't have the solution yet, but we're working on it."

He envisions a collection of communications elements—nanoscale wires, switches, and routers—to move data around the chip. The cores would have standard interfaces to plug into the network. A new generation of tools would support component selection and network optimization.

"Instead of designing links between each circuit, you would plug components into a standardized backbone," Carloni said. "This makes it much easier to design processors. Engineers could continuously upgrade and test new components, then plug them in and know they would work on the chip."

Networked chips would also support multiple cores running at different clock rates. Chips could assign tasks to different cores to optimize speed or reduce energy use. "The path towards green computing systems starts with more efficient communication infrastructures," Carloni said.

*B.S., University of Bologna (Italy), 1995; M.S., University of California-Berkeley, 1997; Ph.D., UC Berkeley, 2004*

Consider the power of global interconnectedness: One person's tweet about a product can influence a purchase half a world away, another person's email to a group about dissatisfaction with rules can lead to a public protest, and someone else's real-time video during a natural disaster can result in an outpouring of aid. All are astounding outcomes from social networking.

Although social networking is flourishing on today's Internet, it does not make the most of our everyday interaction, Augustin Chaintreau argues. "This is because the technology that personalizes the web to your need does not mirror how you make and keep social connections," said Chaintreau. "When you ask a friend their opinion about a good movie, you do not first have to tell her about your most recent purchases, places you have been and the websites you have visited. But that's more or less what today's computers require you to do." Today's social networking software also requires that you are connected at all times to a server on the Internet, even to interact with nearby people (or objects).

"In real life, we collect and communicate useful data sparingly, and we interact much more with our immediate environment," he said. "Why can't we do that to use the Internet socially—to update a Facebook status, email a friend, collaborate on plans?" One challenge is that humans are incredibly efficient at social interaction. By better understanding natural social networking, which predates its online counterpart, we can then mathematically model that to enhance computer networking performance and outcomes.

Chaintreau works on building algorithms that connect online social networkers more efficiently and more intuitively. What makes these algorithms unique is that they use only local information and exploit mathematical models describing users' behaviors and interactions in groups and organizations. It shows in particular that users should not surrender their privacy. "Many believe that handing out your data is necessary to connect efficiently with your friends. We want to give the users a choice," he said.

These techniques could also allow us to interact socially with many more people and objects, reaching new applications. "When you look at most urgent environmental issues, to save water or organize electricity distribution from renewable sources, many of them could greatly benefit from involving people through a fast, mobile, social Internet," he concluded.

*Ancien élève, École Normale Supérieure (Paris), 2002; Ph.D., École Normale Supérieure, 2006*

*Scaling Up the Mobile Social Internet*

# AUGUSTIN CHAINTREAU

Assistant Professor of Computer Science

## Developing Next-Generation Visual Search Engines

# SHIH-FU CHANG

Professor of Electrical Engineering
and of Computer Science

Accurately searching through the glut of visual data available today—digital images produced daily in the thousands or millions—depends upon how closely your verbal description matches the words used to classify the image. It is a frustrating, time-consuming exercise that affects the general user as well as news, media, government, and biomedicine specialists who crave a richer search and browsing experience. An automated visual matching and search technology would not only enhance classification and searching activities, but could also facilitate media forensics, helping to explain if an image has been manipulated, or if it is a natural photograph or computer graphic.

In order for a search engine to visually classify and find images, or determine if images have been tampered with, computers would need to perceive the abundant visual information provided by each individual image. All that data is much like DNA: thousands of genetic concepts of objects, people, scenes, events, and domain-related syntax that make up the individual image.

Shih-Fu Chang, director of the Digital Video and Multimedia (DVMM) lab at Columbia Engineering, targets his research on next-generation search engines for digital images and videos, and has been influential in shaping the vibrant field of content-based multimedia retrieval. His group leads the Columbia ADVENT University-Industry Research Consortium, promoting industrial collaborations with the University's research teams in the media technology area. In addition, his group has actively participated in the development of MPEG-7 and MPEG-21 international standards.

Ranked by Microsoft Academic Search as the most influential researcher in the field of multimedia, Chang's research includes multimedia search, pattern recognition, media analytics, video adaptation, and media forensics. Results include a groundbreaking search paradigm and prototype tools that allow users to find content of similar visual attributes, search videos by a very large pool of visual concept classifiers, and summarize the event patterns and anomalies found in a large collection of video content.

In 1998, he developed one of the first video object search systems, VideoQ, which supported automated spatio-temporal indexing at the object region level. His work has been broadly funded by government and industry and many video indexing technologies developed by his group have been licensed to companies.

Chang is a fellow of the Institute of Electrical and Electronics Engineers and received the IEEE Kiyo Tomiyasu technical field award in 2009.

*B.S., National Taiwan University, 1985; M.S., University of California-Berkeley, 1991; Ph.D., UC Berkeley, 1993*

The underlying impetus to every human interaction is competition, which, in turn, affects our decision making. As individuals, we decide how fast we drive in a specific lane of a highway, alongside other drivers, in order to get to a desired destination at a particular time. In business, a board of directors undertakes merger negotiations with another corporate entity in order to achieve an outcome that is profitable for their shareholders. Governments negotiate diplomatically in order to achieve economic and political benefits. In all these interactions, the need to make good decisions is important. To make good decisions, we need to understand how outside influences impact the process.

Game theorists have traditionally applied mathematics to help understand the competitive behavior of rational agents and the decision-making process in the context of economic systems. It's an area of study that is highly valued: eight game theorists have won Nobel Prizes in economics.

In the past decade, computer scientists have witnessed numerous applications of game theoretic approaches and concepts in the study of the Internet and e-commerce, where an absence of central authority opens a new frontier in understanding decision making. Much interest has centered around the new and rapidly growing field called algorithmic game theory. This theory lies at the intersection of computer science, mathematical economics, game theory, and operations research, and examines new and classic game theoretic models through the lens of computation. The goals of algorithmic game theory are to understand and even predict the behavior of selfish agents in order to make Internet-based applications more successful.

Xi Chen studies algorithmic game theory and theoretical computer science with an emphasis on natural and fundamental computational problems that arise from the game-theoretic study of Internet, e-commerce, and other decentralized systems. His current research examines algorithmic issues related to some of the most classic and fundamental models in game theory and economics, and seeks to understand and characterize the intrinsic difficulties in the computation of classical solution concepts in game theory and economics. He is especially interested in how social influence can change the computational landscape of market equilibrium problems.

Chen has won awards for his work on the computation of Nash equilibria and on the computation of market equilibria.

*B.S., Tsinghua University (P.R. China), 2003; Ph.D., Tsinghua University, 2007*

# *Exploring the Structure of Abstract Graphs*

# MARIA CHUDNOVSKY

Associate Professor of Industrial
Engineering and Operations Research

In many ways, a good theory behaves like a rock thrown in a pond: It makes a splash and then its ripples spread. Maria Chudnovsky's work in graph theory is like that.

"A graph is a good model for many practical problems," she said. "You can think of the Internet as a graph and the computers on it as vertices; some are connected and some are not. Graph theory can tell us about its structure."

Graph theory does not involve what we normally think of as graphs. Instead, it involves groups of points, or vertices. Sometimes they form geometric objects like squares and pentagons. Other times, they are distributed as randomly as cities or cell phone towers on a map.

Graphs are characterized by the properties of their vertices and the lines, or edges, between them. They can be used to answer problems, from finding the best route for a delivery truck to routing Internet traffic to calculating the shortest itinerary on a GPS.

Chudnovsky works at understanding these attributes. In 2002, her team proved a conjecture about perfect graphs, which are graphs roughly defined as being easy to color. They showed that only two types of defects keep a graph from being perfect, and that all perfect graphs fall into a handful of different categories.

Chudnovsky's proof makes it possible to determine if a graph is perfect without coloring all its vertices. While this may sound like a strictly cerebral exercise, perfect graphs were originally conceived in order to solve a problem in communications theory.

Her work is relevant in other fields as well. Engineers could use her proof to locate wireless towers so their frequencies do not interfere with one another. Knowing whether a graph is perfect or not also helps computer scientists choose efficient algorithms to solve certain problems.

Chudnovsky continues to explore the structure of graphs. Her recent work looked at graphs that did not contain a claw. This structure occurs where three lines, or edges, emanate from a common vertex to form a three-fingered claw.

"We've explicitly described all graphs that do not contain a claw," she said. "Now that our characterization is in place, many problems that seemed to be out of reach can be solved relatively easily."

While her work is highly abstract, her results promise to solve some of the most practical of problems.

*B.A., Technion Israel Institute of Technology, 1996; M.Sc., Technion Israel Institute of Technology, 1999; M.A., Princeton, 2002; Ph.D., Princeton, 2003*

With people becoming ever more connected around the globe, statistical natural language processing (NLP), a sub-field of artificial intelligence, has become a critical area of research—as the amount of electronic data increases exponentially, so does the need for translating, analyzing, and managing the flood of words and text on the web. NLP deals with the interactions between computers and human languages, often using machine learning to approach problems in processing text or speech. One of the world's leading NLP researchers has just come to Columbia Engineering from MIT: Michael J. Collins, recently named the Vikram S. Pandit Professor of Computer Science, whose work in machine learning and computational linguistics has been extraordinarily influential.

Collins' research focuses on algorithms that process text to make sense of the vast amount of text available in electronic form on the web. The overarching thrust of his work has been the use of machine learning along with linguistic methods to handle difficult problems in language processing. His research falls into three main areas: parsing, machine learning methods, and applications.

Collins has built a parser that can obtain such unprecedented accuracy levels that it has revolutionized the field of NLP: for the first time, a system was able to accurately handle enormous quantities of text in electronic form. His parser is now one of the most widely used software tools in the NLP field.

His development of new learning algorithms has enabled him to make significant advances in several language-processing applications, greatly impacting speech recognition, information extraction, and machine translation. "A major focus of my work is on statistical models of complex linguistic structures," said Collins. "The challenge is to combine sophisticated machine learning methods with these complex structures."

Collins' research also focuses on "efficient search" in statistical models of language, an important challenge in many NLP applications. For example, in parsing, you have to search through a vast set of "possible" structures for a given sentence, in order to find the most probable structure. In translation, you need to search through a vast number of possible translations for the most plausible structure; in speech recognition, you must search through a vast number of possible sentences for the most likely sentence that was spoken.

"I find linguistics fascinating," said Collins. "I really enjoy developing mathematical models for languages. And the algorithms we're developing to process text in intelligent ways have all kinds of intriguing applications."

*B.A., University of Cambridge (England), 1992; M.Phil., University of Cambridge, 1993; Ph.D., University of Pennsylvania, 1999*

*A Man of Many Words*

# MICHAEL COLLINS

Vikram S. Pandit Professor
of Computer Science

INFORMATION

# Modeling Systemic Risk in Financial Networks

## RAMA CONT

Associate Professor of Industrial Engineering and Operations Research

INFORMATION

In 1987, automated trading programs shoved the market off a precipice. In 2008, a liquidity crisis brought the global financial system to its knees. Rama Cont, who uses probabilistic methods to model financial markets, has studied such system-wide discontinuities for more than a decade. His research on market discontinuities and systemic risk has made him a valued contributor in redesigning financial markets to reduce the impact of major shocks.

"When an epidemic spreads by contact and you cannot vaccinate the whole population, you have to prioritize vaccination resources to prevent further spread," said Cont. "We ask similar questions about market mechanisms that could lead to a financial meltdown."

Cont takes a system-wide view of financial markets. "We cannot understand why several banks failed simultaneously in 2008 by looking at individual bank portfolios," he said. "Instead, we must look at the flow of funds and assets in a network of interlinked portfolios." A theoretical physicist by training, he uses the mathematical language of science to analyze financial networks and identify where they are prone to breakdowns.

In the past, Cont said, regulators promulgated rules that restricted the behavior of individual institutions. "Now, they are trying to look at the market as a whole and assess risks in the entire system. Most markets evolved spontaneously from traders' needs. Some degree of intervention that strengthens their weakest links can make them less vulnerable to disruption," he said.

Cont believes clearinghouses can strengthen the system by acting as intermediaries for trades. They would require trading parties to register their transactions. This would increase market transparency about the price—and risk—of derivatives and other instruments that traded at wildly varying prices in the past.

Clearinghouses would also require deposits on all trades. The amounts would rise as institutions take on more risk. The deposits would act as brakes on risk and help compensate for losses if a party defaulted.

Cont is applying his systemic approach to risk management to the design of new derivatives clearinghouses. He is one of the two academics collaborating with the Market Transparency Working Group, a panel of industry officials and regulators charged with redesigning over-the-counter derivatives markets.

"Some people thought that after the market crash, financial engineering was finished. Instead, it raised awareness about the need for rigorous methods for managing risk," Cont said. "More than ever before, quantitative modeling is in demand now."

*Diplôme, École Polytechnique (France), 1994; D.E.A., École Normale Supérieure (France), 1995; Doctorat, Université de Paris XI, 1998*

Emanuel Derman knows something about models. He practiced physics after receiving his Ph.D., but moved to Wall Street in 1985. At Goldman Sachs, he co-developed one of the earliest interest rate models, and later headed their quantitative strategies group. *Business Week* chose his memoir, *My Life as a Quant: Reflections on Physics and Finance*, as one of the top 10 books of 2004.

*Models Behaving Badly* is Derman's tentative title for his next book. "It's about the different approaches people use to understand the behavior of the world," he said. In it, he distinguishes how theories differ from models, and explains how the unwarranted assumptions of models can lead to incorrect conclusions.

"Theories," Derman explained, "are attempts to grasp the way the world actually is, even if we don't know why. Take Newton's laws. You can't ask why they are correct. That's the way the world is. These are regularities that are always true."

Models are different. "In my view, they are metaphors or analogies," Derman continued. "We say, 'The brain is like a computer,' or 'Stock prices change the way smoke diffuses through a room.' Models are attempts to describe something by using theories that already work in a different field.

"When I first came to finance, I used the principles of physics to try to build something just as truthful. I discovered that although the techniques appear similar, the resemblance is deceptive. When we make analogies, we simplify things," he said.

Many on Wall Street believed their models represented reality. They were disabused of that notion in 2008.

"In physics there may one day be a theory of everything," he said. "In finance and the social sciences, you're lucky if there is a usable theory of anything."

Yet models still have a role to play. "I'm a bit of a Platonist," Derman added. "I think there is some truth out there. I'm trying to distinguish between finding the truth, which is rare, and building models while understanding their inherent limitations.

"Maxwell once remarked that Ampere's experiments could not have led to his results. His experiments seemed to confirm his intuition rather than point to it.

"I believe in intuitive knowledge, but you don't just wake up with it. It comes after a lot of hard work. Models are a step on that road," he concluded.

*B.Sc., University of Cape Town, 1965; M.A., Columbia, 1968; Ph.D., Columbia, 1973*

## *Understanding When Models Behave Badly*

# EMANUEL DERMAN

Professor of Professional Practice
in the Department of Industrial Engineering
and Operations Research

## Testing and Correcting Embedded Processors

# STEPHEN A. EDWARDS

Associate Professor of Computer Science

A car takes a curve too fast. Before it spins out, its stability control system kicks in. Its microprocessors calculate and recalculate the right amount of force to apply to each wheel, adjusting the brakes many times per second until the car comes under control. Such critical systems often juggle several events at once. A car's stability system must calculate speed, momentum, spin, and dozens of other variables before each application of the brakes.

Unfortunately, its embedded processors can only perform one task at a time. To get around the problem, Stephen Edwards said, programmers slice tasks into many little pieces and have the processor hop between slices at such blindingly fast speeds, it presents the illusion of simultaneity.

This illusion—called concurrency—comes at a cost. Most programmers use the C language to code embedded processors. This involves lots of repetitive programming, and errors can creep in. "It's like writing a phone book by hand. People could do it, but there would be lots of mistakes," Edwards said.

Second, concurrent C programs are hard to test. C programs must be translated, or compiled, into the ones-and-zeros language of processors. Their sliced-up nature makes them hard to translate, model, and test. "The only way to tell if they will run fast enough to handle critical calculations is to test and re-test programs until they appear to work," he said.

Edwards has solutions for both issues. First, he has developed a language, Software-Hardware Integration Medium (SHIM), which simplifies programming concurrent events. SHIM reduces the errors that creep into repetitive programs. "We developed algorithms that automate all the bookkeeping necessary to manage simultaneous events," he explained.

He also created a customized compiler that generates testable code. It takes C-like programs and translates the concurrent parts of the programs into a (very long) series of sequential commands. It then re-compiles them back into C.

"This lets you test your program in a model to check its speed and reliability and make improvements," Edwards said. "This will lead to more reliable behavior and maybe fewer huge recalls when embedded processors fail.

"Embedded processors hide in the environment. As hardware plummeted in price, it became possible to put them everywhere. I ask students how many processors they own. They may count their computers or smart phones, but miss their coffee makers, air conditioners, and cars. We made 10 billion embedded processors in 2008."

*B.S., California Institute of Technology, 1992; M.S., University of California-Berkeley, 1994; Ph.D., UC Berkeley, 1997*

There is a big difference between hearing and listening. Listening requires complex auditory processing, which facilitates learning. It's a skill humans use automatically in order to filter out background noise to understand someone's speech; remember a previously heard tune and hum along; or recognize the difference between a ringing phone and ringing alarm and understand what an appropriate response to those sounds would be.

Human listeners are able to handle such mixed signals, but machines—such as automatic speech recognizers—are vulnerable to added interference, even at levels that listeners barely notice. Consider the implications of machines that could respond when called, technology that could classify and retrieve videos by their sound tracks, or applications that could automatically search for audio data the same way we do now for text data.

To make these advances possible, it is important to understand how perceptual systems manage to make precise judgments in noisy and uncertain circumstances. This understanding can then be applied to extracting information from sound commonly encountered in daily life, identifying characteristics of the sounds, classifying them, and matching the sounds to appropriate responses.

Daniel P. Ellis is working on such advances. He is the founder and principal investigator at the Laboratory for Recognition and Organization of Speech and Audio (LabROSA) at Columbia Engineering. This lab is the only one in the nation to combine research in speech recognition, music processing, signal separation, and content-based retrieval in order to implement sound processing in machines.

His chief focus is to develop and apply signal processing and machine learning techniques to extract high-level, perceptually relevant information from sound. His intention is to test theories about how human auditory perception works and enable the creation of machines that can make use of sound information in the same way humans do.

Ellis' work in soundtrack classification pioneered the idea of using statistical classification of audio data for general classification of videos by their soundtracks. Current projects in the research group include speech processing and recognition; source separation and organization; music audio information extraction; personal audio organization; and marine mammal sound recognition.

He is a member of the Audio Engineering Society, International Speech Communications Association, Institute of Electrical and Electronics Engineers, and the Acoustical Society of America.

*B.A., University of Cambridge, 1987; M.S., Massachusetts Institute of Technology, 1992; Ph.D., MIT, 1996*

# Delving into the Science of Listening

# DANIEL P. ELLIS

Associate Professor of Electrical Engineering

INFORMATION

## *Transmitting Information Securely*

# DIRK ENGLUND

Assistant Professor of Electrical
Engineering and of Applied Physics
and Applied Mathematics

The assurance of confidentiality is required in all aspects of transmitting information, from the exchange of banking information and health records to military tactics and trade secrets. The problem is there is no foolproof method to ensure that confidentiality. No matter how encrypted the information is that is transmitted, as long as there is a key to decrypt it, there is a weak security link in the chain of communication.

The solution may lie in quantum photonics, the sending and receiving of data in the form of photons—the tiniest particles that make up light. By sending data encoded in photons, the data stream becomes a single-use, self-destructing key. If the message is intercepted, the stream would change, immediately alerting the receivers to the breach. In addition, by intercepting the stream, the disturbance would automatically scramble the message, making it indecipherable.

Quantum photonic networks could decrypt classically-encoded messages in a matter of minutes, rather than months or years as per today's networks. Such networks would allow for absolute security; even another quantum computer would not be able to secretly crack a coded message sent via a quantum network.

Working in the quantum world, addressing present day problems, requires an in-bred curiosity about the nature and behavior of matter and energy on the atomic and subatomic level, and a desire to develop revolutionary applications. Those are the talents of Dirk Englund, who leads the Quantum Photonics Group at Columbia Engineering. He concentrates on quantum optics in photonic nanostructures, with primary applications in communications, computation, sensing, and energy. His research focuses on implementations consisting of quantum bits (qubits) that are encoded in photons and in spins of electrons and nuclei in semiconductors.

Englund's work includes chip-based quantum networks that promise exponential speedups in computational algorithms and unconditionally secure cryptography as well as highly sensitive quantum-limited sensors. Recent works include time-resolved lasing action from single and coupled photonic crystal nanocavity array lasers, and optical modulation based on a single strongly-coupled quantum dot.

His group is also developing spin-off applications that rely on phenomena from cavity quantum electrodynamics (QED) to substantially lower the power consumption of optoelectronic systems for high-speed, low-power devices. These applications have potential for adaptation in high-performance computing. Related projects include radiation-hard electronics and radiation detectors and thin-film solar cells.

*B.S., California Institute of Technology, 2002; M.S., Stanford, 2008; Ph.D., Stanford, 2008*

W hat happens when a mechanic must work on an unfamiliar piece of equipment? He or she will pull out a manual and keep referring to it while making repairs. Steven Feiner has a better alternative, one that changes how we see the world around us.

His approach to this problem involves augmented reality (AR). Unlike virtual reality, which creates an artificial world, AR adds virtual information to the real world.

AR can guide people through complex tasks. "Instead of looking at a separate manual while disassembling a PC, imagine putting on lightweight eyewear containing a see-through display that graphically highlights the screws in the order you need to remove them," Feiner said.

Feiner has been developing experimental AR maintenance applications for 20 years. This involves delivering information about a system, quickly and naturally, as workers move around a workpiece. He does this by tracking the position and orientation of their eyewear, then aligning information with their perspective.

In recent studies with U.S. Marines at Aberdeen Proving Ground, Feiner's lab found that AR helped professional mechanics find the location of parts they needed to repair faster than using manuals. "With manuals, the documentation is separate from the task. Workers are always going back and forth. AR keeps them focused on the work by integrating the documentation with the task," Feiner explained.

Feiner is also working on better ways to display AR information for people interacting with their surroundings. He has come a long way since 1996, when his lab created the world's first outdoor mobile AR system. Before the era of smartphones, ubiquitous GPS, and Wi-Fi, it consisted of head-worn and hand-held displays—plus a 45-pound backpack stuffed with electronics.

That system let users tour Columbia's campus, overlaying the names and websites of academic departments on their buildings. Within a few years, Feiner's lab had added multimedia news stories and created AR restaurant guides.

Today's smartphones are far smaller and more powerful than those early AR systems. Feiner and his students are harnessing their power, both alone and with other computers and displays ranging from wearable to wall-sized.

AR displays can create a compelling experience. That is why Feiner wants to ensure that every AR system respects the physical environment and the user's relationship to it. "We don't want users losing awareness of the world around them while trying to cross a busy street," he said.

*B.A., Brown, 1973; Ph.D., Brown, 1985*

## *Augmenting Reality*

# STEVEN K. FEINER

Professor of Computer Science

## *Pushing the Limits of Multiscale Science and Engineering*

# JACOB FISH

Robert A. W. and Christine S. Carleton
Professor of Civil Engineering

"Imagine a world free of traditional scale-related barriers between physics, chemistry, biology, and various engineering disciplines; a world where products and processes are designed based on nature's building blocks, a world in which multiscale science and engineering will revolutionize the way engineering design and scientific discovery are conducted in the 21st century," said Jacob Fish, recently appointed as the Robert A.W. and Christine S. Carleton Professor of Civil Engineering.

Considered by many to be a pioneer in multiscale computational science and engineering, Fish has spent much of his career, first at Rensselaer Polytechnic Institute and now at Columbia Engineering, working at the forefront of this emerging discipline that bridges the gap between modeling, simulation, and design of products based on multiscale principles. His research encompasses a wide variety of science and engineering disciplines, from investigating the structural integrity of mechanical, aerospace, and civil systems, to electronic packaging, nanostructured material systems, biological systems, and energy absorption systems. He has an accomplished track record of technology transfer to industry and has worked with such companies as GE, Rolls-Royce, Lockheed Martin, Sikorsky, Ford, General Motors, Chrysler, Boeing, and Northrop Grumman.

Fish, whose research emphasizes the abundance in nature of systems that encompass interacting behaviors occurring across a range of spatial and temporal scales, believes strongly that "tomorrow's technological advances in science and engineering, including materials, nanosciences, biosciences, electronics, energy, and homeland security, cannot tolerate a partitioned view of nature." Together with his University colleagues, and in collaboration with the City College of New York and New York University, he is forming a new interdisciplinary center, Multiscale Science and Engineering Center (MSEC). MSEC, whose mission is to develop the basic science needed to revolutionize engineering practice and scientific discovery based on multiscale principles, will bring together universities in New York City, drawing upon their strengths in modeling, simulation, and experimentation across multiple spatial and temporal scales. As director of MSEC, Fish hopes to promote an ongoing research in multiscale science and engineering, develop new synergies, and pursue new funding opportunities.

"I am passionate about multiscale science and engineering," said Fish, "because I honestly believe that this field is the next frontier that will transform scientific discovery and engineering design. And I'm very excited to be able to do this at Columbia Engineering."

Fish earned his B.S in structural engineering, his M.S in structural mechanics, and his Ph.D. in theoretical and applied mechanics.

*B.S., Technion (Israel), 1982; M.S., Technion, 1985; Ph.D., Northwestern University, 1989*

# GUILLERMO M. GALLEGO

Professor of Industrial
Engineering and Operations Research

Fruits and vegetables are perishable inventory because they spoil if grocers cannot sell them. The same is true of hotel rooms, rental cars, and airplane seats. Unless they are filled by a certain time, these services cannot produce revenue.

Corporations have become adept at selling perishable inventory by varying prices and running sales. These adjustments are called dynamic pricing, and Guillermo Gallego is one of the field's pioneers. He originally explored how customers value such attributes as a flight's departure time, stopovers, seats, and luggage policies. His work is embedded in many of the models used to price perishable services.

Today, Gallego is working on "service engineering," a concept similar to financial engineering. "It is similar to selling options on a stock," he explained. "We take a basic service and create derivative services from it. This can be a win-win for buyers and sellers, and could dramatically change how certain services are sold."

An example is a fulfillment option. Ordinarily, airline customers buy seats on specific flights. Gallego proposes that airlines offer a discount to customers willing to fly within a certain time period, say 9:00 a.m. to 3:00 p.m., and allow the airline to pick the flight. "The buyer gets a discount. The company buys flexibility, so they can accommodate business customers who often book late and must pay a premium price for a ticket," he said.

Callable products are another possibility. Here, the seller discounts a service in return for the right to buy it back at a premium. A concert promoter, for example, might do that if a band becomes wildly popular during a tour. "In exchange for a discount, the provider can take advantage of a rise in prices," Gallego said.

Gallego is also assessing options where consumers pay an up-front fee that gives them the right to buy a service, such as a hotel room, at a discount in the future. "Companies can afford to do this because not all consumers will exercise their options," he said.

"There's an art and science to engineering and pricing services, but it is always easier when they are win-win for buyers and sellers," Gallego said. "I'm using service engineering concepts to help Hewlett-Packard redesign its warranties. We can offer annual warranties or month-to-month warranties that customers can drop at any time. Priced right, monthly warranties offer value to customers who replace products frequently and are profitable at the same time."

*B.S., University of California-San Diego, 1980; M.S., Cornell, 1987; Ph.D., Cornell, 1988*

## *Increasing Control over Cloud and Mobile Data*

# ROXANA GEAMBASU

Assistant Professor
of Computer Science

M odern technology is both a blessing and a curse. While mobile devices and web services can deliver quick access to information and even quicker connection to other people, there is a downside: the loss of control over our data.

Consider the trouble likely to occur if your laptop is stolen: you have no way to erase the sensitive data stored on it, you cannot prevent a thief from accessing that data, and you cannot identify potentially compromised data. Or, consider that you cannot be totally certain that photos, email, or documents you try to erase from online services —like Facebook, Hotmail, or Google documents—are not maintained by these web services long after you have requested they be deleted.

To regain confidence in the privacy and security of personal data, new technology applications need to manage sensitive data rigorously and provide users with strong controls over its ownership, distribution, and properties.

Roxana Geambasu works to identify the security risks inherent in today's mobile and web technology and designs, and she constructs and evaluates systems that address those problems. She designed Keypad, a system that guarantees remote control and auditability for data stored on a stolen device; Vanish, a self-destructing data system that provides control over the lifetime of data stored in untrusted web services; Comet, a system that lets users customize the way data is managed in a storage cloud; and Menagerie, a system that offers a uniform view of a user's scattered web data.

Her interests span broad areas of systems research, including cloud and mobile computing, operating systems, and databases, all with a focus on security and privacy. She integrates cryptography, distributed systems, database principles, and operating systems techniques and advocates a collaborative approach to developing cross-field ideas in order to solve today's data privacy issues.

In 2009, she was the recipient of the first Google Fellowship in Cloud Computing. Her current research focuses on an operating system redesign for mobile devices. She has identified that the principle mechanisms, assumptions, and interfaces of mobile device operating systems have not evolved to match the unique characteristics and workloads they are meant to handle.

*B.S., Polytechnic University of Bucharest (Romania), 2005; M.S., University of Washington, 2007; Ph.D., University of Washington, 2011*

Computing power has grown rapidly, but not as fast as the problems researchers aspire to solve. "We're dealing with enormous problems, problems so large we can't even store all the numbers in computer memory at the same time. We cannot rely on the same methods we used for smaller problems and expect to solve them," said Donald Goldfarb.

His work on extracting movement from surveillance videos provides an example. On surveillance videos, the background never changes. One frame looks very much like the next, except for the people moving through the space. Each frame has roughly 20,000 pixels.

"To extract moving images from a couple of minutes of video, we need to process 50 million variables and 25 million linear equations," Goldfarb said. Doing it by brute force—one computation after the other—would take days on powerful computers. Instead, he developed a systematic optimization procedure, or algorithm, that lets a simple workstation remove the background in under an hour.

Goldfarb has a long history of developing powerful optimization algorithms. Some of his early algorithms are used in commercial software to optimize complex systems. They make it possible, for example, to adjust refinery operations on the fly instead of spending weeks plotting a production schedule.

Goldfarb's work goes beyond just finding fast ways to solve difficult problems. "I try to prove that the algorithms I develop are not just fast for a specific problem, but will work well for any similar problem," he said. "It's like providing a certificate guaranteeing the algorithm's performance."

He also tries to discover properties about different classes of algorithms. Recently, he has focused on convex functions. Like many algorithms, they recast algebraic problems in geometric terms in order to estimate answers more rapidly. Goldfarb likens a convex function to a bowl with the minimum, or optimal, value at the bottom. Constraints usually push the answers to any given problem somewhere along the sides of the bowls.

"If you're sitting on the side, you can see every other point inside the bowl. If you look around and every other point is higher, then you are at the optimal point," Goldfarb explained.

Recently, Goldfarb used convex functions to optimize a method to produce MRI and CT scan images using only one-fifth the radiation. "The algorithm enables us to get an appropriate image with fewer measurements, so patients only have to spend one-fifth as much time in these machines," Goldfarb said.

*B.Ch.E., Cornell, 1963; M.A., Princeton, 1965; Ph.D., Princeton, 1966*

## *Finding a Way Around Too Much Data*

# DONALD GOLDFARB

Alexander and Hermine Avanessians Professor of Industrial Engineering and Operations Research

INFORMATION

# *Studying Decision Making in the Face of Uncertainty*

# VINEET GOYAL

Assistant Professor of Industrial Engineering and Operations Research

In almost every field, decision makers are often required to make important choices in the face of uncertainty. For instance, a financial portfolio manager must make investment decisions without being certain of asset returns. A medical doctor must prescribe a treatment without being totally certain about a patient's response to that particular treatment. An electricity grid system operator must select a set of generators to be switched on without fully knowing what the consumer demand will be and what the state of the transmission lines are. An airline makes pricing and scheduling decisions while facing an uncertain demand. Today's world of free markets, fast communication links, and availability of vast amounts of data makes the study of decision making under uncertainty or dynamic optimization extremely important.

Uncertainty in a decision-making problem is usually modeled in one of two ways: either by a probability distribution in a stochastic model or by an uncertainty set in a robust model. A stochastic model estimates probability distributions of potential outcomes by allowing for random variation in one or more inputs over time. While a stochastic model might be a good approximation of reality, the resulting optimization problem is often very difficult to solve even approximately. On the other hand, a robust model can be solved efficiently in most cases but is considered too conservative to be useful in practice as it optimizes over the worst case.

Vineet Goyal works to address a fundamental question about the relationship between these two diametrically opposite paradigms. His research focuses on providing justification for robust and other tractable approaches as a practical method to solve dynamic optimization problems. His work shows that under fairly general assumptions, the robust optimization approach provides a good approximation of the stochastic problem in many cases.

Goyal's current work focuses on analyzing the performance of various tractable approaches such as affine policies (also referred to as linear decision rules) and piecewise affine policies for dynamic optimization problems. His goal is to better understand the trade-off between tractability and performance of various approaches. This is a fundamental question and has potential for significant impact given the wide applicability of dynamic optimization.

Goyal is especially interested in applications in electricity markets where dynamic optimization is very applicable with an increasing concentration of renewable sources of generation that have a highly uncertain generation capacity. He also applies this research to problems associated with revenue management and inventory management.

*B. Tech., Indian Institute of Technology (India), 2003; M.S., Carnegie Mellon University, 2005; Ph.D., Carnegie Mellon University, 2008*

# LUIS GRAVANO

Associate Professor of
Computer Science

I magine searching for a concert and pulling up the usual web pages, plus untagged Flickr photographs, Twitter remarks, YouTube videos, and Facebook comments. Or, asking when the band will perform again and getting back a table of dates and locations.

Luis Gravano is supercharging search engines to conduct exactly those types of searches. Often, that means tapping the chaos of social media. "It's not so much about just returning a list of individual web pages as it is about combining and making sense of all information on the web to increase the effectiveness of a search," he said.

For example, many online photos are tagged to refer to specific events. Others have time and GPS data that coincide with the time and location of an event. Sometimes photos are forwarded or linked to other people who have commented about an event.

"We analyze these tags, comments, and links, and automatically cluster them to correspond to real-world events," Gravano said. His team has already shown that it can aggregate such information. It is now probing how to fit the data together to develop more powerful searches.

"If there is a concert or political demonstration, people take pictures, tweet, and form groups around these activities," he said. "We want to capture and associate this content with real-world events automatically. We'll return results that correspond to a specific event at a certain time on a particular street in New York City."

Gravano also wants to improve our ability to extract structured information, such as tables from the Internet. Today, he explained, anyone who wants to analyze the characteristics of past infectious disease outbreaks would have to sift through hundreds or thousands of search engine results.

Gravano's extraction technology searches for pages that are likely to contain the desired structured information, which is often embedded in natural language text. It then extracts, analyzes, and puts the information into a table automatically. Unfortunately, the process is prone to errors. Information is sometimes out of date or wrong. Writing is often ambiguous.

Gravano hopes to reduce errors by using such trusted sources as government documents, university archives, newspapers, and specialized websites, as well as by analyzing the frequency and context of the extracted information.

He also taps crowd wisdom to assess the reliability of popular sources. "Popularity is a step in the right direction—if you trust people to go to trustworthy sources," Gravano said.

*B.S., Escuela Superior Latinoamericana de Informática (Argentina), 1991; M.S., Stanford, 1994; Ph.D., Stanford, 1997*

# Predicting the Motion of Materials

# EITAN GRINSPUN

Associate Professor of Computer Science

What do dresses, medical instruments, and the bristles on a paintbrush have in common? Their motion can all be predicted with unparalleled accuracy by techniques developed by Eitan Grinspun.

Grinspun's techniques have broad application. In the movies, they produce stunningly realistic animations of gowns swirling on dancers and animal manes billowing in the wind. "If you can compute motions that obey physical laws, you can make artistic choices about what laws you want to disobey and produce things you would never see in real life," he said.

His work is equally applicable to physics. "Think about how honey behaves when you pour it on a scone," he said. "It is a liquid, but it loops around like a rope. If we can understand how honey moves, we can understand how lava flows or the best way to bottle shampoo."

Bottling shampoo is not a trivial problem. Shampoo entrains air, which reduces its density and increases its volume. "If you can understand how shampoos move, you can reduce entrainment and pack them in smaller containers to reduce costs," Grinspun said.

Physicians have used Grinspun's techniques to test how to steer surgical needles through human tissue. Adobe has leveraged them to simulate each individual paintbrush bristle in its popular Photoshop and Illustrator programs. "Those bristles are really bending, and you get all the effects you would get with a real paintbrush," Grinspun said.

What makes Grinspun's work unique is his deep understanding of the geometry underlying physics. For example, when he looks at a long, thin surgical needle, he sees a flexible curve that bends and twists. "Computers, geometry, and physics are my ingredients. I mix them up in a bowl and what I get is a computer's ability to predict the motion of materials.

"We can visualize the problem by thinking of the boundary of North America on planet Earth," Grinspun explained. "The energy stored in bending is like the continent's perimeter, while the energy stored in twisting is its area. We have a competition between bending, which wants to keep length as short as possible, and twisting, which wants to deform the length to enclose more area."

Understanding the geometry of those forces produces fast and accurate predictions of movement. The results are readily visible in movie special effects and in basic science as well.

*B.A.Sc., University of Toronto (Canada), 1997; M.S., California Institute of Technology, 2000; Ph.D., California Institute of Technology, 2003*

one equation describes many objects

$$\frac{1}{2}\int \alpha\kappa^2 ds + \frac{1}{2}\int \beta n^2 ds$$

J onathan Gross knew little about Celtic knots before he started studying them. "I knew one when I saw it. They are characterized artistically by repetitive patterns and symmetries," he said. "Then, while browsing the Internet, I found a graphic artist's description of them so precise, I could turn it into math."

Gross uses computers to explore algebraic topology, the mathematics of translating geometric forms into algebraic expressions. "We calculate a polynomial from a picture of the knot. Once we represent the shapes with algebra, we can manipulate the math to learn fundamental truths about the shapes," he explained.

"For example, Reidemeister proved that if you make new crossings in a knot without cutting the string, the resulting figure has the exact same polynomial as before. If you hand me a knot, I can either fumble for hours trying to untie it or I can calculate a certain polynomial and quickly know that the string is really knotted," Gross said.

Gross is quick to point out that his research is theoretical. Yet some of his insights have worked their way into practical applications. "Some of my work is related to practical technology," he said. "But what motivates me are mathematical problems that involve spatial visualization and deriving algebraic formulas to count mathematical objects far too numerous and/or too intricate to count by any elementary methods."

Last year, for example, he collaborated with two colleagues in Texas to develop a computer graphics program to create designs in woven textiles. "We designed software whose mathematical models embody key principles of algebraic topology," said Gross. "A graphic artist doesn't have to know any of this to use the software to create a complicated woven pattern very quickly."

Gross has also applied mathematical modeling to social anthropology. Anthropologists used to live with a people and describe what they saw. Their descriptions were typically highly subjective. Gross worked with a team that developed an objective way to measure and compare behavior.

They started with food systems. "There are differing levels of randomness in the way people eat," he said. "When some people eat scrambled eggs, you know for sure it's breakfast. Not quite so for others. To differing extents, meal content reflects the time of day, time of year, and festivities. By measuring the information content in these patterns, we could make comparisons between different peoples."

To Gross, it was just another knot untangled by mathematics.

*B.S., Massachusetts Institute of Technology, 1964; M.A., Dartmouth, 1966; Ph.D., Dartmouth, 1968*

## *Untying Knots with Mathematics*

# JONATHAN GROSS

Professor of Computer Science and of Statistics

INFORMATION

# *Modeling the Irrational*

# XUEDONG HE

Assistant Professor of Industrial
Engineering and Operations Research

Fill a glass half way and some people will call it half filled and others half empty. Either way, the amount of liquid in the glass is the same. Our frame of mind—optimistic or pessimistic—imposes meaning on what we see.

Investors in financial markets are not any different, said Xuedong He. They all view the same financial data, yet they draw different conclusions from what they see. Irrational biases often play a role.

"Classical economic theory assumes that investors evaluate information correctly and make decisions rationally," he said. "In reality, though, they have biases. They may overemphasize or overlook certain types of information, and this affects how they manage their portfolio."

For example, investors often miscalculate the odds of an event because they put too much weight on recent data. One common bias is to go with someone on a winning streak. "Gamblers who win two or three times in a row think they have a hot hand and are more likely to win the next time. The odds are still against them, but they over emphasize their recent success," He said.

Other investors may assess the odds correctly, but hidden biases guide their actions. "Look at people who buy lottery tickets and insurance," he said. "A lottery ticket usually has an expected value lower than the selling price. Buyers know the probability of winning is very low, but take the risk for the reward. On the other hand, people know the probability of their house burning down is low, but they buy insurance because they are risk averse."

He builds mathematical models that show how these twin engines—hope and fear—drive investment strategies. "Hope and fear coexist in investors' minds. When stock prices surge, hope takes control, so investors are more likely to invest in stocks and gamble more. When the market turns down, fear dominates and investors quickly liquidate their portfolios," he said.

"In financial engineering, not much work has been done on irrational biases. We have developed a concrete model of these irrationalities based on extensive research. We want to understand how these biases affect investor behavior and strategies," he said.

He is one of the few financial engineers researching irrational motivations. By taking biases into account, he hopes to create models that better predict market behavior and perhaps even warn when investors are being carried away by irrational exuberance.

*B.S., Peking University (China), 2005; D.Phil., University of Oxford (England), 2009*

Anyone who has ever navigated an interactive voice-recognition system to make a reservation or review a charge knows that anger and sarcasm change nothing. But one day they might, thanks to research by Julia Hirschberg.

Hirschberg studies prosody, the intonation and melody of speech. Often, it conveys subtle differences in meaning. For example, "I like cats" may sound like a statement, but raising the pitch at the end turns it into a question.

"During deceptive speech, you experience emotions like fear if you think you'll be detected or elation if you're getting away with it. This shows up in the prosody of your speech. The best people at judging liars are criminals. Police were worse than average, and parole officers the worst of all, because they assume people are always lying," she said.

Hirschberg's goal is to teach computers to understand such subtle variations and reproduce them in natural sounding speech. This involves understanding how prosody changes under different circumstances.

"When I was at Bell Labs, we did lots of experiments that looked at people's speech, and tried to predict what words he or she would emphasize," Hirschberg related. "We looked at syntax, context, the part of speech being uttered—you use whatever information you have, and usually that's not a whole lot."

At Columbia, she has analyzed the prosody of charismatic and deceptive speech. "Much of the perception of charisma is not about what people say, but how they say it," she explained. "In English, charismatic speakers are very expressive, vary their pitch contour a lot, and speak more rapidly."

She has also conducted extensive experiments in which people either lied or told the truth. In these experiments, the speakers told the truth about 61 percent of the time. Her automated computer system labeled identified truth tellers and liars about 70 percent of the time. Humans got it right about 58 percent of the time, worse than if they had just guessed "truth" every time, Hirschberg said.

She is also working on teaching interactive voice-response systems a technique called entrainment. This occurs when one speaker mirrors back the same vocabulary, pitch, and speed as another. "People like people who entrain to them more than those who do not," Hirschberg said. "We want to teach computers to change their pitch, intensity, speaking rate, and other factors to sound more like the user."

If that doesn't mollify the next generation of callers, at least the computer will recognize their anger when they express it.

*B.A., Eckert College, 1968; Ph.D., University of Michigan, 1976; MSEE, University of Pennsylvania, 1982; Ph.D., University of Pennsylvania, 1985*

*Recognizing the Melody of Speech*

# JULIA B. HIRSCHBERG

Professor of Computer Science

# Finding the Fundamentals of Silicon for Advanced Electronics

## JAMES IM

Professor of Materials Science and of Applied Physics and Applied Mathematics

INFORMATION

Silicon, the second most abundant element in the Earth's crust, is the key material of the modern information age. Microelectronic chips use bulk-silicon wafers to power computers, and silicon is used for increasingly important electronic applications, such as inexpensive solar cells, high-resolution flat-panel displays, radio-frequency identification tags, and 3-D integrated chips. But manufacturers need high-quality crystalline silicon films in which atoms are nicely and periodically arranged.

While it's easy to obtain amorphous silicon films, they are not well-suited for making these electronic devices. Developing efficient ways to generate high-quality silicon films is a key to the proliferation of these micro- and macro-electronic applications. James Im's process for developing high-quality silicon film is playing a crucial role in developing the latest generation of flat-screens for a wide array of electronic devices.

Im has done extensive research that investigates how silicon, solid thin films and nanoscale structures behave when these materials are rapidly heated by laser irradiation, melted, and then subsequently solidify. While his studies look primarily at the scientific and fundamental issues involved, the findings also have led to various technical approaches for realizing high-quality silicon films on various technologically important substrate materials such as glass or plastics.

These laser-induced and melt-mediated crystallization processes, which convert initially amorphous or defective silicon films into low-defect-density silicon films, take place at temperatures above 1400 degrees C. According to Im, understanding how silicon melts and solidifies under these extreme conditions is critical for understanding how the atoms are subsequently packed and positioned.

"Knowing the fundamental details of how Si melts and solidifies makes it a rather straight-forward exercise for us to come up with efficient and effective ways to generate useful materials with periodically arranged atoms that make good electronic devices," said Im.

The fundamental findings and technical approaches generated at Columbia are powering the evolution of the field of thin Si-film based electronics. One method, called Sequential Lateral Solidification (SLS), is used to manufacture high-resolution LCDs, and has recently emerged as the leading method for the next generation of flat-panel TVs, which use organic LEDs.

Top display makers, including LG Display, Sharp, and Samsung, have already licensed this technology. The innovation is also applicable to smart cards, RFIDs, image sensors, and 3-D integrated circuit devices.

In addition to laser-based approaches, Im is also investigating other beam-induced crystallization techniques that could provide unconventional, yet effective solutions for various electronic devices and applications.

*B.S., Cornell, 1984; Ph.D., Massachusetts Institute of Technology, 1989*

Garud Iyengar is helping to unlock the secrets of how colonies of bacteria work together, though he is not a biologist. "I'm a problem solver, rather than someone who focuses on one particular research area," said Iyengar. "My particular interest is in understanding how simple components can produce complex behavior when networked together."

Iyengar's varied background in mathematical modeling and optimization enables him to tease out insights that classically-trained biologists might miss. "My particular strength is in building mathematical models to guide experimentation by blending tools, often from different disciplines, that together work better than any single tool used independently," he said.

"Most scientists have a set of pet mathematical tools. Someone trained in statistics immediately thinks about regression to model experimental data. A computer scientist builds a combinatorial model," he explained. "An electrical engineer wants to use information theory. I've been exposed to many of these disciplines, and so my bag of tricks is bigger."

Lately, Iyengar has been trying to discover how colonies of unicellular organisms communicate in order to exploit their environment. Density sensing in Pseudomonas aeruginosa, a bacteria that inhabits the lungs of patients with cystic fibrosis, is an example. "These bacteria only turn virulent when their local density crosses a certain threshold. At lower densities, the host's immune system would overwhelm it," he explained.

It is well understood that bacteria use certain signaling molecules to sense density. A positive-feedback biochemical network triggers a switch when the signal concentration is high enough. According to classical control theory, there are many possible networks that yield the same density dependent switching behavior. Evolution, however, has selected one particular network in many different bacterial species. Iyengar is interested in understanding the reasons underlying this selection.

A more complex problem is how bacteria determine the colony's average temperature in order to optimize their metabolism. This is more difficult than it sounds. Each cell perceives only the temperature around it. Many factors, such as nearby water or chemical reactions, create microclimates that vary significantly from the average.

Iyengar speculates that bacterial colonies use a technique called belief propagation to measure spatial averages. Belief propagation is a well-known paradigm from statistical physics that describes how a particle adjusts its behavior based on the behavior of its neighbors.

"If it is used by bacteria, there are measurable consequences that logically follow," he said. "We are using our models to guide the type of experiments we need to do to quantify these consequences."

*B. Tech., Indian Institute of Technology, 1993; M.S., Stanford, 1995; Ph.D., Stanford, 1998*

*Deciphering the Mysteries of Microbial Communications*

# GARUD N. IYENGAR

Professor of Industrial Engineering and Operations Research

INFORMATION

# Finding Patterns in
## a Complex World

# TONY JEBARA

Associate Professor of Computer Science

Most of the data created in human history was actually generated in the past handful of years. "Every person in the world on average generates and consumes gigabytes of text, video, Internet media, images, and music every year," Tony Jebara said.

Jebara's specialty is developing machine learning programs that sift through massive amounts of data to discover underlying patterns and make accurate predictions. "I work at the intersection between statistics and computer science, applying machine learning tools to massive data sets where the relationship between variables is often not deterministic. Our algorithms must be fast, because computer speeds are not growing as rapidly as the amount of data they must handle," he said.

Computers slice through data that would take humans years to analyze. Yet their capabilities are only as good as the underlying algorithms—the set of rules used to classify and analyze data. Computers, for example, find it hard to identify faces, a task babies master within months.

This is an area where Jebara made his start by building one of the top face recognition algorithms. His approach to face recognition used probability distributions to calculate the likelihood that two images were of the same individual. Jebara also worked on extending the standard Bayesian algorithms to minimize error rather than maximize likelihood.

Most recently, Jebara has been working on matching and graph algorithms, two promising ways of learning from massive datasets, such as those generated by social networks and the web. Viewing large amounts of data as a graph often provides a faster and powerful way to solve problems such as data labeling and partitioning.

Also, graphs allow algorithms to be implemented very efficiently by such techniques as message passing, which Jebara has worked on extensively. He has built programs that automatically visualize, label, partition, and match data in large data sets, ranging from images to social networks.

Similar algorithms also power Sense Networks, a startup Jebara founded in 2006 to analyze data from telecommunications companies. By tapping smartphone calls and GPS data, Jebara's algorithms can classify people by behavior patterns. Users can then query the network to see where people with similar tastes go to eat, drink, or shop. The phone company can use the data to filter recommendations and provide targeted advertising.

It is one more example of machine learning finding patterns in a world awash with data.

*B.S., McGill University (Canada), 1996; M.S., Massachusetts of Technology, 1998; Ph.D., MIT, 2002*

We are witnessing an emergence of a variety of large-scale man-made information networks, including the wireless or wired Internet, World Wide Web, social, and economic networks. Similarly, on a microscopic scale, large biological protein networks inside the cell and inter-cellular neuronal networks are just being uncovered.

While these networks operate on entirely different temporal and spatial scales, address unrelated applications, and use diverse mediums to represent information, many of them are governed by the same underlying mathematical principles. Most commonly, these networks exhibit very high variability of their parameters, either in their connectivity, the statistical properties of information they carry, or the delays for processing and transferring the information.

Predrag Jelenkovic uses the mathematical theory of heavy-tailed and power law distributions to capture the highly variable characteristics of these networks. His research focus is on mathematical modeling, analysis, and control of large-scale information networks with heavy-tailed characteristics.

His recent research resulted in a discovery of an entirely new phenomenon in communication networks that shows that retransmissions can cause long (heavy-tailed) delays and instabilities even if all messages and files in the network are relatively short (light-tailed). This finding is important in general since the retransmission-based failure recovery is at the core of the existing communication network architecture, and especially in wireless networks where communication link failures are frequent.

In addition, he focuses on developing the statistical ranking mechanisms for rapidly growing information webs (e.g., the World Wide Web, scientific data, biomolecular and neural networks, social networks, news, and e-commerce). Given that the scale and complexity of these information sets will continue to increase in the future, a new statistical approach for their ranking and understanding is needed in the same way that statistical mechanics were needed for understanding large sets of molecules. Interestingly, this research reveals that the ranks of pages on the World Wide Web, according to Google's page ranking, follow heavy-tailed power law distributions as well.

Jelenkovic is a member of the Communication & Networking and System Biology groups in the department. Within these groups, he works to advance the mathematical foundation of the underlying design principles of both man-made and biological information networks. Furthermore, his work on heavy-tailed distributions applies more broadly to insurance risk theory, financial mathematics and economy, where heavy tails are widely used.

*B.S., University of Belgrade (Serbia), 1991; M.S., Columbia, 1993; M.Phil., Columbia, 1995; Ph.D., Columbia, 1996*

*Unwinding Heavy Tails*

# PREDRAG JELENKOVIC

Professor of Electrical Engineering

INFORMATION

## Understanding the Dynamics Behind Pricing

# SOULAYMANE KACHANI

Associate Professor of Professional Practice in the Department of Industrial Engineering and Operations Research

Some prices never sit still. Retailers discount clothing and technology products seasonally. Traders bid stocks up and down daily. Airline and hotel prices fluctuate by the hour. These are examples of dynamic pricing, where companies price goods based on cost, customer behavior, and competitive dynamics. Soulaymane Kachani's research in the field has taken him in some interesting directions.

"We are applying traffic flow theory used in transportation networks to blood rheology to prevent blood clots," he said. "Existing models are hard to calibrate for elderly patients because they require too much ultrasound data. Our models are simpler, and appear to better predict where clots will form. Our next step is to conduct clinical trials."

One recent project assessed lifecycle pricing for different generations of technology products. He found that to maximize long-term profits, companies should not discount old technology too deeply.

"These companies interact repeatedly with their customers," Kachani explained. "Once they set a price, it affects the reference price. So if they start driving down the price of older goods, they cannot go back and ask for a dramatically higher price for their next-generation product. In fact, long term, many tech companies are better off discontinuing old products than discounting to sell off inventory."

Real estate, on the other hand, could benefit from more dynamic pricing. "Imagine you're developing condominiums," Kachani said. "What price do you assign each unit?

"You don't want to sell out all the units with upper floors, good views, or two bedrooms first. If you do that, it means you did not put the right premium on the more desirable units. If the premiums are set correctly, all your different units should sell at roughly the same pace," Kachani explained.

To find the right premiums, Kachani looks at both unit sales and also what units visitors view. He uses their actions as input for a computer model that modifies prices based on real market input. This gives developers a realistic way to set prices to maximize returns.

His work also extends to fashion. Kachani compared retailers who emphasize innovation and design with those who focus on pricing. The innovators, with short product runs and high turnover, had higher profits than retailers with larger product runs who relied on periodic discounts to clear the shelves.

Yet Kachani urged the innovators to consider dynamic pricing. "They would do even better if they managed their pricing strategy better," he said.

*Diplôme d'ingénieur in Applied Mathematics, École Centrale de Paris (France), 1998; M.S., Massachusetts Institute of Technology, 1999; Ph.D., MIT, 2002*

Software systems have a complex lifecycle, and Gail Kaiser likes to work on all aspects of it. Her research ranges from creating systems that make recommendations to finding flaws in "non-testable" programs. "I like to find solutions in one domain and then generalize them," she said.

For example, she is working on three "recommender" systems. One system monitors how biologists use tools for genomic analysis, and then gives novices recommendations based on the workflow of more experienced users. A second mines past experience to help programmers convert software to parallel code for multicore processors. The third helps computer science students solve certain errors in the code they write.

"We built all three systems independently, then noticed that they all used essentially the same architecture," Kaiser said. "This let us derive a general reference architecture that might be useful in building future recommender systems."

Kaiser is also interested in testing so-called "non-testable" programs. These include machine learning, simulation, data mining, optimization, and scientific computing systems. "I come from a software engineering background, but work at the borders of my discipline and operating systems, databases, and security," said Kaiser. "I'm concerned with how to build systems—not just coding software, but how to design and test systems over their full lifecycle.

"Ordinarily, you can look at a program's input and see if the output is correct. But what if you can't tell? After all, non-testable programs are written to answer questions whose solutions are unknown. What if the answers are wrong in some cases, but not others? These programs could have all sorts of arbitrary errors, but how would we know?"

Kaiser has developed a number of approaches to test machine learning programs. One is a technique many math students will remember. She provides a problem, then changes the order of inputs to see if the program still generates the same answer.

"We found a lot of bugs in certain packages widely used in the machine learning community by using these approaches," Kaiser said.

She has also developed methods to test for errors on computers deployed in the field. Field tests look at the widest possible range of software operating conditions. With so many variations, she can find subtle errors that elude even the most comprehensive lab testing programs.

"You can never get all the bugs out of them," she said, "but the more bugs you remove, the better."

*B.S., Massachusetts Institute of Technology, 1979; M.S., MIT, 1980; Ph.D., Carnegie Mellon University, 1985*

## Testing What Cannot Be Tested

# GAIL E. KAISER

Professor of Computer Science

## *Indexing Videos Automatically*

# JOHN KENDER

Professor of Computer Science

**M**any colleges videotape classes so students can review lectures, notes, equations, pictures, presentations, computer screens, and simulations. Yet students rarely use videos to review for exams. Why? Because it takes too long to find the topics and references they need.

John Kender hopes to solve that problem with software that automatically indexes videos. Just like in a book, his index enables people to find exactly what they want in a video. "It is hard to index a video," said Kender. "Most presenters move around and change the subject. Those taping them often lack training. There are none of the classical clues, like fades or establishing shots, to indicate a change in topic. We are developing software to find those clues and create an index."

Kender has tested the software on videotaped lectures at Columbia. "We have shown that our tools helped students effectively locate the parts of lectures they wanted to study," he said. "After we gave them the tools, their grades improved between midterm and final exams. If you have a good way of reviewing educational videos, it pays off in your grades."

Indexing videos is no simple task. "A professor may start a lecture with a slide, move to a website, then stop to answer a question. That may trigger something he or she forgot to say earlier. They may start four new ideas without finishing previous ones," Kender related.

Kender's team found several ways to keep track of this convoluted discourse. One student developed software that recognized and indexed programming languages when they flashed across the screen. "Students can ask for all examples of software code and quickly page through them to find what they want," Kender said.

Another program reads words from presentations, handwriting from white boards, and captures spoken words using speech-to-text software. Although handwriting and speech-to-text identification is not highly accurate, speakers repeat key concepts often enough to locate them in the video. Another program matches the resulting index with textbook chapters and articles that cover the same material.

A current project involves gestures. Instructors typically use different gestures when reviewing old material, introducing concepts, or working through difficult problems. These gestures vary from teacher to teacher. Kender hopes to decode their meaning by correlating them with such actions as showing new slides, writing on a board, or introducing new words.

Visual indexing could change how people use videos. "It's like providing a table of contents and index for a book that didn't have them before," Kender concluded.

*B.S., University of Detroit, 1970; M.S., University of Michigan, 1972; Ph.D., Carnegie Mellon University, 1980*

"The barbarians are no longer at the gates," Angelos Keromytis said about computer security. "They are inside the doors and there are not enough guards to repel them."

Most security systems are designed to keep bad guys out, and can do little once they are inside, Keromytis explained. "We start with the proposition that attackers will compromise your system, despite your best efforts to keep them out. The only solution is to make systems that are self-healing and self-protecting," he said.

Keromytis' approach is to teach computers to act like the best human experts, if they had all the time in the world to react to an attack. "We want the computer to recognize an attack, see what happens, and come up with a way to modify the system so that it blocks the attack," he said.

Most attackers take advantage of the fact that nearly all computers on a network run the same software. If an attacker finds a vulnerability in one computer, it can attack all the computers. Keromytis turns this into an asset. His software monitors each system, noting when attacks fail or succeed and looking for unusual behavior.

When the alarm sounds, his security system isolates the infected computer. Then it analyzes recent events to find the trigger—an e-mail virus, a malicious download, a tainted document—that set it off. The system automatically attempts to write software code to fix the problem, testing different approaches until it finds one that works. It then rolls back the computer to a time before the attack and inserts the fix. The entire process takes only fractions of a second.

The newly inoculated computer also passes information about the threat around the network. Each computer then builds its own fix. This build-your-own approach prevents hackers from somehow attaching viruses to fake fixes.

"What we're trying to do is build systems where the individual computers and servers collaborate to prevent attacks, fix attacks that succeed, and then send information to other parts of the network about the vulnerability so they can fix it too," he said.

Keromytis is currently testing the software and plans to scale up to larger systems soon. He is also looking at ways to find viruses that wait weeks or months until erupting.

The barbarians may have gotten through the gates, but in the future they will find the doors barred by a new generation of persistent guards.

*B.S., University of Crete-Heraklion (Greece), 1996; M.S., University of Pennsylvania, 1997; Ph.D., University of Pennsylvania, 2001*

*Protecting Computers After the Barbarians are Inside the Gate*

# ANGELOS KEROMYTIS

Associate Professor of Computer Science

## *Accelerating Processing's Family Van*

# MARTHA KIM

Assistant Professor of Computer Science

According to Martha Kim, the typical computer processor is like the family van. It is a good all-around machine, but it achieves its flexibility by sacrificing power and performance. It will get you there, but it's not made for off-road adventure or hugging the curves at Le Mans.

Modern computers have the potential to act as vans, sport cars, and motorcycles—all on the same chip, Kim said. It is just a matter of getting under the hood and adding accelerators, small chips-within-a-chip designed to process certain types of data very efficiently.

Accelerators are possible because today's chips are so large. Many contain several separate processors and upwards of two billion transistors. "We have transistors to burn," she said. "If we could organize a few hundred thousand of these transistors into a specialized accelerator, we could handle certain types of data 100 times faster and with 100 times less power."

Those gains are possible because everything needed to process information would reside in the accelerator. "Instead of reading and decoding software instructions specifying how to manipulate the data, the accelerator could start processing immediately without waiting for software instruction," said Kim.

"Today's integrated circuits offer an embarrassment of transistors," she added. "The challenge is how to translate efficiently these raw resources into easy-to-use, high performance, low-power processors. Spending some transistors on special purpose data processors, which store and manipulate structured data types, could simultaneously boost performance and conserve power. "

Accelerators are relatively simple to define in hardware but can be very difficult to use in software. "With accelerators, the programmer not only has to write the code, but has to coordinate what parts of the program should run on which accelerators, and then reassemble the results. Also, if the number and type of accelerators differs from chip to chip, programming becomes even more complex," Kim explained.

Kim's goal is to create common interfaces and tool chains to protect the programmer from this complexity. "The programmer would write code normally. A compiler would track the libraries and data structures used by the application as well as the accelerators available on the chip" she said. "It would do the job of matching parts of the computation with the available accelerators."

In other words, Kim does not want to make her van into a Formula 1 race car. She wants to keep all of the van's flexibility and still take those turns at ridiculously high speeds.

*B.A., Harvard, 2002; M.E., University of Lugano (Switzerland), 2003; Ph.D., University of Washington, 2008*

We live and work in a digital society, surrounded by cell phones, laptops, cameras, iPods, and other electronic devices constantly in use. And the desire for more automation, more information, and more broadband access with better, faster, cheaper mobile infrastructure continues to increase exponentially across the globe. But the physical world around us is analog. Music, speech, images, physiological signals, radio waves, any physical signal is continuous in time and in value. As our information society transitions to more and more digital media and communications, the need for interfaces between real-world analog signals and digital signals (bits) keeps growing drastically. For instance, voices need to be converted to digitized pulses and vice versa on cell phones, music has to be translated into bits for storage and converted back to sounds we can enjoy, and images on digital cameras need to be changed to digitized pixels and then reversed.

The challenge is how to keep all our digital devices connected to the real world with better quality, more pixels, more bits, while needing less—less space, less energy, and less cost. Peter Kinget is one of the researchers leading the way in, as he puts it, "connecting bits to life."

Kinget's research is focused on designing efficient integrated circuits ("chips") that connect digital electronic circuits to the real world. The relentless scaling of semiconductor devices to nanoscale dimensions, a.k.a. Moore's law, has brought a tremendous performance improvement and cost reduction to digital electronics. But the design of interface circuits using nanoscale devices is becoming progressively harder while the performance demands keep increasing. Inventing new circuit techniques is key to keeping electronics, along with all the systems that rely on them, progressing.

These innovations are important enablers to a large variety of applications in which Kinget's group is involved. Novel wireless links using very short pulses to communicate require so little power that they can operate perpetually on energy harvested from the environment, rather than needing batteries. Such highly energy-efficient communication capabilities are key to the realization of EnHANTs (Energy Harvesting Networked Tags), a new type of tags that will enable us to connect and network everyday objects that are part of our daily lives, like wallets, keys, toys, clothing, produce, and even furniture.

But novel integrated circuits reach far beyond communications. For instance, smart power circuits used in combination with new materials and fabrication techniques to make high quality printed capacitors can also be used to convert electrical wall AC power efficiently to DC power for "greener" types of lighting, employing LEDs to replace wasteful incandescent bulbs.

*M.S., Katholieke Universiteit Leuven (Belgium), 1990; Ph.D., Katholieke Universiteit Leuven, 1996*

## Connecting Bits to Life

# PETER KINGET

Professor of Electrical Engineering

## *Linking Domino Theories to Real-World Pricing*

# STEVEN S.G. KOU

Professor of Industrial Engineering
and Operations Research

Many blame structured financial instruments, such as credit default swaps and collateralized debt obligations, for the 2008 recession. Yet similar products traded for decades without problems. Even now, billions of dollars in structured debt trade daily. Steven Kou has made it his mission to make these products safer.

"As an engineer, I'm interested in linking economic theory to real-world pricing of structured financial products," said Kou. "Economists understand the structure of economic forces, and statisticians understand how one event triggers another, like the aftershocks of an earthquake. We're trying to apply both to the details of financial products."

Structured instruments reduce risk, he said. He points to instruments that pool corporate bonds. Instead of buying a bond from one company, investors can buy a diverse portfolio of bonds from companies in different industries.

Financial firms typically divide this basket of bonds into risk categories, or tranches. The top tranche has the lowest risk but the lowest returns. It loses money only if 30 percent of the bonds default. This is highly unlikely, and it trades like a highly rated bond. The bottom tranche has the highest return but loses money if only a smaller percentage of bonds default.

"There's a value to this," Kou explained. "Pension funds, for example, cannot invest in bonds rated less than AAA. Many strong companies have lower credit ratings. If their bonds are included in the top tranche, a pension fund can buy them without great risk and still receive a higher return."

Many investors were lured by that combination of higher returns and lower risk. They believed that even if conditions in one industry forced a company to default, diversification would keep their investments safe.

In 2008, though, that assumption was upended. "The model we had been using was no good. During a severe crisis, we found that when one company defaults, others outside its industry are more likely to default," Kou said.

Kou calls this "default clustering." To understand how it affects risk and value, he builds models that draw on both economics and financial engineering.

Kou said the models will help set more realistic prices for structured financial instruments. Initial results are promising. Just before Lehman Brothers went bankrupt, conventional models set the cost of insuring the top tranche of corporate bonds at about $7,000. His model priced it at around $52,000.

"That's more consistent with what happened in the market," he said.

*M.A., Columbia, 1992; Ph.D., Columbia, 1995*

Automobile collisions account for tens of thousands of fatalities in the United States annually. While the most expensive automobiles have on-board collision avoidance systems, such technology is priced out of the market for most drivers. The cost has much to do with the technologies that are currently used to implement these systems. Current sensors rely on multiple integrated-circuit chips based on compound-semiconductor technologies, resulting in systems that are large, bulky, power-inefficient, and expensive.

Silicon-based millimeter wave technology could make automobile collision avoidance systems as common as seatbelts in the cars of the future. Millimeter waves deliver good directionality, and offer a large amount of available bandwidth not currently being used, making them functionally comparable to fiber optics without the financial and logistical challenges. Silicon-based technologies offer the opportunity to integrate complex sensors onto a single chip, greatly reducing power, cost, and size. This technology's utility is wide ranging and includes collision warning systems, blind spot analysis, and pedestrian detection. It also is being explored for high-data-rate personal area networks for future "wireless homes," non-invasive medical imaging, airborne chemical sensing, and concealed-weapon detection for security systems.

Integrating extremely high frequency electronic circuits and systems into silicon-based technologies is one of the grand challenges of electronics, and where Harish Krishnaswamy is applying his research efforts. He pioneered silicon-based, nonlinear, multifunctional circuits, and systems which, when coupled with millimeter wave technology, allow multiple simultaneous functions to be performed on a single, compact, power-efficient chip. A nonlinear, multifunctional phased-array transceiver chip won the prestigious Lewis Winner Award for Outstanding Paper at the 2007 IEEE International Solid-State Circuits Conference. Krishnaswamy is also working on new Multiple-Input, Multiple-Output (MIMO) radar concepts that use multiple transmitting and receiving antennas to capture a more detailed and accurate image of the scene around the vehicle.

The Krishnaswamy Group at Columbia University analyzes, designs, and experimentally verifies novel integrated devices, circuits, and systems for a variety of radio frequency and millimeter-wave applications. His research efforts blur the boundaries between circuits, electromagnetics, device physics, and communication/signal processing theory. Results include a variable-phase ring-oscillator based architecture for radio-frequency (RF) and millimeter-wave phased arrays, architectures and circuits for single-chip MIMO radar, timed arrays for ultra-wideband beamforming, and high-performance RF and millimeter wave building blocks for wireless transceivers.

*B. Tech, Indian Institute of Technology (Madras), 2001; M.S., University of Southern California, 2003; Ph.D., University of Southern California, 2009*

## Designing Ways to Account for Foreseeable Financial Risk

# TIM SIU-TANG LEUNG

Assistant Professor of Industrial Engineering and Operations Research

In order to attract and retain top executive talent, many firms develop sophisticated compensation arrangements that include employee stock options (ESOs) and securities. In fact, almost half the compensation for corporate CEOs is usually in the form of stock options.

But what's the true value of these ESOs? It's difficult to determine because value is dependent upon fluctuations in the stock market and when an ESO owner exercises the option to cash in those compensation vehicles. Because timing is variable, valuation of ESOs can be somewhat random. Without a viable model for ESO valuation, the actual and true costs of these compensation vehicles cannot be correctly reflected in any company's financial bottom line. This puts a burden on other shareholders, the company, and the economy.

Tightening the gaps in accepted practice of valuation for compensation vehicles like ESOs can have direct impact on businesses as well as the stabilization of the economy. Key to accomplishing that is the application of mathematical acumen and practical financial knowledge—components of financial engineering.

Financial engineering is both the art and science of evaluating, structuring, and pricing financial instruments and designing strategies to reduce risk and maximize opportunities. Through innovative, analytical procedures, financial engineers help individual and institutional investors as well as regulators understand and manage financial risk.

Tim Siu-Tang Leung uses financial theory, engineering methodology, and mathematics to build reliable models that account for foreseeable financial risks. His research interests are in financial engineering, especially in the valuation of ESOs and credit derivatives. The National Science Foundation is underwriting his research in stochastic modeling of risk aversion and its implications for derivative pricing and risk management.

He has made significant contributions to the field with a revised ESO valuation model that takes into account the complex contractual features and the realistic behaviors of ESO holders (i.e., due to their heightened risk perceptions—fear of market crash or job termination—ESO holders usually exercise options to cash in early). He has also developed strategies to help employees hedge some of the risk involved with owning ESOs. His research has led to interesting mathematics including analytical and numerical studies of several combined stochastic control and optimal stopping problems. The mathematical tools from his research are also being applied to tackle other financial engineering challenges.

*B.S., Cornell, 2003; Ph.D., Princeton, 2008*

During Richard Longman's sabbatical in 1984 he initiated research in three new fields, becoming one of the very early contributors to each. With support of ex-doctoral student Robert Lindberg at the Naval Research Laboratory, an Egleston Medal recipient, he started research on robotics in space. The shuttle arm can handle a load of mass similar to the shuttle, and this creates a question: Which end of the arm is the base and which is the load? Two of his early papers appeared in the first book on space robotics produced by the Carnegie Mellon Robotics Institute.

With German collaborators, he started research on time optimal control of robots, something that challenges numerical solution methods. One research focus was a press chain on the Mercedes production line near Stuttgart. The objective was to increase productivity by making the slowest robot get its job done faster. A series of publications progressed from idealized investigations to ones including detailed hardware constraints. Similar productivity problems appear in the production of semiconductor chips.

When a robot is commanded to follow a trajectory, it will repeatedly follow a somewhat different path. Robots often do the same operation hundreds of times a day, making the same errors each time. Longman considered this a bit stupid—can't we make a control system that learns from its experience to do what we ask? He started work on this at the University of Newcastle in Australia. Since then, this problem has developed into the fields of iterative learning control (ILC) and repetitive control (RC).

Longman has produced some 250 publications in this area, and is known for advancing the theory in a way that produces improved real-world performance. Experiments on a robot at NASA improved tracking accuracy by a factor of 1000 in just 12 iterations for learning. The methods can apply to a very large number of feedback control systems, creating high precision motion by improved algorithms instead of higher precision hardware.

At Seagate Technology, experiments reduced the repeatable error in computer disk drives by 98 percent. Similar experiments improved paper handling in copy machines at Xerox. Experiments also demonstrated improved beam focus at the 8 GeV (one thousand million electron volts) accelerator at Jefferson National Accelerator Facility. Longman is currently working on similar experiments at the Naval Postgraduates School on jitter control in laser optics on spacecraft.

ILC and RC aim for high precision motion and optimal control aims for fast motion. Longman is working to develop a marriage between these research areas to simultaneously get the benefits of both—aiming for higher quality products created with improved productivity.

*B.A., University of California-Riverside, 1965; M.S., University of California-San Diego, 1967; M.A., UC San Diego, 1969; Ph.D., UC San Diego, 1969*

*Making Robots Learn*

# RICHARD W. LONGMAN

Professor of Mechanical Engineering and Professor of Civil Engineering and Engineering Mechanics

INFORMATION

# Securing the Lock after the Key is Stolen

# TAL MALKIN

Associate Professor of Computer Science

From online transactions and ATM machines to databases and voting, cryptography lets us share critical information while keeping it safe. Yet cryptographic systems have a weakness. They rely on keys to code and decode messages, and keys can be cracked or stolen.

"Traditional cryptography depends on the assumption that an attacker has no access to secret keys," Tal Malkin said. "Yet sometimes an attacker can hack into a computer or tamper with your hardware. Part of my work is to maintain security even against such adversaries."

She envisions systems that respond when attacked. "We can build systems where the key evolves to protect against an adversary who reads or changes part of the key. Even if an adversary reads the entire key, we can protect future transactions," she said.

Another assumption underlying cryptographic systems is that there is some hard problem that no attacker can solve. For example, the public key software used for secure Internet transactions often relies on the assumption that it is hard to factor the product of two very large prime numbers.

"No one can prove the factoring problem is hard to solve," said Malkin. "We assume it is because people have worked on this problem for decades. They have developed sophisticated techniques that are much better than the more obvious approaches, but even those procedures require as many operations as the number of atoms in the universe. But if someone does find an efficient solution, it would break all encryption on the Internet."

As part of her research, Malkin also studies the mathematical foundations of cryptography, searching for the minimal assumptions needed to guarantee security. This starts with studying primitives, such as one-way functions, that act as cryptographic building blocks. "Primitives are small, simple to describe, easy to compute, and hard to crack," Malkin said. "Cryptographers can combine small primitives to form complex, multilayered security systems."

Malkin has also focused on general systems for secure computation among two or more parties, as well as optimizing their performance for specific purposes. One example is the no-fly list. The government wants to keep it secret, while airlines want to protect passenger privacy. Malkin has developed a fast way to exchange critical information without showing compromising data. Other applications of secure computation include online voting, sharing national intelligence, and bidding on projects.

In today's increasingly interconnected world, Malkin's work on provably secure cryptographic protocols could help protect some very important secrets.

*B.S., Bar-Ilan University (Israel), 1993; M.S., Weizmann Institute of Science (Israel), 1995; Ph.D., Massachusetts Institute of Technology, 2000*

At first glance, the nine-year-old Columbia Newsblaster website (newsblaster. cs.columbia.edu) looks like Google News. Both feature the day's top stories plus sections on national, world, financial, and science/technology news.

The difference is their technologies. Google lists the first few sentences of one news article and links to similar stories. Newsblaster publishes summaries of a dozen or more articles—all written and edited by software developed by Kathleen McKeown.

"Newsblaster summarizes multiple news articles," said McKeown. "We're using similar technology to answer questions from information on the web. Today, users read the documents their search returns to see if they are relevant. Our software takes the next step. It looks into the documents, pulls out the relevant information, and summarizes it in a paragraph."

McKeown's software starts by scraping 25 different websites for news every night. It uses key words to cluster articles and categorize topics, counting the number of articles in each cluster to determine its importance.

Once classified, the software uses several approaches to generate summaries. First, it extracts sentences from important sources, such as stories from prominent newspapers and wire services.

It also pairs each sentence with every other sentence in the cluster. It analyzes their similarity and groups related themes together. "The software lines up the sentences in each group side by side and looks at where they overlap or intersect," McKeown explained. "It is looking for phrases that say the same thing, where words overlap or there is paraphrasing.

"The software parses the sentences for grammatical structure, so it knows that this phrase functioned as a noun and that phrase acts as an adjective. This helps it align similar sentences and fuse phrases to create summary sentences. It then generates the summary by ordering the sentences, using information about chronological order of the events. It also edits for coherence, substitutes proper nouns for pronouns, and adds or removes references, depending on whether a person or place is well known or not," she said.

The core technology has found other uses. A small company is using it to power smartphone applications that track and create timelines for breaking news on specific topics. Another application responds to open-ended questions, generating summaries of information about, for example, a particular event or a particular person. A third creates English summaries from news sources in other languages.

While some Newsblaster stories read like newspaper articles, others are choppier. Still, the technology could become an important tool for making sense of all the information on the web.

*B.A., Brown, 1976; M.S., University of Pennsylvania, 1979; Ph.D., University of Pennsylvania, 1982*

## Summarizing the News (Automatically)

# KATHLEEN MCKEOWN

Henry and Gertrude Rothschild
Professor of Computer Science

INFORMATION

# Boosting Profits with Peer-to-Peer Networks

# VISHAL MISRA

Associate Professor of Computer Science

Peer-to-peer (P2P) networks exploded onto the scene around 2000. That is when Napster, LimeWire, BitTorrent, and similar services made it possible for anyone to download libraries of music and movies for free over the Internet. The new technology gutted music industry profits and led to massive layoffs and downsizing.

Yet peer-to-peer networks are not inherently bad for profits, Vishal Misra argued. In fact, they may prove the most efficient and least expensive way to share media over the Internet.

In 2000, large peer-to-peer networks were something new. Instead of warehousing information on a central computer, they took advantage of files distributed on PCs throughout the network to store and send files to other users.

"Smartphones need lots of bandwidth," said Misra. "Wireless providers want us to buy femtocells, small broadcast towers to improve performance in our homes and offices. Instead, they should give us femtocells. Then they could offload traffic from their cell towers and reduce the number of new towers they need to build to support their smartphones.

"Everyone agrees P2P is a great technical solution. The more users, the more resources the network provides and the faster it responds to requests," Misra said. This is the opposite of today's centralized client-server model, which must keep investing in more servers as network demand grows larger.

"There shouldn't be this war between P2P users and people who own music and movie copyrights on the other," he continued. "We need an economic reboot so that the system works for both camps."

To understand how that might be possible, Misra used game theory to analyze the problem. Ordinarily, models that involve cooperative interactions are extremely hard to calculate, especially for millions of users. Misra simplified those calculations by applying theories based on fluid flow to the continuum of users and peers. "It's like analyzing a glass of water as a fluid instead of trillions of water molecules. By representing millions of peers as a fluid," he said, "it is easier to see their behavior and compute the right incentives."

For example, Misra estimates that providers of such content as live TV and video-on-demand could save over 90 percent of their Internet distribution costs through user-based P2P networks. "The stores could save lots of money, and people who own legal copies of media might be willing to share them if they receive part of those savings," said Misra.

"Peers, or users, can help providers reduce costs, as long as incentive structure are in place to reward them," he concluded.

*B.S., Indian Institute of Technology, 1992; M.S., University of Massachusetts-Amherst, 1996; Ph.D., University of Massachusetts-Amherst, 2000*

Computer Networks

COUNTEREXAMPLES IN

A First Course in Proba

IN GAME THEORY

Shree K. Nayar's work is all about seeing things differently. "The basic principles of photography have remained unchanged since the earliest camera obscura," Nayar explained. "Cameras use an aperture to capture light, a lens to focus it, and some medium to capture the familiar linear perspective image. In the 1990s, I started asking whether we could use new optics and a computational processing to produce new types of images."

One of Nayar's first inventions was the Omnicam. Its combination of lenses and mirrors captures panoramic 360 degree images in a single click. "The image is distorted, since you can't map a sphere to a flat surface without distortion, but we corrected that with mapping software," he said. "In fact, a single 360 degree image could be used to generate any number of traditional views of the scene.

"Placed in the middle of a table of people, it gives the illusion of multiple cameras pointed at individuals during a video conference, although it is one camera with no moving parts," Nayar said. The camera is also used for surveillance.

Nayar's next invention, a high dynamic range camera, takes better photographs of scenes that mix dark and light areas. "Let's say you try to take a picture of a scene with shadows and a bright sky. Today's digital cameras cannot reveal details within the shadows and the sky. If the sky comes out well, the shadows do not, and vice versa," Nayar said.

Nayar's solution is to use an image sensor with a patterned optical mask on it. The mask ensures that neighboring pixels on the sensor have different sensitivities to light. His software decodes the captured photo to produce one that captures the shaded clouds in the sky and the objects in the shadows. Sony has prototyped the technology for use in its digital cameras.

A third camera enables photographers to focus on close-up details without blurring background features. Nayar does this by physically sweeping the image sensor of the camera through an entire focal range, during the exposure of a single photo. The captured photo is again processed by software to obtain one where everything appears in focus.

Nayar has also launched a project to help children around the world learn science, art, and culture by assembling and using a digital camera. His Bigshot Camera has panoramic and stereo imaging capabilities, and makes it easy to post photos on the web.

"Each picture is a window on another culture, and youngsters can learn about those cultures from their peers," he said. To Nayar, it is just another way of seeing things differently.

*B.S., Birla Institute of Technology (India), 1984; M.S., North Carolina State University, 1986; Ph.D., Carnegie Mellon University, 1990*

*Picturing the World in New Ways*

# SHREE K. NAYAR

T. C. Chang Professor of Computer Science

INFORMATION

# Delivering Desktop Computing from the Cloud

# JASON NIEH

Associate Professor of Computer Science

Cloud computing—delivering software and services from a central computer to desktop terminals—is arguably the hottest topic in computing today. The reasons are economic. PC hardware prices continue to fall, but maintenance costs continue to rise.

"If you're a large corporation with 50,000 or 100,000 desktops, you're fixing broken hardware, guarding against viruses, and patching and upgrading software for each one of them. The costs are astronomical," explained Jason Nieh.

If the PC-on-a-desktop paradigm is broken, what will replace it? "Most analysts believe we are moving to cloud computing, where corporate computers run only in secure data centers where they are protected, secure, and easier to manage and service. If a desktop fails, it doesn't matter because all the memory and files actually reside in the data center," said Nieh.

But cloud computing has a weakness: speed. Centralized applications run slower than the same program on a local PC. This is especially true for programs with graphical displays.

"A modest display has 1024 x 768 pixels, and each pixel has 32 bits of data," added Nieh. "Displays update 30 to 60 times per second or more, so you're potentially sending a gigabyte or more of data per second to each PC on the network, and that can slow response times."

Computer scientists have tried to compress data to reduce the load. This helps, but it requires additional computing power and fails to handle gracefully today's complex graphical interfaces.

Nieh uses intelligent software to reduce data flows and response times from the cloud. In Nieh's scheme, the application draws the screen on a virtual display. Then his program analyzes what is on the display, and sends commands to the desktop terminal, instructing it on how to redraw the screen. Many of the most common commands are embedded in the graphics card's hardware, so they operate very fast. The system updates the terminal by sending only those portions of the display that change, enabling very fast response times.

The big payoff comes when connecting to the Internet. Data centers almost always have the fastest Internet connections. "They update web pages much faster than local desktops, laptops, or smartphones," Nieh said. "If a carrier uses this technique, you don't have to settle for the limited functionality of smartphones that run some software but not others.

"You get improved functionality and improved performance that makes you feel like you're right there, and you get it on your smartphones, desktops, and laptops."

*B.S., Massachusetts Institute of Technology, 1989; M.S., Stanford, 1990; Ph.D., Stanford, 1999*

For decades, computer processors were typically organized like marching bands: a conductor kept time and band members stepped to the beat. In processors, a clock's pulse determined when all computations and data movement occurred. Today, that paradigm is breaking down, Steven Nowick explained.

Modern processors consist of a handful of smaller processors, or cores. "When you have four separate cores, it is difficult for one clock to keep them in lockstep," Nowick said. The problem will only worsen when future processors have dozens of cores.

Today's transistors also pose problems. As they shrink to a few tens of nanometers, they become much more variable. "Their speeds vary depending on temperature, voltage, and how they are manufactured. Their unpredictability is a major design challenge," Nowick said.

Nowick and colleagues at other institutions have been pursuing an alternative approach: eliminate the clock and let digital components operate at their own speeds. "Let them communicate as conditions require, and make their own decisions with their neighbors about when they need new data and when they will output results," he stated.

"Most digital systems have clocks running at billions of cycles per second. Everything operates in lockstep with that clock," he continued. "As circuits get larger and more complex, imposing fixed timing on billions of transistors and millions of components is a huge design effort. We think we can solve these problems with asynchronous, or clockless, circuits."

It sounds chaotic, but the Internet works the same way, Nowick said. "People around the world add, update, and remove web pages individually, without any centralized control mechanism."

In addition to solving timing issues, asynchronous digital systems could provide other advantages. In synchronous chips, even idle components are activated every clock cycle, like band members marching in place. In contrast, the on-demand components in asynchronous systems respond only when necessary. This conserves energy and can prolong battery life in laptops, smartphones, and other portable devices.

Asynchronous processors are potentially easier to design, since new circuits do not have to be synchronized with the entire chip. "It's a Lego-like system, which can be snapped together," Nowick said. Hurdles remain. Engineers need new software tools to design asynchronous circuits, and face subtle issues in designing these circuits correctly.

Nowick is currently working on both challenges, including projects to design a flexible asynchronous interconnection network for future desktop parallel computers, and ultra-low energy signal processors for hearing-aids and medical implants.

*B.A., Yale, 1976; M.A., Columbia, 1979; Ph.D. Stanford, 1993*

## *Marching Without a Beat*

# STEVEN NOWICK

Professor of Computer Science and of Electrical Engineering

INFORMATION

## *Searching for a Heavy Tail*

# MARIANA OLVERA-CRAVIOTO

Assistant Professor of Industrial Engineering and Operations Research

Search Google and within a fraction of a second it will return a list of the most popular websites on the subject. Or will it? Mariana Olvera-Cravioto has been trying to answer that question by understanding what makes a website popular on Google.

The principles behind Google's page-ranking system are well known. It weighs links to and from a page, as well as links of other pages on the same website. Yet the details remain unclear. For example, what counts more, a few links from such important websites as Wikipedia or Technorati, or many links from less significant pages? And what happens to the rankings if you change Google's search algorithm ever so slightly?

To probe those questions, Olvera-Cravioto relies on a form of probabilistic theory called heavy tail theory. To understand it, consider a normal bell curve. Most samples are grouped close to the center, or mean, and decline rapidly towards the ends of the curve.

Heavy tails have far more outliers at the ends of their curves than normal distributions. They are surprisingly common. They show up in the distribution of wealth (few people own more assets), oil reserves (a few have the most value), insurance payouts, and the time supercomputers spend completing tasks.

"Internet video transmission is an example of a heavy tail distribution," she said. "Streaming video only transmits pixels that change. Most of the time, that's relatively few pixels. But then the camera changes angles and the whole screen is refreshed. It happens less often, but accounts for most of the transmitted data." Google search results also have a heavy tail distribution.

"The mathematical techniques needed to solve heavy tails are completely different from what we use with well-behaved distributions," Olvera-Cravioto said. Those techniques provided some deep insights into Google's page rankings.

"Before we started our analysis, it was not obvious what determined the relative rankings of websites," Olvera-Cravioto said. Heavy tail analysis, for example, shows how large numbers of links outweigh important links in popularity rankings.

"Once you understand how it works, you can engineer search algorithms for specific purposes," she said. "Maybe you want to rank stores by number of sales rather than links, or measure the importance of a paper by how many times it is cited by reliable websites. Adding these things to a search algorithm could make it easier to find the page you're after."

*B.S., Instituto Technológico Autónomo de México, 2000; M.S., Stanford, 2004; Ph.D., Stanford, 2006*

When disaster strikes, the interdependent complexity of the environment (utilities, transportation, communication infrastructures, homes, and office buildings) can result in a cascading effect that quickly exacerbates the crisis. Large-scale disasters, such as Hurricane Katrina and the earthquake in Haiti, have graphically demonstrated the need for reliable initial disaster preparedness, response, and recovery. In such cases, the immediate availability of critical real-time data is crucial to saving lives.

Feniosky Peña-Mora, dean of The Fu Foundation School of Engineering and Applied Science at Columbia, has developed a new disaster response framework—Collaborative Preparedness, Response, and Recovery (CP2R)—that makes a significant difference in the outcome of such disasters. As part of this framework, he and his research team have created a mobile workstation using an all-terrain, heavy-duty Segway personal transporter outfitted with a payload that can include a Tablet PC, infrared and thermal still and video cameras, Global Positioning System receivers, and other advanced data collection technology. These instruments can collect, archive, analyze, and report large quantities of data to provide better situation awareness of an emerging disaster response scenario, and automatically generate digital models that can be used for disaster response.

By deploying these modified chariots manned by civil engineers, real-time data from first responders can be transmitted to coordination centers by wireless voice and data communication infrastructures. "This new cohort of first responders will provide accurate, real-time information to support technically sound decision-making processes during both the initial disaster response and the recovery phases," said Peña-Mora. "With a legion of mobile workstation chariots, we will be able to mitigate the dynamics of the disaster by improving the dynamics of the disaster response."

Recent testing of the mobile chariot has shown the potential for its success in the field. Despite additional weight from mounted instruments, the unit retained its stability on uneven surfaces and in differing weather conditions. Using digital images collected at the disaster site, decision-makers in coordination centers can evaluate infrastructure stability, study how the first responders are reacting to changing situations, and collect data for future analysis.

Peña-Mora holds appointments as professor of civil engineering, computer science, and earth and environmental engineering, is the author or co-author of more than 150 scholarly publications, and holds five patents, one provisional patent, and one technology disclosure.

*B.S., Universidad Nacional Pedro Henríquez Ureña, 1987; Post-Graduate, Universidad Nacional Pedro Henríquez Ureña, 1988; S.M., Massachusetts Institute of Technology, 1991; Sc.D., MIT, 1994*

*Improving Large-Scale Disaster Response*

# FENIOSKY PEÑA-MORA

Morris A. and Alma Schapiro Professor and Professor of Civil Engineering and Engineering Mechanics, of Earth and Environmental Engineering, and of Computer Science

INFORMATION

# Creating Nanoscale Devices

# ARON PINCZUK

Professor of Applied Physics and Applied Mathematics and Professor of Physics

Creating the next generation of electronic devices—be they computers, smartphones or displays—will depend on understanding the properties of materials on the nanoscale—one-billionth of a meter.

Aron Pinczuk's research projects employ advanced optics methods in condensed-matter science, with a focus on understanding the properties of novel materials and the physics of exotic states of matter that emerge in semiconductors at extremely low temperatures. His research findings address issues used by scientists seeking the development of quantum computing and cryptology. The research on graphene, a single atomic layer of graphite, contributes to the quest to initiate a new era in the creation of electronic components.

Pinczuk conducts his research at the Nanoscale Science and Engineering Center at Columbia, in the Department of Applied Physics and Applied Mathematics, and in the Department of Physics. His laboratory had support from the Keck Foundation and his research is funded through the National Science Foundation, the Department of Energy, and the U.S. Office of Naval Research, which support projects that span disciplines in science and engineering.

His research has explored the properties of gallium arsenide, a semiconductor, which is used in advanced optoelectronics, lasers, microwave circuits, and solar cells. To determine material properties in condensed matter systems, he subjects gallium arsenide to temperatures below 0.1 Kelvin, a temperature at which almost everything freezes. At these temperatures, the electrons cool down to make a liquid, emit light, and exhibit new, unexpected behaviors.

His research with gallium arsenide also has added to the basic science needed to develop a quantum computer, in which computational operations are executed in quantum bits. Theoretical studies show that quantum computers can solve certain problems quicker than classic, digital computer systems.

His findings also have assisted those looking to develop ways to use complex quantum states to build a key used to encrypt computer information. Such encrypted keys could be used to improve the security of computer systems.

Pinczuk's research with the carbon material, graphene, is part of the effort to develop a new generation of electronics that use carbon components. He studies the properties of carriers of an electric charge as it travels through a single layer of graphene, which is two-dimensional. Scientists are working on larger scale integration of these layers, which will create multi-layer structures with new properties.

"In the case of graphene, there are new properties that develop when you put all the layers together," said Pinczuk. "It's a field that is rapidly evolving."

*Licenciado, University of Buenos Aires (Argentina), 1962; Ph.D., University of Pennsylvania, 1969*

The volume of data we want to analyze is growing even faster than computing power. Kenneth Ross is looking for ways to close the gap. "People are coming up with ever-more challenging database projects, like analyzing the differences in genomes, which have billions of base pairs, among thousands of patients," Ross said.

Until now, computer scientists have relied on raw increases in computer power to crunch more data. Today, those advances have been harder to achieve. To keep moving forward, engineers reinvented the microprocessor, dividing it into two or more smaller processors, or cores.

Dividing tasks among cores works best when the answers do not depend on the previous step. Databases are like that. "The work you do on one record is pretty much what you do on another, you can process them in parallel," Ross said.

Yet parallelism comes with its own set of problems, such as cache misses and contention.

Cache misses occur because computer processors have fast and slow memory. They waste hundreds of processing cycles retrieving data from slower memory. Those lost cycles—cache misses—waste half the time needed to perform some tasks.

Ross wants to reorganize data to take up less space in memory. The hard part, he said, is doing this without spending too much time or resources.

"I'm trying to take advantage of relatively recent changes in computer architecture to make database software more efficient," said Ross. "Computer processors are now made up of four to eight smaller processors, or cores. We have to take advantage of those cores by developing code that runs in parallel."

Contention occurs when several parallel jobs all need to update a single item. "Each of those jobs needs exclusive access to the item for a short time to keep them from interfering with one another. If the item is sufficiently popular, those jobs get stuck in line waiting for their turn to access the data rather than working in parallel," Ross explained.

Ross' recent research seeks to automatically detect contention and then create several clones of the busiest data items. "We want to distribute processes among the clones and then combine results. Again, the key is to do this without using more computer resources than we are saving by eliminating contention," he said.

From genomics to climate, the sciences are accumulating data at a faster rate than ever before. Ross' work will help make it possible to analyze that data and see what they really mean.

*B.Sc., University of Melbourne, 1986; Ph.D., Stanford, 1991*

*Processing Parallel Insights*

# KENNETH ROSS

Professor of Computer Science

INFORMATION

## Networking Your Wallet, Credit Cards, and Keys

# DAN RUBENSTEIN

Associate Professor of Computer Science

Imagine a world where library books tell you they are on the wrong shelf and fruit reports it has gone bad to grocers. It is a universe where you can always find your keys or remote control.

This world is under construction in Dan Rubenstein's laboratories. His team is working with small tag-like devices that attach securely to everything from books to baseball bats. "They will let you track all the things you want to track without being tracked by entities you don't want to track you," Rubenstein said.

The devices are called EnHANTs, which stands for energy-harvesting active network tags. "They're designed to soak up energy from the environment to form a network with the tags around them. The networked tags then keep track of one another," said Rubenstein. "Unlike similar radio frequency identification (RFID) tags, which turn on only when activated by powerful radio transmitters, EnHANTs would generate their own power by harvesting energy from ambient light, tiny vibrations, or temperature changes.

Unfortunately, this is not enough power to stay turned on all the time, communicate more than 10 feet, or send lots of information at a time. To get around those limitations, EnHANTs must network with other nearby EnHANTs and devices.

"Existing network protocols waste too much power to work with devices of EnHANTs' size. We have to be more efficient," Rubenstein said.

He imagines a room with 10 tagged possessions. The devices sleep to conserve energy, but turn on periodically to see what devices are nearby. Over time, the EnHANTs identify the other devices in the room.

A more powerful device, such as a home wireless network or smartphone, would query the EnHANTs and ask them what they see. Over a period of time, the network would build a map of the room's contents and any sensor data the EnHANTs had to communicate.

"If you start to leave your house and your wallet knows it should be with your belt, coat, and keys, it could tell the network to text a reminder to your cell phone," Rubenstein said.

Meanwhile, Rubenstein's group continues to work on shrinking prototypes to postage-stamp size. "We are really scaling back the components that go into a tag to see how small we can make it," he said. If he succeeds, we may never forget our wallet, keys, or bank cards again.

*B.S., Massachusetts Institute of Technology, 1992; M.A., University of California-Los Angeles, 1994; Ph.D., University of Massachusetts-Amherst, 2000*

The latest smartphones automatically plot your location and update traffic and weather. If a Facebook friend calls, they automatically find and display his or her picture. Slowly, we are weaving together the different strands of the virtual world. Henning Schulzrinne wants to make that fabric richer by making it easier to connect those services and adding sensors to the mix.

Sensors let computers measure and interact with the physical world. "Imagine you're driving home," Schulzrinne suggested. "If the temperature is above 80 degrees F, your GPS-enabled cellphone could turn on your air conditioner. It would then turn it off when the last family member leaves home."

Working behind the scenes, Internet-enabled automation could use sensor data to tailor its response to the situation. Interconnected sensors could warn when household appliances need repairs, water the lawn only when it is dry, analyze traffic so you leave home with enough time to make your dinner reservation, and even check for signs of disease.

"Today, many of these web services are available to other applications," Schulzrinne continued. A savvy developer could query a calendar program for today's appointments or a weather program for a forecast.

"We want to leverage these services into more interesting and comprehensive systems," Schulzrinne said. "We want to program anything that can be controlled through the Internet, from your lighting and heating to your e-mail and smartphone. We want to make it easier to build smart offices and homes, and to link your calendar with your phone."

To make that happen, Schulzrinne is focusing on two first steps. One is to develop simple ways to interconnect services, sensors, and applications. "Today, you have to learn Java or other programming languages, or rely on tools from Internet companies. We want to make it easy for the nontechnical to moderately technical users to link things together in interesting ways," he said.

He is also pushing for standardized interfaces that make it easy to plug sensors into the web. "There is no reason why every sensor maker should not use the same format to convey information," Schulzrinne said. "We want to develop a standardized interface, a platform that other people can create modules that use sensor and Internet data to trigger events like services. For example, a module might trigger a stock sale depending on its performance. Another might see if it is going to rain before watering the lawn."

Ultimately, it could lead to a physical world as interactive as the virtual world that ties it together.

*B.S., Technical University of Darmstadt (Germany), 1984; M.S., University of Cincinnati, 1987; Ph.D., University of Massachusetts-Amherst, 1992*

## *Sensing Our Connected World*

# HENNING G. SCHULZRINNE

Julian Clarence Levi Professor of Mathematical Methods and Computer Science and Professor of Electrical Engineering

INFORMATION

# Improving Human Health with Low-Power Cyber Physical Systems

## MINGOO SEOK

Assistant Professor of
Electrical Engineering

Technological innovation on the health care front means better data management—like being able to monitor multiple vital signs of a patient on an operating table—as well as enhanced patient outcomes, such as the use of implanted pacemakers that use electrical impulses to prompt a heart to beat at a normal rate. Now, science is exploring how to take technology to the next level in order to further improve human health. That step will require the design of complex, interoperable medical devices that would be able to vary their operation to suit changing body conditions, detect minute physiological changes that signal disease, and transmit such data to medical professionals, who could take remedial action before the disease is significantly developed.

The development and use of cyber physical systems that interconnect the human body and external computers (and thus medical professionals) will be dependent upon several things: minute scalability of the system and power source, long-term operability, functional robustness regardless of environmental factors, and security of the transmitted information. Creating nearly invisible implantable medical devices is challenged by conventional circuitry and system-design techniques that fail to deliver energy efficiency to satisfy a lifetime of service.

Mingoo Seok works to combine new circuitry and architectural design elements with ultra-low-voltage systems to make the possibility of millimeter scale implantable medical devices possible. He has demonstrated a very small (1 mm$^3$) computer that consumes pico- to nano-watts of power—consumption that is more than 1,000 times smaller than previous state-of-the-art technology.

His research interests are in low-power digital and mixed-signal design and methodology, and he has devised approaches that deliver record-setting energy efficiency in microcontrollers, embedded memories, power conversion circuits, and DSP accelerators. As part of the technical staff at the research and development centers of Texas Instruments, he focused on developing ultra-low-power security-enhancing circuit techniques.

*B.S., Seoul National (South Korea), 2005; M.S., University of Michigan, 2007; Ph.D., University of Michigan, 2011*

I n "20 Questions," one player thinks of an object and the others get 20 yes-no questions to guess its identity. "That's easy, but what if you let the answerer lie three times? That makes it much more difficult," Rocco Servedio said.

That is the type of problem researchers face when false signals, or noise, corrupt data. Servedio's goal is to develop robust algorithms that learn complicated rules even in the presence of noisy data. Such algorithms could learn patterns that improve sensor performance, predict earthquakes, or forecast financial markets.

One of Servedio's most powerful tools is geometry. "When you cast a learning problem in a geometric framework, you're often on the way towards solving it," he said.

Imagine, for example, a piece of paper with red plus signs and green minus signs on opposite sides of an unknown dividing line. A few pluses are mixed with the minuses and vice versa. "In this two-dimensional example, you can eyeball the data and see which points don't belong. In higher dimensions, where each point has many coordinates, this is much more difficult, though we can sometimes pull it off with tools from high-dimensional geometry," he said.

"The way people understand something is by drawing pictures. I'm usually working in high-dimensional Euclidean spaces where it's tough to draw accurate pictures," he said, "but thinking geometrically still provides useful insights."

Servedio also takes a geometric approach to studying rules used to classify information. One popular approach is the decision tree. Like "20 Questions," it uses a sequence of yes-no questions to decide how to label data points.

"If you think of this logical representation geometrically, you can sometimes see properties that would have otherwise remained hidden. These insights can lead to better learning algorithms," Servedio said.

Servedio also uses geometry to compensate for missing data. Imagine that it takes 1,000 coordinates to describe a data point completely. What kind of learning is possible if only one of those coordinates is available?

"There are ways to compensate for massive amounts of missing data," Servedio said. "It might sound impossible, but doctors do something like this all the time. They could potentially run thousands of clinical tests on a patient to fully describe his or her condition, but a good doctor can make a useful diagnosis from just one or two tests."

*A.B., Harvard, 1993; M.S., Harvard, 1997; Ph.D., Harvard, 2001*

*Playing "20 Questions" with Geometry*

# ROCCO A. SERVEDIO

Associate Professor of Computer Science

## Designing Secure Hardware

# SIMHA SETHUMADHAVAN

Assistant Professor of Computer Science

All computer software has one thing in common: it runs on computer hardware. But what if you could not trust the hardware to securely run software? That's the question posed by Simha Sethumadhavan. "If the hardware is hacked, then it can subvert all software and software security countermeasures," said Sethumadhavan. "Since hardware is the root of trust, attacks on hardware are potentially very dangerous."

Until recently, computer scientists never suspected that someone could tamper with hardware. Yet investigators have found unusual additions in military chips. One way to prevent hardware hijackings is by passing tokens every time data moves within hardware. Sethumadhavan likens this to sending a thank you card after a gift.

"Let's say Charlie wants to contribute $100 to Alice's charity, but has to send it to Bob first," he said. "Bob takes $10 for himself and pays the rest to Alice. One way to find out if there is a problem is for Alice to write Charlie a thank you note for the $90 donation. When Charlie sees the discrepancy, he asks accountants to trace the missing money."

Sethumadhavan proposes creating similar triangle-like structures within a computer processor. "They would monitor any irregularities. We want to create a chain of monitored data and sound the alarm if any of the links break. These lightweight monitoring additions incur very little processing overhead," he said.

"We are taking a clean slate, ground-up approach to designing secure systems," he added. "As a foundational step, we have designed methods to protect processors, the core of all computing infrastructure. Once processors are secure, we can securely build out support for protecting other hardware and software."

Sethumadhavan is also working on other techniques for securing processors. "All hardware back doors have triggers and payloads. The triggers are usually time or data input values that activate the payload," he said.

"We are working on ways to silence the trigger," he said. "For example, we might be able to reset the processor's counter so it never reaches the threshold value needed to trigger an event. Or we could use lightweight encryption to obscure data values." Only when we fully trust our processor can we fully trust other security procedures, Sethumadhavan concluded.

Sethumadhavan is leading a project on rethinking security, making it a priority instead of an afterthought, with three other Columbia Engineering professors and a team from Princeton University. The project, titled "SPARCHS: Symbiotic, Polymorphic, Autotomic, Resilient, Clean-slate, Host Security," is funded by a federal grant for more than $6 million.

*B.S.E., University of Madras, 2000; M.S., University of Texas, 2005; Ph.D., University of Texas, 2007*

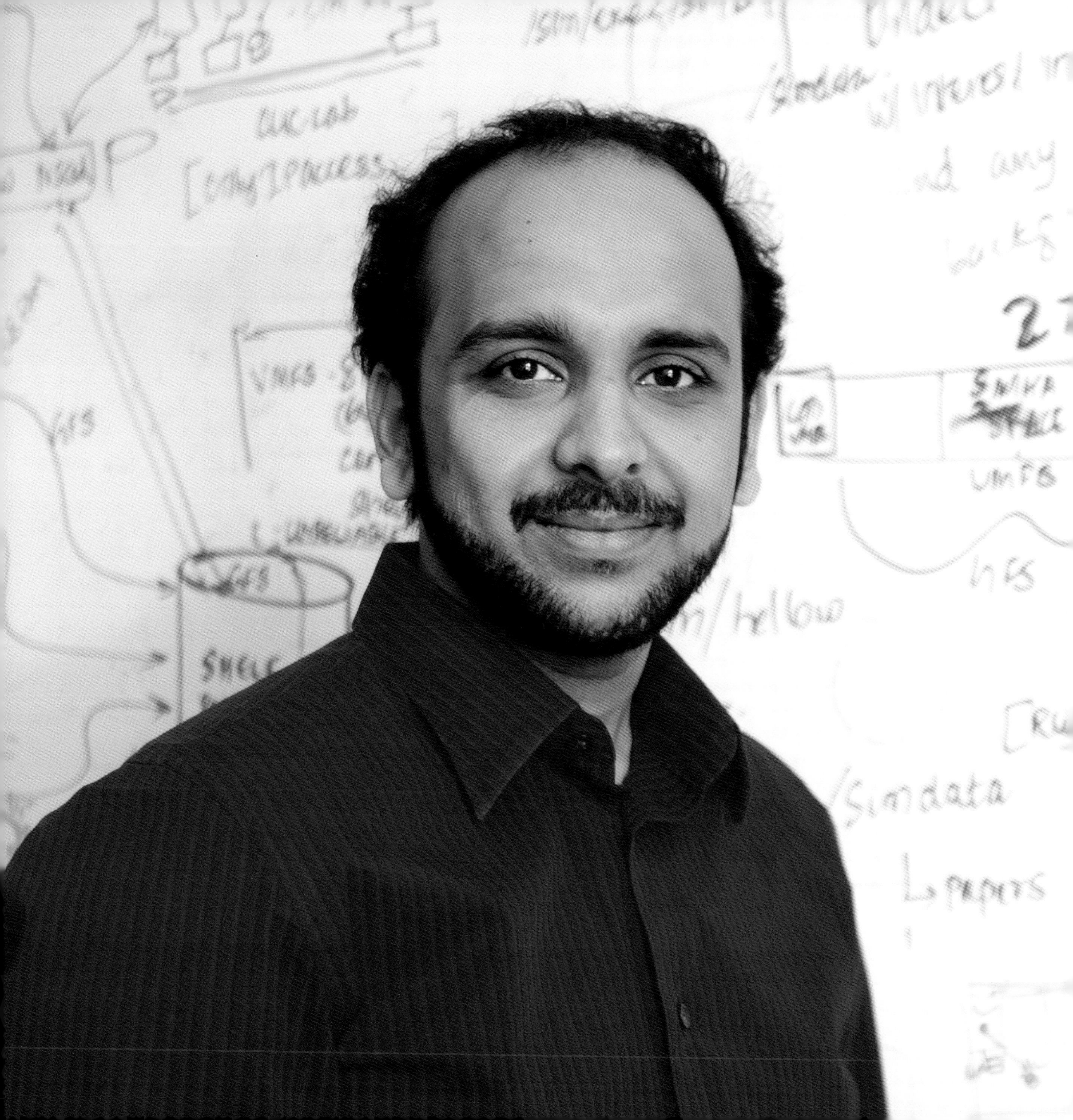

Jay Sethuraman began his career by matching sets of jobs with machines to improve factory performance. More recently though, he has used operations research to find the fairest way to admit students to top public high schools.

To Sethuraman, the two problems are similar, with one major exception: "In a factory, the machines don't care what job they do. But schools do care about which students they admit," he said.

New York City's selective schools choose students based on admissions test scores. Students who do not get into their top choice can appeal. In fact, schools may set aside a certain number of seats for appeals, in addition to those seats lost when students they admitted leave for another school.

Resolving appeals fairly and efficiently discourages students from gaming the system, Sethuraman said. They may be willing to go to several schools, but list only one school if that increases their chance of placement. Or they may list schools that are unlikely to admit them if it improves their odds of getting into the school they want.

"A better system would give students an incentive to list their true preferences without penalizing them for doing it," Sethuraman said. "We want to maximize the number of students who get into their top choice, but treat all students in a fair, systematic way."

Under Sethuraman's approach, each student starts with a seat in a school that he or she wants to trade. Rather than trade individual seats, students exchange their seat for a fraction of a seat in the schools they want to attend. Those fractions, which add up to a full seat, are computed based on seat availability plus the desirability of the student's existing seat.

"At the end of this procedure, a student may have one-half a seat in school A, one-third a seat in school B, and one-sixth a seat in school C. This determines their probability of getting a seat in the lottery," Sethuraman said. Students who do not complete a trade move onto the next round of lotteries, where their odds are reset to account for the remaining available seats.

"Listing all the schools you are willing to attend increases your chances of staying in the game longer and getting into a school you really want," said Sethurman. "We give students an incentive to list all their acceptable schools without trying to game the system."

*B.E., Birla Institute of Technology and Science (India), 1991; M.S., Indian Institute of Science, 1994; Ph.D., Massachusetts Institute of Technology, 1999*

*Predicting the Probability of Congestion*

# KARL SIGMAN

Professor of Industrial Engineering
and Operations Research

When people refer to the World Wide Web as an information superhighway, they rarely consider traffic jams. Yet congestion slows the movement of information around the web, and appears naturally in systems as diverse as highways and hospitals.

Karl Sigman uses probability tools to build and analyze mathematical models of congestion, also known as queueing. A simple example is an ATM machine, where people arrive randomly and sometimes find themselves waiting in line to use the machine.

Successfully analyzing queueing models can help optimally route requests to a set of web servers, staff a call center, process jobs in a manufacturing plant, and schedule surgeries in a hospital.

The mathematics of probability gives Sigman many insights into a model's evolution. Still, many models remain breathtakingly complex due to the inherent randomness involved in the real world.

"Randomness, such as when the next request arrives or when something breaks, affects all these systems," said Sigman. "The further you look into the future, the more random it can become. It's like stock prices. Tomorrow's price is likely to be similar to today's, but the price next week is less certain.

"I'm interested in the relationship between what system users see and what the system actually does," he explained. "A user might click a link on a website. How long he or she waits to see the page is a measure of congestion from the user's perspective."

A system observer's viewpoint is different. "He or she looks at the web server over time and asks, 'How many users are trying to access a given page?' It does not look at the experience of any given user," Sigman said.

"This is also a measure of congestion and system performance, but from different perspectives," Sigman added. Yet the two views are interrelated. In fact, the solution to a problem from one perspective can sometimes be transformed into the desired solution from the other perspective.

Sigman has spent years teasing out those connections. "Sometimes the model looks very complicated from the perspective of a user, but it proves easier to solve from the perspective of an observer," he said.

Sigman joined Columbia Engineering in 1987. He was the recipient of the Distinguished Faculty Teaching Award both in 1998 and in 2002. He teaches courses in stochastic models, financial engineering, and queueing theory. Before joining Columbia, Sigman was a postdoctoral associate at the Mathematical Sciences Institute at Cornell University.

*B.A., University of California-Santa Cruz, 1980; M.A., University of California-Berkeley, 1983; M.S., UC Berkeley, 1984; Ph.D., UC Berkeley, 1986*

Aging infrastructure is a major problem around the world and monitoring the health of structures, from bridges to dams to buildings, is critical to our modern society. Andrew Smyth specializes in structural health monitoring, using the dynamic signature of a structure to determine its condition. This can include assessing a structure's day-to-day performance, locating and quantifying potential areas of damage, or calibrating a model that can be stressed in a computer simulation for a heretofore-unseen loading event.

One of Smyth's recent projects has focused on monitoring vibrations on New York City's Manhattan Bridge. To assess the bridge's performance subsequent to a major retrofitting and strengthening program, and to calibrate a mathematical model of the bridge to predict its performance in the event of a potential seismic event, Smyth and his team placed a variety of different sensors that detected dynamic motions on the bridge over a two-month period. With the recorded data and their newly developed data fusion algorithms—a new technique that combines data from multiple sources— the team was able to identify the dynamic characteristics of Manhattan Bridge.

Smyth has also pioneered the use of differential GPS technology in conjunction with the data fusion technique to obtain highly accurate measures of low-frequency bridge deformations. He continues to develop data fusion algorithms for other civil and mechanical systems that combine information from a network of different kinds of sensors used to measure the dynamic response of a system. He says that, by taking advantage of the various levels of data redundancy, one can get high-fidelity virtual-sensing information that plays to the respective strengths of different types of sensors.

"Basically our work allows us to better understand the condition and performance of the built environment," said Smyth. "This really is our society's most valuable physical asset and the backbone of our way of life. Structural health monitoring allows us to better allocate our resources to maintain and improve our infrastructure, and keep us safe."

In 2008, Smyth was awarded the prestigious Walter L. Huber Civil Engineering Research Prize of the American Society of Civil Engineers. The award recognizes notable achievements by younger faculty members in research related to civil engineering. Smyth was recognized "for fundamental contributions in the highly efficient identification and modeling of nonlinear deteriorating structural dynamics." The selection committee commented that his research is characterized by "thoroughness, novelty, relevance, and intelligent breakthroughs."

*B.A./B.Sc., Brown, 1992; M.S., Rice, 1994; Ph.D., University of Southern California, 1998*

## Monitoring Structural Health with Sensor Data Fusion

# ANDREW W. SMYTH

Professor of Civil Engineering and Engineering Mechanics

INFORMATION

# Estimating Solutions to Difficult Problems

# CLIFFORD S. STEIN

Professor of Industrial Engineering and Operations Research and of Computer Science

Cliff Stein has built a career on finding algorithms to solve difficult problems—but not precisely. Stein specializes in algorithms that estimate the answer to problems that are difficult to solve. In operations research and computer science, these are problems that grow exponentially more complex as the number of inputs grows.

This contrasts with simple problems, like alphabetizing words. Double the number of inputs—words—and it takes only about twice as long to accomplish the task.

A well-known difficult problem is calculating the most efficient route for a salesman to visit different cities. To find the most efficient route, a computer must calculate all possible outcomes. For five cities, there are 120 potential paths. For 10 cities, 3.6 million. "For 80 cities, there are roughly as many possible answers as there are atoms in the universe," Stein said.

"No conceivable advance in computing power would enable us to solve that problem precisely," Stein noted. "But if you're willing to solve it approximately, you can do so more easily and efficiently."

Many algorithms already exist for estimating the solution for the traveling salesman and other difficult problems. Stein prefers to break new ground, studying the fundamental structure of problems to develop new algorithms.

"There's a collection of algorithmic tools that are commonly used to solve many problems," he said. "But often there are problems that are important to solve. It is worth investing the time to study their mathematical or combinatorial structure to come up with a solution specific to that problem."

Much of his work deals with scheduling everything from computer systems to factories. Scheduling starts with jobs and the machines needed to complete them. Constraints—jobs take different amounts of time, some are more important than others, some tasks depend on others—add to the difficulty. So do different objectives, like fast completion, minimal resources, and rapid response.

Stein is looking at ways to apply scheduling to computer processors in order to save energy. "Most chips can run at four or five different speeds," he said. "If you run at half speed, you decrease energy use by roughly a factor of four. But no one has figured out how to give chips the intelligence to know when to slow down, so they typically run at top speed all the time."

By estimating a chip's workload, constraints, and performance goals, Stein believes he can achieve significant energy savings. Even if his estimates are not precise.

*B.S.E., Princeton, 1987; M.S., Massachusetts Institute of Technology, 1989; Ph.D., MIT, 1992*

If your credit card company ever called to confirm a purchase, you have entered Salvatore Stolfo's world. Stolfo specializes in detecting anomalies, events that stray too far from expected patterns. In addition to fraud, anomaly detection can be used to monitor engineered systems, sensor networks, ecosystems, and computer security.

Stolfo entered the field after inventing an algorithm that let marketers merge lists of consumers and purge bad records. "I realized I was aiding and abetting people who pierced personal privacy. It was an ethical dilemma," he recalled.

His interest in privacy led to cybersecurity and eventually to the study of insider attacks. "Most security breaches are the fault of the humans. Someone didn't implement something, or stole an identity, or had a grudge against an organization," Stolfo said.

This differs from most security research, which aims to keep out hackers. University researchers are more ambitious, developing inherently secure programming languages and self-repairing systems. "These are important aspects of security, but they don't matter if your adversary is already inside," Stolfo said.

"There are many different types of insiders, and they all do things in different ways," he added. "We think of it as a chess game. What if insiders can control system access? If they can blind the system to their actions, they can get away with anything. We want to stop them."

The most common type of insider threats is unintentional users. They may disable security measures to do their job more easily, or inadvertently push two buttons and erase a day's work. "These are the most prevalent and least dangerous insiders," Stolfo said.

Masqueraders include credit card thieves with stolen credentials. "The credentials make them insiders," Stolfo said. He works with banks to model consumer transactions. "We're always looking for ways to use more data to find problems sooner," he said.

Maliciously intentful insiders use their own credentials to copy secret government or corporate documents, steal money, and even sabotage the system. Highly privileged insiders have a similar agenda, but they are the ones responsible for detecting other intruders.

To foil these intruders, Stolfo looks at how their behaviors vary from company norms. By plotting how users interact with software and documents, he hopes to find patterns that suggest malicious intent. He has also developed decoys to ensnare bad guys.

"Ultimately, we want to define metrics for what it means to be secure," he said. "Then we can start to build a science of security."

*B.S., Brooklyn College, 1974; M.S., New York University, 1976; Ph.D., NYU, 1979*

# Using Anomalies to Defend Against Insiders

# SALVATORE J. STOLFO

Professor of Computer Science

INFORMATION

# JOSEPH F. TRAUB

Edwin Howard Armstrong Professor of
Computer Science

Joseph Traub is best known as a pioneer in the computational complexity of continuous problems. This involves understanding the least amount of resources—time, memory, communications—needed to solve a computing problem.

"My strategy is to start a new area of research or get into something fairly early," he said. "Then I can just walk along and pick up diamonds of knowledge and insight. I never have to strip mine for them."

It is probably as good a background as any for his investigations into the potential of quantum computing. It is a quest at the intersection of physics, mathematics, and computer science.

Quantum computing stands conventional computing on its head. For example, bits are the basic unit of information in today's computers. They can have one of two values, either zero or one, which microprocessor transistors represent as on or off.

Quantum computers are built around qubits, which have a property called superposition. This means they can be in many quantum states between zero and one, all at the same time. The more qubits a processor has, the more potential states it allows.

Qubits also have a property called entanglement. For reasons not yet understood, changing the quantum state in one of two entangled particles instantaneously changes it in the other. "That enables qubits to work together without wires," Traub said.

Because quantum computers are not limited to on-off states, they can calculate many possible answers at once. This could make it possible to calculate very complex problems rapidly.

"What I'm trying to do is ask, 'Where are the big wins?' In particular, what kind of problems could a quantum computer solve that physicists and chemists are really interested in solving," Traub said.

One of those problems is calculating the lowest energy state, or ground state energy, of a large number of particles. "This is a central problem in computational chemistry, and it would allow us to predict chemical reactions better," Traub explained.

The problem, he explained, is that ground state energy calculations are difficult and soak up computer resources. A quantum computer's ability to make multiple calculations simultaneously could give chemists the tool they need to predict particle interactions in large systems.

"We're theoreticians, trying to understand the type of problems quantum computers might be able to solve. Physicists may never succeed in building one, but if they do, we want to be ready," Traub concluded.

*B.S., College of the City of New York, 1954; M.S., Columbia, 1955; Ph.D., Columbia, 1959*

While the transistor revolutionized the field of electronics and paved the way for personal computers, it made way for several perpetual challenges: deliver more power in smaller sizes, enable real-time interaction with the real world, and constantly adapt to technological change. Solutions to those challenges can make possible, for example, biomedical ingestible pills, containing chips that aid, or give information about, the body; sensor networks that provide information about the environment or physical infrastructure; or wireless communication technology that uses less battery power but provides more range.

One of the challenges in making this new era a reality lies in advancing the development of single silicon chips that perform both analog and digital signal processing. Analog and digital signal domains have significant technical differences, yet new technology demands more and more complex mixed-signal design. The development pace is relentless, driven by demands for increased performance. New techniques need to be invented, and fundamental limitations must be better understood, to make such analog/digital circuits with improved performance possible.

Yannis P. Tsividis has been an important contributor to the field of silicon chips that mix analog and digital circuits. He and his students have done extensive research in this field at the device, circuit, system, and computer simulation level.

In 1976, Tsividis designed and built the first fully integrated MOS operational amplifier and demonstrated its use in a coder-decoder for digital telephony. These results were widely adopted by the industry in the first massively produced mixed-signal MOS integrated circuits, which incorporate both analog and digital functions on the same silicon chip.

Tsividis and his students have since been responsible for several important contributions, ranging from precision device modeling and novel circuit building blocks to new techniques for analog and mixed-signal processing, self-correcting chips, switched-capacitor network theory, RF integrated circuits, mixed analog-digital Very Large Scale Integrated (VLSI) computation and the creation of computer simulation programs. This work has resulted in several patents in several countries, and has been incorporated by the industry into products we use every day.

Tsividis is a fellow of the Institute of Electrical and Electronics Engineers.

*B.E., University of Minnesota, 1972; M.S., University of California-Berkeley, 1973; Ph.D., UC Berkeley, 1976*

## Creating New Circuits for Interfacing the Computer to the Physical World

# YANNIS TSIVIDIS

Charles Batchelor Professor of Electrical Engineering

INFORMATION

# Unlocking a Complex World Mathematically

# VLADIMIR VAPNIK

Professor of Computer Science

"When the solution is simple, God is answering," Albert Einstein once commented. He believed we could discover nature's laws only when they connected a few variables, like the relationship between temperature and pressure or energy and mass. "When the number of factors coming into play is too large, scientific methods in most cases fail," Einstein said. Of course, Einstein did not have computers. Vladimir Vapnik does.

Vapnik works in machine learning, a discipline that uses algorithms to detect automatically those laws of nature that depend on hundreds or even thousands of parameters. This enables computers to make better predictions, and also provides insights into the elusive nature of human learning.

Today's machine learning technology requires many examples to generate accurate rules. Yet humans clearly learn to understand their complex world from far fewer examples. This led Vapnik to consider how teachers provide students with what he calls "privileged information," holistic knowledge often delivered as metaphors and comparisons.

Master classes for musicians are an example. "The teachers cannot show students how to play an instrument because their technique is not as good," he said. "Instead, teachers may use metaphors or comparisons to show students how to understand a piece. This may sound like nonsense in terms of musical technique, but it helps them play better."

Vapnik has shown mathematically that privileged information could slash the samples needed for machine learning by the square root of the original number. "Instead of 10,000 examples, we would need only 100," he said.

He demonstrated this using privileged information to help a computer identify handwritten numbers. He asked Professor of Russian Poetry Natalia Pavlovitch to write a short verse describing her feelings about each number sample. The information was subjective and not available by analyzing only the numbers. Including it during training yielded more accurate results than training with the numbers alone.

Vapnik also used surgeons' descriptions of biopsy pictures—from "quiet" to "wide aggressive proliferation"—to improve the classification of tumors. The notes were impressionistic, but improved the computer's ability to identify cancerous cells.

Humans frequently use such holistic privileged information to make sense of complex phenomena. Providing it to machines could open a new door onto a complex universe.

"For 2,000 years, we believed logic was the only instrument for solving intellectual problems. Now, our analysis of machine learning is showing us that to address truly complex problems, we need images, poetry, and metaphors as well," Vapnik concluded.

*M.S., Uzbek State University, Samarkand, 1958; Ph.D., Institute of Control Sciences, Moscow, 1964*

Advancing wireless communication technology to a new generation of application and service is one of today's prime research disciplines. Demands for higher capacity drive the need to create novel signal transmission techniques and advanced receiver signal processing methods. Challenging design requirements are compounded by the complexity of the nature of the transmitter and receiver: a complicated system consisting of radio frequency, analog and mixed-signal components. Plus, heated competition in the development arena forces tight time-to-market deliverables.

To develop effective next-generation wireless technology under the constraint of thousands of variables, it is important to use mathematical modeling and analysis, computer simulations, fast calculations, and data summaries to thoroughly account for manufacturing process variations before build-out. Using these tools to analyze production provides a comprehensive transistor-level statistical design and verification framework. With it, designers can troubleshoot and devise design enhancements to solve the issues of fading, impulsive noise, and co-channel interference in the concept phase.

Xiaodong Wang is a leading researcher in signal processing, computing, and communications. His broader research interests include information theory, algebraic coding theory, wireless communications, optical communications, communication networks, statistical signal processing, and genomic signal processing. Results of his research have included extensive publication in these areas, most recently in the areas of chip-level asynchronism on a Code Division Multiple Access (CDMA)-based overlay system for optical network management; modulation classification via Kolmogorov-Smirnov test; Generalized Likelihood Ratio Test (GLRT)-based spectrum sensing for cognitive radio with prior information; and blind frequency-dependent I/Q imbalance compensation for direct-conversion receivers.

Wang also has become active in the emerging field of genomic signal processing (GSP). The aim of GSP is to integrate the theory and methods of signal processing with the global understanding of functional genomics, with special emphasis on genomic regulation. He took part in a National Science Foundation-funded multidisciplinary collaborative project to develop a structural health monitoring (SHM) system using a wireless piezoelectric sensor network.

Wang is a fellow of the Institute of Electrical and Electronics Engineers (IEEE). He received the 1999 NSF CAREER Award and the 2001 IEEE Communications Society and Information Theory Society Joint Paper Award. He has served as an associate editor for the *IEEE Transactions on Signal Processing*, the *IEEE Transactions on Communications*, the *IEEE Transactions on Wireless Communications*, and *IEEE Transactions on Information Theory*. He is listed as an ISI-Highly-Cited researcher.

*B.S., Shanghai Jiao Tong University, 1992; M.S., Purdue, 1995; Ph.D., Princeton, 1998*

## Devising a Design Framework for Next-Generation Wireless Technology

# XIAODONG WANG

Professor of Electrical Engineering

## Predicting Waves Mathematically

# MICHAEL WEINSTEIN

Professor of Applied Physics and
Applied Mathematics

INFORMATION

Understanding the behavior of waves in complex environments holds the key to advances in a wide range of applications—from optical communications and computer technology to the prediction and detection of seismic, atmospheric, and oceanic phenomena. Wave phenomena are described using partial differential equations, which are a mathematical encoding of physical laws.

But significant challenges arise because phenomena are both multiscale—they derive from activity and interactions among very small spatial scales all the way up to very large scales—and nonlinear, which leads to waves that distort dramatically and "scatter" differently as their size is changed. These general features limit the solvability of problems on even the fastest computers.

Michael Weinstein develops hybrid analytical/computational approaches, which combine asymptotic mathematical analysis with computer simulation. Asymptotic analysis yields approximate, but fairly explicit and detailed information, on the very small-scale phenomena. With these degrees of freedom "solved for," the computer can then focus on the larger scales and efficiently give approximate, yet very accurate predictions.

Applying these approaches to the partial differential equations of optics, Weinstein has discerned how "soliton" light-pulses travel and interact within communications lines. This work has a wide range of practical applications: from determining the stability of optical pulses to ideas on how to robustly encode information in streams of optical pulses.

He has proposed designs of novel optical media to slow or even stop light pulses in micro-structured waveguides, and has proposed their application to optical buffering of information. A recent project exploits parallels between the equations of electromagnetics with those arising in the theory of shock waves in supersonic flight, to understand the generation of broadband, multi-colored light from laser light of a single color. Broadband light sources have applications ranging from communications to imaging science.

Other recent work he is addressing concerns metamaterials: specially engineered microstructures, which act as a macroscopic device, and achieve properties not possible using naturally occurring materials. One application studied by Weinstein is the attainability of the cloaking effect. Cloaking involves surrounding a region of space by an appropriate metamaterial. Anything in the surrounded region is undetectable by exterior sensors, and anything within the shielded region is isolated from the exterior world. Other application areas of metamaterials envisioned include improved solar energy cells, secure communications and sensors.

Weinstein is a fellow of the Society for Industrial and Applied Mathematics (SIAM), elected for his "contributions to the analysis and applications of nonlinear waves".

*B.S., Union College, 1977; M.S., Courant Institute of Mathematical Sciences at New York University, 1979; Ph.D., Courant Institute, 1982*

Anyone who has driven on highways understands that random events affect congestion. Even in relatively light traffic, with no accidents or obstructions, cars will suddenly bunch up, slow, and then speed up again.

Ward Whitt studies the enigma at the heart of this process. His discipline—queueing theory—examines how random fluctuations in flow, waiting, and processing cause congestion in complex systems.

Examples are everywhere. "We all spend too much time waiting on lines, from physical lines in a supermarket or bank to invisible lines on hold for a call center or waiting for a web page to load," Whitt said. Queues are equally present in the waiting times of a computer processor or the movement of parts through a factory.

One major goal of queueing theory is to reduce waiting. Understanding congestion helps engineers specify the right number of telephone switches, Internet servers, and even call center personnel.

Despite their wide use, queuing models have a significant weakness. "The standard queueing models assume random flow, but the rate of that random flow is assumed constant. In reality, the arrivals to a system occur randomly, but the rate of that random flow is not constant," Whitt said.

Whitt tries to capture that systematic variation in the flow rate together with the uncertainty about that flow rate. He builds and analyzes models that reflect both these features of everyday queueing phenomena. "This produces high fidelity descriptions of congestion that go far beyond standard textbook queueing models," he said.

Whitt is also applying these insights to complex networks. "Queues do not appear in isolation, but appear in networked systems with multiple flow paths and queues," he said.

One way to tackle complex, networked systems is to see how they would behave as they scale up. "Sometimes," Whitt said, "a larger model tells a clearer story. Toss a coin 20 times and you expect to average 10 heads and 10 tails, but you may see from seven to 13 heads. But toss the coin one million times, you are likely to get closer to a 50-50 split."

He has developed mathematical techniques that show how congested systems behave at larger scales. He then compares the model with computer simulations of the system or data from that system.

"When you do this, you can end up with a fairly simple story that tells you a lot about your system," Whitt said.

*A.B., Dartmouth, 1964; Ph.D., Cornell, 1969*

*Unraveling the Mysteries of Congestion*

# WARD WHITT

Wai T. Chang Professor of Industrial Engineering and Operations Research

INFORMATION

# *Bringing Order to High-Dimensional Datasets*

# JOHN WRIGHT

Assistant Professor of
Electrical Engineering

I t's a data-driven world out there. Every day, streams of data in the form of images, videos, biomedical observations, Internet links, and more are fed to scientific organizations, businesses, and governments worldwide. And while management and warehousing of these prodigious amounts of data are important, equally important is developing the technological capability to understand the structure of the datasets.

Much of the data collected today is in digital imagery, each made up of several million pixels. With millions upon millions upon millions of pixels residing in any given dataset, finding order within those datasets is critical to being able to efficiently search and find specific data. Add to that the challenge when data in any set is unreliable (e.g., "dead" pixel(s), a disguised face, shadows, or occlusions), and the classical algorithms used to search and find specific data break down.

John Wright considers the area of high-dimensional data analysis a gold mine for great mathematical and algorithmic problems, with the potential for profound impact on applications that can deal intelligently with imagery data.

His research has developed new theory and algorithms for uncovering several important types of low-dimensional structure in high-dimensional datasets, even in the presence of gross observation errors. This combination of efficient algorithm and good theoretical understanding has led to new, highly accurate algorithms for recognizing human faces, even with occlusion or disguise; for recovering the shape of three-dimensional objects from two-dimensional images; and for building three-dimensional models of urban environments.

He is currently working on new techniques for finding good representations of data—searching for a "dictionary" that can most compactly represent a given set of data samples. Recent results have shown that if it is possible to find efficient data representations, those representations can be used to acquire signals and images more accurately, and using fewer resources. Through collaborations at Microsoft Research, he is investigating the use of these techniques to efficiently acquire images for cultural heritage preservation.

Wright is a member of the Association for Computing Machinery, the Institute for Electrical and Electronic Engineers, and the Society for Industrial and Applied Mathematics.

*B.S., University of Illinois at Urbana-Champaign, 2004; M.S., University of Illinois, 2007; University of Illinois, Ph.D., 2009*

Even the best written software contains errors. Junfeng Yang wants to unmask and correct those often subtle defects. The software bugs are costly. In 2002, the National Institute of Science and Technology put their cost at $60 billion annually. Bugs do more than crash computers. They contributed to the northeast power blackout in 2003, and delivered lethal doses of radiation to hospital patients.

"My research involves finding ways to make software more reliable," Yang said. In graduate school, he developed an automated method to detect storage system errors. "Past tests were like throwing darts and hoping to hit a problem area. We developed systematic ways to test all possible storage states," he said.

After joining Microsoft, he extended his work to distributed storage systems on large networks. "People knew they were losing data, but not why. Our tool helped them find those bugs," Yang said. His work led to numerous patches for Microsoft's production systems and the Linux Operating System.

Now Yang is focusing on the reliability of multithreaded programs. Unlike programs that run all their instructions sequentially, multithreaded programs consist of segments, or threads, that run concurrently. Multithreaded programs are significantly faster than sequential code.

They are also more difficult to write, test, and debug. "This is because they are not deterministic," he explained. In other words, a multithreaded program may behave somewhat differently each time it runs. "It may act correctly or buggy, depending on such variables as processor speed, operating system scheduling, and what data arrives when during operations," Yang said.

Lack of determinism makes it difficult to reproduce errors, much less fix them. Yang's research makes multithreaded programs execute deterministically, so programmers can isolate problems.

Explaining his approach, Yang likens threads to cars driving down a four-lane highway. "The cars drive in parallel lanes. During nondeterministic execution, they can change lanes whenever they want. When they do, sometimes they collide and cause the program to crash.

"To make threads execute deterministically, we've placed barriers between the lanes. We only allow threads to change lanes at fixed locations, following a fixed order. This prevents random car collisions," he said.

Yang records this path and makes every subsequent group of cars follow it. "Because we know the path causes no collisions, there should be no collisions when another group of cars use it," he said. By attacking multithreading, Yang hopes to weave more reliable software.

*B.S., Tsinghua University (Beijing), 2000; M.S., Stanford, 2002; Ph.D., Stanford, 2008*

# JUNFENG YANG

Assistant Professor of Computer Science

INFORMATION

## Calculating What Is Possible

# MIHALIS YANNAKAKIS

Percy K. and Vida L. W. Hudson
Professor of Computer Science and
Professor of Industrial Engineering
and Operations Research

Computers are solving ever more complex problems, yet some problems have resisted intense efforts for many decades. How can we tell which problems can be solved efficiently and which cannot? How do we find the most efficient algorithms? And for intractable problems, how do we find the best solutions possible in reasonable amounts of time? These are some of the challenges taken on by Mihalis Yannakakis.

One line of his research seeks to understand the inherent computational complexity of problems. "It turns out that many computational problems from diverse fields are intimately related to one another," he said. For example, optimizing network designs, scheduling jobs, and folding proteins all exhibit essentially the same type of computational difficulties. Yannakakis seeks to find the underlying features that characterize the complexity of different problems and identify their unifying principles.

Many optimization problems are computationally hard, in the sense that we cannot compute efficiently the optimal solution. For these cases, Yannakakis has been working on algorithms that compute near-optimal solutions. His goal is to design efficient approximation algorithms with provable performance guarantees.

Yannakakis' third research thrust involves trade-offs when making decisions. "We care about a design's quality and also its cost, or a health treatment's benefits and risks. Typically, there is no one solution that is optimal for all criteria, but rather many incomparable solutions that encapsulate the trade-offs between different criteria," he explained.

For two criteria, Yannakakis visualizes these trade-offs as a curve on the plane. As the number of criteria rise, the trade-offs form a surface in a higher dimensional mathematical space. "It is generally impossible to generate all the points on the trade-off surface because there are usually an exponential or even infinite number of them," he said. "But we wish to generate enough points to represent the whole design space, so decision makers have an accurate enough view of the trade-offs to make an informed choice."

Yannakakis' approach is to design algorithms with guaranteed succinctness and accuracy to compute a carefully selected small set of solutions that offer the best possible representation of that space.

"Computers could work forever on a task," he summarized. "We try to characterize what we can actually compute efficiently for a specific task and in general. Like trying to understand the physical world, we're trying to find the laws that govern the computational world. We want to determine the powers and limitations of computation."

*Dipl., National Technical University of Athens (Greece), 1975; M.S., Princeton, 1979; Ph.D., Princeton, 1979*

What do hospitals, airlines, supply chains, and the Internet all have in common? According to David Yao, they are all complex networks that must bring together multiple services and assets to accomplish any task. They must also share these same resources among different classes of customers, who pay different amounts for service.

Organizations want to manage their resources efficiently to maximize profits. But if they are too efficient—Yao likens it to filling a highway with cars so traffic slows to a crawl—they sacrifice quality of service. Balancing efficiency and service across complex networked resources is an exercise in extreme juggling. Yao wants to help by giving organizations the tools to do it in real time.

He points to airlines as an example. They must divide a limited number of seats among first, business, and several types of economy classes. Each class sells for a different price.

Airlines maximize revenue when they fill every seat. They can do this by discounting and by overbooking flights, since they know there will always be some no-shows. They also reserve some tickets to sell at higher last-minute prices.

That leads to problems. "The price they pay for overbooking is that they may have to ask people to get off the airplane. They also don't want to hold too many last-minute tickets, or they will have unfilled seats," Yao said.

Airlines estimate how many seats to sell and reserve by looking at past data. "That does not capture the real-time dynamics of the network," Yao stated. "On a particular day, a plane might be delayed and those passengers will need new connecting flights. Now their planes must carry their own customers plus passengers from the delayed flight."

Yao's models capture that type of real-time information and use it to optimize the entire system rather than a specific resource, like a single flight, a bank of servers, or a hospital bed. On airlines, his models assign all seats a shadow price, the revenue they could potentially earn if they sold a reserved ticket, and compare it with the probability of delays and other events as they evolve. It shows them the most profitable way to reroute passengers and flights.

"We look at the probability of events, but also at how we can hedge our bets if that probability is wrong," said Yao. "We want to create models that are predictive but robust, so if you're off, you won't walk away from money on table."

*M.A.Sc., University of Toronto (Canada), 1981; Ph.D., University of Toronto, 1983*

## Optimizing Networked Resources

# DAVID YAO

Professor of Industrial Engineering and Operations Research

## Turning Students into Entrepreneurs

# YECHIAM YEMINI

Professor of Computer Science

Dell, Yahoo, Google, and Facebook were founded by college students, Yechiam Yemini tells his Principles of Innovation and Entrepreneurship class. He wants to teach students how to create innovative technologies and transform them into successful startups.

Yemini has combined academia with serial entrepreneurship. His first company, Comverse Technology, co-founded in 1984, revolutionized voice messaging technologies. Ten years later, System Management Arts created the first products to diagnose network failures automatically.

Startups, he explained, are another way of disseminating basic knowledge. "High-tech startups distill the value in raw, basic technologies by creating innovative products and introducing them to the market," he said.

Yemini's course rests on three legs. The first is understanding how to identify opportunities. The most fertile areas are those where new ideas disrupt established ways of doing things, such as integrated circuits, the Internet, and wireless networks.

"Today, the biggest transition is from cellular phones to mobile computing. Now your phone is a tool to go shopping, access content, play video and read books. It's a wonderful opportunity to launch companies that exploit this," Yemini said.

The course's second leg involves startup mechanics. "We look at the engines of value creation," Yemini said. "Different engines make products, exchange information with the market, and manipulate the flow of financial resources. We look at how to design these engines to optimize the value they create while minimizing risks and errors."

Yemini's third leg is product development. "Many companies fail because they spend all their time creating a product and then look for a market," he said. "They didn't manage the risk that customers wouldn't like their implementation, or that market needs might change." He advises students to begin talking with customers from day one, and to keep improving products incrementally until they are happy.

Yemini is focusing on managing mobile services. "Mobility presents a disruptive change in delivering network services. It presents research opportunities to create new technologies, which may one day lead to new startups," he said.

"A startup company is a bunch of engines that express the value of a technology," said Yemeni. "Think of it as a mechanism, a black box. There are ways to build a better box, ways to engineer it to better distill the value of the underlying technology. My course on innovation and entrepreneurship tries to teach how to engineer a technology company, much as one engineers other innovative constructs."

*B.Sc., Hebrew University of Jerusalem (Israel), 1972; M.Sc., Hebrew University of Jerusalem, 1974; Ph.D., University of California-Los Angeles, 1978*

Computer chips are the building blocks that allow billions of transistors to fit in a small area. These chips have enhanced everyday life, and enable the design of electronics of increasing functionality and lower cost, making most modern-day technology possible. But as transistors continue to become smaller and faster, new challenges for circuit designers constantly arise. The research field of Very Large Scale Integration (VLSI) addresses these challenges.

One of those challenges is transistor current leakage, which is becoming a bigger problem as transistors in computer chips continue to shrink, leading to problems with power and reliability. While current leakage and power dissipation in each transistor remain quite small, they can add up to a significant amount over billions of transistors, potentially limiting function and performance. Solving this problem could have a big impact on industry, and the feasibility of critical future applications of electronics.

Charles Zukowski, past chairman and current vice chairman of the Department of Electrical Engineering, has worked in the area of VLSI throughout his career and has contributed to the progress of integrated circuit technology in a number of areas. His chief focus now is twofold: circuit techniques such as monotonic logic to reduce the impact of current leakage in future integrated circuit technologies; and special-purpose hardware prototypes for the simulation of gene regulatory networks. Through this work, his intention is to further the capability of integrated circuit technology and to explore new applications.

His research has covered both circuit design and circuit analysis, results of which include a patented circuit technique for generating high data-rate serial data from a number of lower data-rate channels, and an approach for mixing digital and large-signal analog computation for simulation. He derived a number of results for bounding the behavior of digital integrated circuits that were compiled into a research monograph, and based on this work, he received a National Science Foundation Presidential Young Investigator Award. He later developed a technique for measuring the convergence of waveform relaxation algorithms for simulating digital circuits. He also proposed a technique for significantly reducing the power consumption in certain content-addressable memories and investigated the use of various memories and circuit techniques in internet routing hardware. Throughout, he has consulted for industry in the field of Complementary Metal Oxide Semiconductor Integrated Circuit (CMOS IC) design.

*B.S., Massachusetts Institute of Technology, 1982; M.S., MIT, 1982; Ph.D., MIT, 1985*

# CHARLES ZUKOWSKI

Professor of Electrical Engineering

INFORMATION

# Improving the Efficiency and Resiliency of Wireless Networks

# GIL ZUSSMAN

Assistant Professor of Electrical Engineering

The design and deployment of mobile and wireless networks has undergone an extraordinary transformation. While this technology already forms the backbone of crucial systems such as health care, disaster recovery, public safety, manufacturing, and citywide broadband access, it has even greater potential. The flexibility inherent in cellular, sensor, mobile ad hoc, mesh, and wireless local area network technologies delivers an almost endless range of applications, including mobile banking, inter-vehicle communication, space exploration, and climate-change tracking.

Despite their promise, efficiently controlling wireless networks is a challenging task, due to interference between simultaneous transmissions, mobility of the nodes, limited capacity of the wireless channel, energy limitations of the devices, and lack of central control. Such distinct characteristics set wireless networks apart from other networking technologies and pose numerous challenging theoretical and practical problems.

To tackle those problems, Gil Zussman focuses on designing new wireless networking architectures and on improving the performance and resilience of existing networks. Due to the special characteristics of these networks, Zussman designs architectures and algorithms that are optimized across multiple layers of the networking protocol stack. For example, he has been working on energy-aware protocols that take into account energy consumption and battery status while making joint decisions regarding routing and scheduling. Zussman has been recently focusing on developing algorithms and prototypes for Energy Harvesting Active Networked Tags (EnHANTs). These tags harvest their energy from the environment and can be used in various tracking applications, and particularly, in disaster recovery applications.

Moreover, in order to enable the efficient operation of distributed algorithms which usually have inferior performance to centralized algorithms, Zussman has been working on identifying topologies in which distributed algorithms obtain maximum throughput. His results in this area enable the partitioning of networks to subnetworks in which distributed algorithms operate very well, thereby improving the overall network performance.

Other research projects of Zussman's group focus on controlled mobility of wireless nodes, dynamic spectrum allocation and cognitive radio, interfaces between wireless and optical networks, and resilience of networks to geographically correlated failures. Results regarding the latter include identifying vulnerabilities of networks to large-scale attacks, such as Electromagnetic Pulse (EMP) attacks, and mechanisms to mitigate the effects of such attacks.

Zussman was a postdoctoral associate with the Massachusetts Institute of Technology as a Fulbright Fellow and Marie Curie Fellow. He is a senior member of the Institute of Electrical and Electronics Engineers.

*B.Sc., B.A., Technion-Israel Institute of Technology, 1995; M.Sc., Tel Aviv University, 1999; Ph.D., Technion-Israel Institute of Technology, 2004*

*Engineering as the Newest Liberal Art*

As a faculty member at Columbia Engineering for more than a half century, I would like to share with you my perspective on the School's history and future. Since 1956, Columbia Engineering has been my academic and professional home.

As a newly appointed professor in the Department of Civil Engineering and Engineering Mechanics, I joined a faculty that boasted many of the top names in their fields—Rudolf Kalman, known for the Kalman filter; Lotfi Zadeh, who invented fuzzy logic; Ferdinand Freudenstein, father of modern kinematics; Raymond Mindlin, known for his work in the theory of elasticity; Cyrus Derman, known for optimization of stochastic systems; and Elmer Gaden, the father of biochemical engineering.

As you read about our current faculty, you can see that today we have similarly outstanding and innovative researchers who themselves are, or are becoming, the equals of the legendary faculty giants who were here when I arrived more than 55 years ago.

What has changed is the nature and practice of engineering, which has now become central to almost all human intellectual activities, ranging from pure science to business and economics. In fact, engineering is now sometimes called the newest liberal art.

This change has served to encourage, and even demand, that a great university such as Columbia have an engineering school ever stronger in its engineering-based programs. This impetus has spurred the creation of additional departments—Applied Physics and Applied Mathematics, Computer Science, Biomedical Engineering, and Earth and Environmental Engineering—and many new programs, such as financial engineering, fusion energy, stem cell research, biological systems research, materials and process research at the atomic and molecular levels.

Engineering and applied science research now plays a greatly expanded role in the rapidly advancing biological, physical, chemical, and mathematical sciences, and as such, in the intellectual life of the University.

I am privileged to be a member of this vibrant Columbia Engineering faculty and I know you are as proud as I am of its accomplishments throughout its history and of the bright future that lies ahead.

*Morton B. Friedman*

Morton B. Friedman
Senior Vice Dean and Professor of Civil Engineering and Engineering Mechanics

# FACULTY INDEX

# Credits and Acknowledgments

Columbia Engineering
The Fu Foundation School of Engineering and Applied Science
Columbia University in the City of New York

Feniosky Peña-Mora, Dean and Morris A. and Alma Schapiro Professor

Senior Editor: Margaret R. Kelly, Columbia Engineering Publications
Senior Designer: Sandy Kaufman, Columbia University Publications
Senior Photographer: Eileen Barroso, Columbia University Photographer
Senior Production Manager: Dan Simpson, Columbia University Publications

Associate Editor: Melanie A. Farmer, Columbia Engineering Publications
Associate Designer: Junie Lee, Columbia University Publications
Associate Photographers: Bruce Hemingway, Alan S. Orling
Associate Production Manager: Donna Snyder, Columbia University Publications

Profile Writers: Jeff Ballinger, Amy Biemiller, Alan S. Brown, Holly Evarts, Ken Kostel, Anna Kuchment, Alex Lyda, and David M. Wilson

To Gareth Williams, Violin Family Professor of Classics, we owe our book's title, *Excellentia, Eminentia, Effectio* (Excellence, Leadership, Impact) and the Latin translations that appear on our Endowed Professorship Medallion. We are grateful for his cheerful willingness to share his expertise with his colleagues at Columbia Engineering.

Thanks also to Susanne Braham, Fredrik Palm, Margaret Griffel, Elaine Ragland, and Dana Vlcek for their editorial and production support in the preparation of this book.

We are deeply grateful to the engineering and applied science faculty of Columbia Engineering for making this book possible. Their research and scholarship highlighted in these pages are leading to innovative solutions to some of the most challenging global problems in health, sustainability, and information. The faculty, together with the School's researchers, students, and administrators, make Columbia Engineering the leading institution for innovative research, progressive thought leadership, and great scholarly achievement that it is.

COLUMBIA | ENGINEERING
The Fu Foundation School of Engineering and Applied Science